THE COMPLETE FUNDRAISING handbook

4th edition

Nina Botting
Michael Norton

DIRECTORY OF SOCIAL CHANGE

In association with
the Institute of Fundraising

Published by
Directory of Social Change
24 Stephenson Way
London NW1 2DP
Tel. 020 7209 5151; Fax 020 7391 4804
E-mail books@dsc.org.uk
www.dsc.org.uk
from whom further copies and a full books catalogue are available.

Directory of Social Change is a Registered Charity no. 800517

First published 1992
Second edition 1993
Third edition 1997
Reprinted 1999
Fourth edition 2001
Reprinted 2003

ISBN 1 900630 84 5

British Library Cataloguing in Publication Data
A catalogue record for this book is available from the British Library

Cover design by Keith Shaw
Text designed by Sarah Nicholson
Typeset by GreenGate Publishing Services, Tonbridge
Printed and bound by Page Bros., Norwich

Other Directory of Social Change departments in London:
Courses and conferences 020 7209 4949
Charity Centre 020 7209 1015
Charityfair 020 7391 4875
Publicity & Web Content 020 7391 4900
Policy & Research 020 7391 4880

Directory of Social Change Northern Office:
Federation House, Hope Street, Liverpool L1 9BW
Courses and conferences 0151 708 0117
Research 0151 708 0136

The Institute of Charity Fundraising Managers (ICFM) is now called the Institute of Fundraising. All references to ICFM in the text should be treated as references to the Institute of Fundraising.

CONTENTS

FOREWORD

Fundraising is a little bit like map reading. As soon as you think you have totally mastered it and your confidence is right up there, you get lost. You then have to revert to reminding yourself of the fundamentals and key principles to guide you back again. This book covers those essentials of fundraising in a way that is informative, accessible and engaging.

Keeping an eye on the key principles, the much quoted 'back to basics', has been a major feature of fundraising over the last few years. The pendulum has started to swing away from an over reliance on technique and greater emphasis has been placed on the quality of honest communication with supporters and ensuring they are treated as individuals.

This edition provides us with some welcome developments to support us in our work. The overall structure of the book has been improved to make it even easier to use as a reference tool. It is now divided into three main parts, covering an introduction to fundraising, sources of funds and an analysis of fundraising techniques. A new chapter draws together developments in the field of direct marketing, and in particular the recent success of approaching potential supporters face-to-face. Additional new material recognises and illustrates the key role that individuals can play even as relatively modest supporters through committed giving and legacies. A useful and up-to-date section covers the different ways an individual can now give in a tax-efficient manner and the benefits that this can bring.

To be a successful fundraiser requires more than the information contained in this book. It is important to network and to share experiences and ideas with others – and despite the increasing competition for support, fundraisers remain a generous lot. Furthermore, training provides a sound basis on which to build up experience. The reference sections at the end of each chapter and at the back of the book provide some useful sources of both networking and training. Follow them up.

Fundraising is a marvellous career. To be successful requires a wide range of admirable attributes. A fundraiser is at the very core of an organisation's work, its cause and the people caught up in that cause. If we can communicate the very essence of that cause and treat our supporters with respect and honesty, then we really can make a difference and be an agent of change.

Lindsay Boswell
Chief Executive
The Institute of Fundraising

ABOUT THE AUTHORS

Michael Norton founded the Directory of Social Change in 1975. He is no longer directly involved with DSC, but has gone on to found the Centre for Innovation in Voluntary Action and to chair Changemakers, a charity which works to promote voluntary action among young people. Changemakers is part of the consortium which set up unLTD, the foundation for social entrepreneurs, which bid successfully for the £100 million endowment previously controlled by the Millennium Commission. unLTD will use the fund to make awards to individuals to set up projects which will benefit their communities. Michael Norton also spends about a third of his time working on projects which relate to the development of the voluntary sector in India, where he has set up the charity Books for Change.

Nina Botting is currently Planned Giving Manager at Tate. She has worked in the supporter development area since 1993, and prior to Tate promoted regular gifts and legacies at Shelter and Amnesty International UK. She started her fundraising career as an account handler at Pell and Bales, the telemarketing agency. Nina is a member of the ICFM and sits on their standards committee. She was on the working party that produced the Code of Practice for Legacy Fundraising and chaired the group that produced the Code for the Personal Solicitation for Committed Gifts. She was also a member of the board which organised the 2001 National Fundraiser's Convention.

Introduction

Of all the fundraising clichés around – and there are lots of them – my favourite is that 'fundraising is simple, but not easy'. Fundraising techniques are important; it would be perverse to say otherwise. Saying the right kind of thing in the right kind of way greatly increases your chances of success. Having a basic understanding of how things work and avoiding common mistakes will save lots of time chasing after money you are never going to get.

However, the key elements of fundraising are generally pretty simple. Fundraising is mainly about people, whether they are donors, volunteer event organisers, users of your service, local reporters, management committee members, sporting celebrities and such like. The really good fundraiser knows – and is known, liked and trusted by – the right kind of people, whoever they may be in each particular situation. This takes time; it can be hard work; it can be hit and miss. But fundraising is about trust, and trust works best between people who know and like each other.

Fundraising is also about the grind as well as the glamour. However star-studded or not your fundraising event may be, the essential thing is that it is well-organised and runs smoothly. This means checking and re-checking that all the basics have been taken care of. There is no quick fix for this. Someone has to do it all, and really carefully.

This book is all about getting fundraising right by focussing on the essentials. We try to tell it how it is, without getting too bogged down in jargon or undue complexity. Maybe we should have called it 'The Naked Fundraiser', although that may have been misinterpreted!

The book has been radically restructured and is now divided into three parts: an introduction to the general principles underlying successful fundraising, a section on the main sources of funds, and a third part which presents and discusses fundraising techniques. New material has been added, particularly on tax effective giving, plus new examples and case studies; we are grateful to all the fundraisers who contributed their experiences. There are new appendices, and the lists of resources and further information now appear at the end of each chapter so that they are easier to refer to.

We owe a lot to many people in bringing this book together, and their contribution is acknowledged below. However, the book primarily remains the work of three people: Michael Norton and Nina Botting, the authors, and Alison Baxter, its editor. It is clear from the final product the great experience and professionalism that each has brought to bear on the book. They have done a terrific job.

And finally, we wish you the reader every success in your fundraising. Just as this edition has been a collaborative effort, so will the next one. You could play your part by letting us know of your successes and failures, where you found the book particularly helpful or where you found it lacking, and anything else you think it could usefully do to help fundraisers in the future.

Many thanks, and good luck!

Mike Eastwood
Former Director
Directory of Social Change

Acknowledgements

The publisher and authors are grateful to the following individuals and organisations who have given so freely of their time and experience in order to provide text, examples, case studies and advice:

Mark Astarita (National Deaf Children's Society), John Baguley (The Medical Foundation for the Care of Victims of Torture), David Barker (British Heart Foundation), Jim Barker (Friends of the Earth), Alison Benjamin (editor of *Corporate Citizen*), Michael Berg (Crusaid), Jo Bolitho (The National Art Collections Fund), Harry Brown (NSPCC), Charities Aid Foundation, Simon Collings (Oxfam), Jennifer Cormack (Tate), Beth Courtier and Karen Spreadbury (BT), Joanna Gilson (Amnesty International UK), Ann Hanson (Help the Aged), Tim Hunter (NSPCC), Howard Lake (Fundraising UK Ltd), Roger Lawson (WWF-UK), Dyrol Lumbard (The Media Trust), Deborah McLean (Greenpeace UK), National Centre for Volunteering, Clare O'Brien (National Theatre), Anne Pilling and Liz Webb (ITDG), Judith Polkinhorn (Compton Hospice), Maia Sanders (Shelter), Neil Skinner (ICOM), Tom Smith (Smee & Ford), Andrew Watt (ICFM), Laurence Wattier (IDs), Darrell Williams (Shared Experience Theatre Company).

We are also grateful to the following organisations for permission to reproduce their copyright material as illustrations:

Amnesty International UK, Crusaid, Greenpeace UK, Help the Aged, The Medical Foundation for the Care of Victims of Torture, NSPCC, Oxfam, Shelter, WWF-UK.

The chapter on government funding was contributed by Susan Forrester and the appendix on data protection by Paul Ticher; we would like to acknowledge their help (and thank them for keeping to our very tight deadlines!).

This edition also draws extensively on material in previous editions and we gratefully acknowledge the contribution of Sam Clarke, the original author.

PART
one

GETTING STARTED

1 BACKGROUND

In this chapter we look at the importance of fundraising to your organisation, the main challenges facing fundraisers, the intended readership, and the structure of the book.

1.1 Fundraising today

Few charities can finance themselves exclusively from the interest on huge endowments or investment portfolios. Nor do many voluntary organisations have the kind of routine annual surplus to enable them simply to absorb new work without the need for additional external finance. And given the short-term nature of most current grants regimes, many organisations find themselves on a kind of financial treadmill – how do we pay for this activity or that piece of work once the three-year grant has run out?

Rightly or wrongly, fundraising is a fact of modern voluntary sector life. For some it is a necessary chore; for others a marvellous and stimulating opportunity; for most of us, it is something in between. However you feel about it, fundraising is critical to the success of your organisation's work. The main reasons are set out below.

Survival

Every organisation needs money to keep going from this year to the next – to meet project costs and develop programmes for the future; to pay the wages and office overheads; to keep buildings and vehicles in a good state of repair, and to pay for new equipment. And the stark truth is that if the money is not raised, the organisation will not be able to do its work, and if the work is not done, pressing needs in society will not be met.

The tool you will use to manage your fundraising is your annual budget. This will show the amount of money you plan to spend. It will also indicate the amount of money that has already been raised or has been promised, and what extra support still needs to be raised during the year so that you can meet your outgoings.

You will monitor your progress in fundraising through keeping records of all money received or promised, and by preparing and discussing management accounts at regular management meetings. If your income isn't coming in as planned, then you will need to take some sort of action – put more effort into your fundraising, find and develop new sources of funds, cut costs, defer planned projects, or agree to subsidise the deficit out of your reserves.

Expansion and development

If your organisation is to meet the challenges of the future, you may need to expand and develop your work: improve your services; extend your work into other regions and areas; evaluate your impact; undertake research and campaigning alongside your basic service delivery work; experiment and innovate. This all requires more money – money that will need to be raised.

You will probably want to prepare a business plan, or at least an outline budget, for the next few years so as to identify the resources you will need for your ongoing programme of work and any proposed major developments. Remember, fundraising always takes longer than you think. The more you plan ahead, the more successful you will be in getting the resources when you need them.

Reducing dependency

Many organisations are funded by only one or a handful of major donors. This can put the organisation into a state of dependency. If one of the grants is withdrawn, this can create a financial crisis. It may also be difficult to determine your own agenda if you are constantly having to adapt to the priorities of a key donor.

Broadening your fundraising base can reduce this dependency. You need to decide whether your organisation is too dependent on any one source. You might then see if you can build some stability by negotiating some form of long-term commitment from them, or you could try to develop alternative sources of income.

Building a constituency

Fundraising is not just about money; it is also about numbers of supporters. Each supporter is important to you. Many can be persuaded to give again and to give even more generously. They may be able to volunteer or to find friends who are willing to support you. They provide an indication of the level of support that your organisation is attracting, and therefore can add strength to your lobbying and campaigning work.

You need to think about the sorts of constituencies that you would like to mobilise and who your work will appeal to. Is it a particular type of business or profession? Or students and activists? Or women? Or retired people with time on their hands? Or parents? Or some other category? You will need to think about how best to reach them, and the sort of message they will respond to.

Creating a viable and sustainable organisation

Fundraising is not simply about generating the resources you need to survive from this year through to next year, or finding the funds for any expansion and development. It is also about helping create a viable and strong organisation which is able to sustain itself into the future.

There are many ways of doing this. One is to build a substantial and active donor base – getting people to support you who sympathise with your aims, and who will continue to give their support over a long period of time. Other ways include: organising fundraising events (which can create a regular and continuing source of income); creating capital within your organisation, such as a capital fund or buildings and equipment (especially when this reduces your need for running costs or can help you generate an income); and developing income generating schemes for the organisation itself.

Many organisations are addressing long-term needs – for example through community development which will not yield immediate results, or in looking after disabled or elderly people where there is a continuing commitment to provide care well into the future. You need to create an organisation that is financially strong in the long as well as the short term, rather than one that is plagued by annual deficits and is at or near bankruptcy. Financial concerns can affect the morale of the whole organisation. Crisis fundraising is time-consuming and increasingly difficult – and in the end you will find you run out of good will. You need to find ways of strengthening the financial position of your organisation and this means developing a sensible fundraising strategy for the future.

1.2 The challenge for fundraisers

Responding to growing need

The UK along with many other countries is facing growing needs and rising expectations of what should be provided. There is a shortage of resources to meet health, welfare and educational needs. Greater life expectancy, persistently high levels of unemployment and family poverty in some regions, changing family structures, rising costs of service delivery, the need to introduce high technology solutions, new issues and problems such as CJD, are all making it difficult to respond to every need.

All the evidence shows that despite rising national wealth, the poor are growing relatively poorer year by year, and a disproportionate number of our children are growing up in poverty. There is also an expectation that voluntary organisations will intervene as providers of last resort, since the state seems to have withdrawn from this role.

It is not just a matter of raising more money to provide more or better services. The challenge for voluntary organisations is to develop solutions to people's needs rather than simply provide services that while improving the quality of people's lives, leave the fundamental problems unresolved. If they can create more imaginative and effective approaches to the problems that exist in society, they can respond to the growing levels of need without necessarily increasing the demand for funding that is just not there. This role as innovator is one of the strengths of the voluntary sector. It is also something that many funders welcome.

Recognising the competition for funds

The fundraising world is extremely competitive. More and more organisations are started. They then need to think about fundraising and how to develop independent sources of income for themselves. This means that all the more obvious sources, such as grant-making trusts, the larger local companies and rich individuals, are receiving increasing numbers of requests for funding – and they can't respond positively to them all, however worthwhile the cause.

Your job is to try to show that your organisation is successful, effective, cost-effective and lively – in short that it is the best recipient for a donor's funds. Alternatively, you can think about developing new sources of money that nobody else is yet exploiting – the large trust that nobody seems to have heard of and which is not yet listed in any of the grant guides, a rich individual who has 'just made it', a new and exciting way of raising money before everyone else has tried to imitate it.

Keeping up to date

The fundraising world changes continually. In April 2000 the tax structure changed completely to encourage people to give more tax-effectively. New technology offers major opportunities both for fundraising and liaising with donors. There are also new laws on Data Protection and Freedom of Information. Every week new government programmes are being introduced, some of which dwarf more traditional sources – for example the Children's Fund will be distributing £40 million a year through 50 local funds by 2004. The fundraiser needs to keep on top of these changes and developments.

Scrambling for funds

'There is intense competition for funds. Groups feel they must apply for whatever funds are available, although they know that their chance of success is low. There are so many initiatives from central and local government that it is difficult for voluntary organisations to respond without a full-time fundraising department. There is that sense of scrambling for funds whether or not they are appropriate for the organisation's current needs. Small groups are told they should market themselves, when they are already fully occupied providing services in often impossible circumstances. Most voluntary groups cannot confidently see beyond the short term. It is very difficult for them to get funds for long-term development, and they continue to hang on in the hope that somebody – the Single Regeneration Budget, the Lottery, a future government – will rescue them.'

[Tim Cook, formerly Clerk to the City Parochial Foundation]

Developing long-term solutions for your fundraising

There is an increasing emphasis on financial sustainability. Many trusts and companies, for example, don't like the organisations they support to continue to be dependent on them for more than a few years. They want to be able to withdraw their support so as to be able to back new ideas and new projects. At the same time, you can find that you have accessed all the ready sources of money, and that fundraising is becoming more and more difficult. At this stage, if you can develop mechanisms for bringing money into your organisation on a continuing basis, then this will provide you with the financial strength and confidence for a more successful future.

Different organisations deal with this problem in different ways. A committed membership paying subscriptions or giving by monthly direct debit; a major fundraising event which can be run annually; a network of local supporters groups; service agreements and other forms of funding partnerships with local authorities – these are all ways of developing continuing income and reducing the need to fundraise.

Generating your own income

Income generation is another way of bringing income into your organisation. Charging for services, selling training and publications, hiring out services, can all pay their way or even contribute towards overheads. But to develop this successfully requires new thinking, new approaches and new skills. There is, as yet, insufficient prominence given to this, and much of the emphasis of fundraising is still on the actual raising of money. But there is a body of experience building up and more organisations are becoming happier with the idea of a more 'commercial' approach.

1.3 Who should read this book?

The simple answer is that everyone who has any sort of fundraising responsibility needs to understand the fundraising process.

- Board members (the generic term used for trustees and management committee members) may in small organisations be responsible for fundraising themselves and in any case will want to know what to expect of fundraisers, how to employ them, what qualities they should have and what support they will need to succeed. They will also want to know the options for income generating schemes.
- The director and other senior managers may also be involved in fundraising and developing a fundraising strategy for the organisation. They will want to know when it is time to employ a specialist fundraiser or a fundraising consultant and how to manage them to achieve the best results.
- Fundraisers will of course need to have a good background guide to the many techniques that are available, and an understanding of which are likely to be the most relevant to them.
- People in other departments should be encouraged to find out more about the fundraising process and its impact on their work.
- People who are looking to move into fundraising (from inside or outside the voluntary sector) will find that this book will show them how fundraising works and which of their current skills may transfer.
- Volunteers involved in raising money could generate good ideas for improving their own contribution.
- Independent consultants and advisers, who are specialists in one area of fundraising will get a broader perspective so as to advise their clients better.
- Trainers may wish to use some of the material as handouts for their courses.

This book has been written from as many points of view as possible, taking into account the perspectives of both large and small organisations, those with some experience of fundraising and those considering the possibility for the first time.

1.4 How this book is structured

The book is divided into three main parts, and within these it is divided into chapters. Each chapter has a summary at the beginning of what it covers and a list at the end of resources and further information, covering the organisations and publications most relevant to the chapter.

Part 1 Getting started

Chapter 1 Background, which is this section, sets out why fundraising is important and what the challenges are for fundraisers.

Chapter 2 First principles describes some of the key principles of fundraising (to give a better understanding of the process) and some of the personal skills required in a fundraiser (so you will know your strengths and weaknesses for the job). It also shows how to construct your case, which will underpin all your fundraising efforts.

Chapter 3 Developing a fundraising strategy describes some of the factors to take into account and suggests ways of developing a fundraising strategy for your organisation, so you can decide where to put your fundraising efforts. Resourcing your fundraising is also dealt with here; alongside having a strategy, it is equally important to have the resources available to implement your fundraising plans successfully. Equipping a fundraising office, recruiting a fundraiser and using a consultant are all discussed. This section also covers testing, evaluation and control, to enable you to be more cost-effective in your fundraising.

Part 2 Sources of funds

Chapters 4–11 cover getting support from individuals, grants from trusts and foundations, company giving and business sponsorship, grants from government and other statutory sources and programmes, the National Lottery and the European Union, and a range of other possible sources for you to consider. This section will give you an understanding of how money is given away, the ways donors can give, and will help you identify opportunities for getting support for your own organisation.

Part 3 Techniques

Chapters 12–16 cover a range of fundraising techniques that you can use with different kinds of donor, covering everything from house-to-house collections and direct mail to organising a fundraising event, running a capital appeal or writing an application to a trust. There is also advice on using the media and working with volunteers. The full list of topics covered in this section is given on the contents pages.

The book ends with:

- appendices, covering data protection and a list of the codes of practice produced by the Institute of Fundraising;
- a list of the key sources of information and advice;
- an index.

2 FIRST PRINCIPLES

This chapter covers some of the key aspects of fundraising. It will help identify the people, the attitudes and the approaches that you will need to get a successful fundraising programme under way.

Details of organisations and publications referred to in this chapter are on p. 33.

2.1 The key principles of fundraising

You have to ask

A major charity once asked non-supporters what was their main reason for not giving. The answer was simple – they had never been asked. The whole purpose of fundraising is to raise money. It is often forgotten that the call to action, communicating the punch-line that actually asks people to give, is the essential piece of the message.

When asking for money you need to be clear exactly what you want, while also being aware of what that particular donor is able and willing to give. You also must make it as easy as possible for the donor to respond.

> 'All of the reading of fundraising literature, planning, strategising, writing case statements and attending fundraising training cannot and will not raise money. Only implementing your plan – taking action – will raise money. So make this your motto: "Today someone has to ask someone for money".'
>
> [Kim Klein, *Fundraising for Social Change*]

The personal approach

The general rule is that the more personal you can make your approach, the more effective you will be. So:

- asking someone face-to-face is better than …
- telephoning someone to ask for support, which is better than …
- writing a personal letter to someone asking for support, which is better than …
- giving a presentation to a group of people, which is better than …

- putting out a request on the internet (at least the people who visit your site are interested in what you are doing), which you can consider alongside …
- sending an appeal to lots of people.

Many fundraisers prefer to send letters asking for support and this is sometimes the only way to reach a large group of people. However, it is not the most effective way of asking, especially when compared to:

- a meeting at your project where the prospective donor can see your work and meet some of the beneficiaries;
- a request from someone who has given or from someone important (such as a business leader or expert in the field). These can be far more effective than a request from a fundraiser or from the project director. Part of the skill in fundraising is knowing who is the best person to do the asking.

Understanding the donor's viewpoint

In making a decision to give, a whole range of feelings and thoughts may be aroused in the donor. It is important for the fundraiser to understand this process.

The act of giving includes elements of faith, hope and charity: faith that the fundraiser truly represents the cause and will act as an efficient conduit for the donor's money; hope that the gift, however small, will make some difference; and charity, which is an act of altruism, a gift without the expectation of any material return.

The donor may have a personal reason for wanting to give. People may support a cancer charity, for example, through fear that they might get the disease, or because a family member or close friend has recently died of it. They may feel strongly about an issue – such as the environment – and want to do something about it. In supporting your cause they are also supporting their cause, doing something that they feel needs doing and that they want to see done. You need to recognise this and build on it.

Fundraising is a people business

People do not give to organisations or to abstract concepts. They give to help other people or because they want to create a better world. Your job as a fundraiser is to show how you help them to achieve this. One way of doing this is through case studies – illustrating your work with examples of who you have been able to help, how you have been able to change their lives and the difference a donation can make.

Another is to focus your fundraising on particular aspects of your work: the community care project you are planning to introduce on the housing estate, and how it will transform people's lives; the YouthBank programme that is getting underway, that enables young people to act as grantmakers in their local community and where you are all full of enthusiasm and excitement about its potential. By focusing on specific projects rather than the overall work of the organisation, it makes it easier to excite and enthuse your donors.

Fundraising is selling

Fundraising is a two-stage process. It is about showing people why your work is important and only then persuading them to give.

You must show people that there is an important need and that you can do something useful about it. Then, if they agree with you that the need is important and that something should be done, and if they agree that your organisation is capable of doing something to make a difference, and if you can show them how the support you are asking them for could be used – then asking for money becomes easy. Once people have been sold the idea, then they will want to give.

Credibility and PR

People prefer to give to organisations and causes that they have heard about and think well of. So your organisation's credibility and reputation are important. Press coverage of your work, trumpeting your successes in the newsletters you send to supporters, getting endorsements about the quality of your work from experts and prominent figures. These can all help give people confidence that you are doing a worthwhile and successful job – which then makes it much easier when you come to ask for support.

How much to ask for

Donors often don't know how much to give. They may not want to give much. Equally, they may not want to give too little and so seem mean. There are various ways of asking for money, some of which give more guidance than others.

- Ask for a specific sum to cover a particular item of expenditure (for example, £500 to sponsor a park bench at a nature reserve).
- Give a shopping list of different items at different prices (for example, if you are equipping a hospice, you can list all the items you will need to purchase, put a price against each and ask a donor to contribute to one or more). The price does not have to be just the direct cost of buying the item, but can include a reasonable overhead allocation as well.
- Show the cost per client as a unit cost, and ask the donor to support one or more units (for example, at a homework club, show how much it costs for

a child to attend for a week or a term, and ask a supporter to sponsor a child for a week, a term or a year).

- Give examples of gifts already received.
- Break down your appeal total into numbers of gifts of different sizes that you need if you are to reach your target. This technique is commonly used in major capital appeals.

Example of a shopping list

ITDG (Intermediate Technology Development Group) is a British development agency which provides practical answers to poverty in the Third World. By giving through ITDG's project sponsor scheme you will be bringing long-term security to poor people across the world.

The following are a few of the projects your donation can support:

- In eastern Sudan, ITDG is working with brick-makers to increase their wages. Project staff are improving their working conditions, introducing appropriate technology to produce a high-quality product. A sum of £90 will purchase new shovels for the brick-making cooperative, £300 could pay for the moulding of 100,000 bricks, and £718 could buy a manual brick press.
- Running your own business is one way of earning a living, and in Bangladesh ITDG is assisting local organisations to provide business advice and technology for women's groups. Businesses range from food-processing and fish cultivation, to black-batik and dyeing and candle-making. Creating new employment opportunities is vital to rural areas. A donation of £75 could buy a bombay mix machine, £100 could buy a wooden block for printing, and £350 could provide essential skills for a group of people from organisations working in local villages.
- The mode of transport in Nepal is usually by foot, with people carrying heavy loads on their head or back because of the difficult terrain. The lack of appropriate means of transport isolates villages from markets and from essential services such as health and education. ITDG is working in Nepal to improve transport options. A donation could help this project. For instance, the sum of £70 could buy a bicycle trailer, £200 could pay for a training programme, and £750 could cover the cost of a baseline transport survey to assess the needs of poor people.

[ITDG – Intermediate Technology Group]

Saying thank you

Saying thank you is extremely important. It recognises and values the donor's generosity. It makes them feel better about your organisation. And it may also prompt them to give again.

A former director of a major aid charity made a point of telephoning donors who had given £500 or more at home in the evenings to thank them personally. 'We're thrilled with your support. We're going to put it to good use immediately by using it to help establish a new health clinic for the Turkana. And we'll keep you in touch with progress.' This makes the donor feel that the charity is doing a good job and that their money is having a real impact. But it is amazing how many charities still never even bother to thank their donors. See chapter 4, section 4.7, for more on looking after your supporters.

Long-term involvement and commitment

What you really want are people who will give to you regularly and substantially. All the effort to find a donor and persuade them to give will really only bear fruit if they continue to give over many years, maybe increasing their level of giving over time. To achieve this means getting them involved with the work of the organisation and committed to its success by:

- saying thank you immediately and telling them what you plan to do with their money
- regular reporting back showing them what you have achieved with their money
- sharing your ideas and hopes for the future
- encouraging them to visit you and meet some of the people that they have been helping
- inviting them to meet with the staff and volunteers who are actually doing the work, and with prominent personalities associated with the cause.

Involvement and commitment

The difference between involvement and commitment is well illustrated by the Bacon and Eggs story. A hen and a pig were discussing the upcoming breakfast in which they were both to play a part. The pig said crossly to the hen, 'It's all very well you being so cheerful. You're just involved. I'm committed!'

Accountability and reporting back

When you take money from somebody, you are responsible for seeing that:

- the money is spent on the purposes for which it was raised – failure to do this is a breach of trust;
- the money is well spent and actually achieves something.

You should always report back to the donor to show them that you have used their money effectively, and what difference their support has made. You can do this by sending a personal letter or a project report or a newsletter, by post or by e-mail. This is not only polite, it is good fundraising practice – an enthusiastic donor who has seen the money make a difference may consider becoming a more committed supporter.

If it turns out that the project has not worked, you can still present this positively. Many voluntary organisations are in the business of innovation, and this inevitably involves risks and occasionally failure. But you will have tried, and you will have learned. The experience can lead to new ideas and new ways of working. Even if you have made a serious blunder (for example purchased an unroadworthy vehicle from a dealer that then went out of business), admit what has happened and put it down to experience. Truthfulness is one of the key skills needed in a fundraiser, as we discuss below.

2.2 The skills required in a fundraiser

Successful fundraisers need a number of key skills and qualities. It is helpful to reflect on what these are and whether you have them.

Enthusiasm and commitment

Commitment is one of the most important qualities in any fundraiser. You must really believe in the cause you are addressing and in the work that your organisation is doing. Your enthusiasm and commitment will encourage others to become equally committed through their giving.

The starving baby syndrome

You are watching TV. There is a programme about a refugee camp in the Sudan. People have arrived there with nothing, absolutely nothing. They have walked days to get there and are near starvation. A picture flashes up of a starving baby, who seems to be crying out to you 'Help me. Please help me. Please.' How can you resist giving your support to the aid charity running the feeding programme at the refugee centre? Then you think about the cause you are working for. 'If only I were having to raise money for starving babies, it would be so much easier', you think.

But your cause is important too. You have to make it seem as important to yourself and to others as saving starving babies. Interestingly the fundraiser for the starving baby charity probably believes that it would be much easier to be raising money to save endangered animals from being poached, and the animal fundraiser would much prefer to be raising money for a cancer charity.

You have to believe whole-heartedly in what you are doing, and make your cause compelling to others. If you can do this, fundraising will become very much easier.

The ability to ask

If you feel uncomfortable with the notion of asking for money, it will make your fundraising life difficult. Whether the task in hand is to write a four-page appeal letter, make a speech at a meeting of the Rotary Club, telephone a business executive to ask for an in-kind donation, organise a committee to run a fundraising event, or pay a personal visit to seek the support of a major donor – all this requires an ability to ask effectively for what you need.

Persuasiveness

People have lots of competing demands on their money. Your job is to persuade them that supporting your organisation is a really worthwhile investment of their hard-earned cash. You need to make a good case and use selling and communications skills to present it in a persuasive way. You need to be able to marshal compelling arguments, write letters which excite interest, talk fluently and interestingly about your cause in public or in private, create a sense of excitement through your enthusiasm, and share your hopes and visions for the future.

Confidence and dealing with rejection

When you are asking for money, you need to radiate confidence. If you are apologetic or hesitant, people are less likely to give to you.

'Some years ago I produced an environmental colouring book for children for a schools education programme. I thought that this might be sold to the public, so I decided to see whether bookshops might be interested in taking copies. I went first to my local bookshop. "Not our sort of book", they said. "No thank you." I had a similar experience at the next three bookshops I visited. I really was beginning to feel that nobody wanted the book. But I decided to go to one more bookshop before giving up. It was just as well that I did. "That's just the book we've been looking for. We'll take 70 copies for our Christmas table. What's the next title in the series, as we'd also be interested in that?" I felt elated. It is exactly the same with fundraising. Your next approach might be your big success! So keep trying.'

[Michael Norton on his book *Colour in Your Environment*]

One of the biggest problems is maintaining your confidence in the face of rejection. Since more people are likely to say 'No' than say 'Yes' – that's a fact of fundraising life – it is very easy to get downhearted. Many approaches will be unsuccessful, whether because of the enormous competition for funds, or just through bad luck. After a couple of rejections, you may begin to believe that nobody wants to support you. You might then start acting as if nobody wants to support you. You become apologetic and you talk as if you expect to be refused and maybe you even avoid asking – so as not to be rejected.

A good fundraiser has to be able to cope with rejection, starting each fresh approach as if it were the first, and learn from experience – so that the next approach is better than the last.

Persistence

Most fundraisers give up too soon. People often take 'no' to mean 'no' – rather than as a challenge to try to convert the 'no' into a 'yes'. If you give up immediately, then there's no chance at all. If you feel that they really should be supporting you, you will try to find a way of getting them to change their mind, or find something else that they might like to support. You approached them in the first place because you need support and you felt they might give it. Don't just give up at the first setback; persistence really does pay.

Persistence pays

I asked a group of fundraisers who were approaching charitable foundations to telephone them when they had received a letter of rejection to find out why they had been turned down, whether there was any possibility of their application being reconsidered, or what else they might apply for. What was interesting was how many eventually succeeded in getting a grant. If you are a donor receiving hundreds of applications, there is a tendency to say 'no' as an immediate response to any request. It is far harder to continue to say 'no' to someone who feels that they have a good project which you really should be interested in and who has the courage to come back and try to enter into a discussion with you – especially if your project falls within their priorities.

Truthfulness

Fundraisers have to be truthful at all times. The need to persuade people creates a pressure to tell partial truths and to claim more for your work than you can deliver. There is also a tendency to present the beneficiary as a victim because this makes it easier to elicit sympathy and support. This is true for people with physical disabilities or families needing support as it is for those suffering from hunger or disease in the less developed world.

Attempting to present a sensitive but truthful case, whilst making it powerful enough to persuade donors to give, can cause conflicts within your organisation. Potential beneficiaries may object to the way in which you have portrayed them. Project workers may feel you are putting them under too much pressure to deliver impossible results. Beneficiaries may feel that they are being patronised. To resolve this demands sensitivity and understanding from the fundraiser.

Understanding your donors

'A fundraiser should never give up. Much depends on their approach and personality. To ask for financial or other support for people who are in need does not mean that you should look unhappy or ugly. Your good appearance, open smile, courage and challenge should light a beam in the heart of your donor. Your belief in the people you are helping should convince the donor. It is useful to remember that the donor is also a human being who lives in the same world as you, and is anxious to do their bit to improve the community. My modest experience in fundraising says that it is very important to create feedback with your donor. Generous people do not necessarily need to be praised up to the sky, but they will be delighted to know that their support has helped improve something or made a better world for somebody. We have become close friends with many of our donors and try to build long-term relationships with them.'

[Contributed by Ekaterina Kim, Contacts-I, a group with disabilities working for people with disabilities in Moscow]

Contacts and the ability to make contacts

A lot of fundraising boils down not just to who you know, but also who can you get to know. One key contact can open up a hundred fundraising doors either by making introductions or, better still, by doing the asking for you. Ask yourself who you need to know in your local area or in the business networks you are trying to break into. Then ask yourself how you can get access to them. Then do it!

Good organisational skills

Fundraising can involve keeping in touch with thousands of supporters, ideally in a way that makes all of them think that they are special and that you have a personal relationship with them. Good organisation is essential. Fundraisers have to keep massive files of correspondence and information on all donations made. These files and your database, if you have one, must be organised and kept up to date so that no past event or piece of generosity is forgotten.

Good social contacts

A good fundraiser needs confidence, patience and tact. Confidence, because a confident appeal is harder to refuse. Patience, to deal with the particular concerns of donors (for example, when they ask to hear about the income ratios of the organisation for the third time). Tact and sincerity, when asking a supporter face to face for a legacy, or to suggest a variation in a will. A good fundraiser should really enjoy meeting and dealing with people. A good memory for names and faces helps too.

Imagination and creativity

Imagination is an invaluable fundraising asset. It will enable you to dream up new activities to inspire existing supporters and create events to enthuse the public. You should aim to present your work in an exciting and imaginative way. Since the work of your organisation is constantly evolving and new opportunities are emerging, you can use this to identify new approaches instead of simply relying on what has been done in the past.

Opportunism

You should be ready to grasp every opportunity that presents itself. For example, when a well-known supporter is awarded libel damages, should your letter asking for support not be in their in-tray next morning? Or if a leading company has just announced a major hike in profits or has been awarded a major construction contract in your area, then a cleverly constructed appeal for funds might just succeed.

The annual calendar provides opportunities at different times of the year. For example in Christian communities, Christmas and the New Year provide extremely good fundraising opportunities. Other faiths have similar points in the year. There are also anniversaries, centenaries or events such as a Jubilee, which can be used as a basis for major appeals.

Example

How Zubin Mehta, the Indian-born international conductor and Music Director for Life, became involved with the Shalom India-Israel Centre in Bombay

'Having nurtured the dream of an India-Israel Centre, I visited Israel in 1991, tramping the offices of umpteen cultural institutions, following up on every tenuous connection, meeting with Israeli government officials. Finally on my way back to the airport, I felt the kind of empty fatigue that comes with carrying a load of promises but nothing tangible. I knew we needed a respected and powerful patron, and many names came up, including Zubin's. But it needed both familiarity and courage to access high places. That first time, in 1991, I'm not sure I had both. Suddenly, there was Zubin before me in the bustling airport. On impulse I went up and congratulated him, and said that he had done every Indian proud. He thanked me politely, then it was over. "In that crowded place", I anguished with myself, "I could have done more". Two hours later, airborne, I noticed Zubin up front, reading glasses perched on his nose. I mustered the courage to send a polite note requesting to talk to him. From that and many subsequent meetings I realised that I was with a very special human being. Zubin's warmth and easy accessibility, his ability to get as excited as a child with an idea, astonished me. Here was something he had always wanted to do – to bring the people of the two countries he loved together culturally.'

[Salome Parekh, Hon. Director and Trustee, the Shalom India-Israel Centre, Bombay]

The key skills: how do you rate?

	have	don't have	could do better
enthusiasm and commitment	❏	❏	❏
the ability to ask	❏	❏	❏
persuasiveness	❏	❏	❏
confidence/ dealing with rejection	❏	❏	❏
persistence	❏	❏	❏
truthfulness	❏	❏	❏
contacts	❏	❏	❏
good organisational skills	❏	❏	❏
good social skills	❏	❏	❏
imagination and creativity	❏	❏	❏
opportunism	❏	❏	❏

You may not have all the skills that you will need. You will find the following helpful:

- assess your strengths, so you concentrate on doing the things you are good at;
- learn what skills you need to acquire, and set about obtaining the necessary training or experience;
- find ways of compensating for your weaknesses by getting others to help.

2.3 Making your case
Fundraising for projects

It is far easier to raise money for something specific than to appeal for administrative costs or general funds. As we saw with the 'shopping list' in section 2.1, donors prefer to feel that their money is going to fund something that they are genuinely interested in, whether it is saving a local woodland or buying play equipment for disabled children to use. Thinking of your work in project terms and designing projects which will attract support is the basis of successful fundraising. This simply means focusing each time on a particular activity or piece of work rather than on your organisation as a whole. A fundable project should be:

- specific: an identifiable item of expenditure or aspect of your work;
- important: both to your organisation and to the need it is meeting – long-term impact is an added bonus;
- realistic and achievable, giving the funder confidence that you will be able to deliver the intended targets and outcomes;
- good value, so that it stands out in a competitive funding environment;
- topical, looking at current issues and concerns;
- relevant to the donor, meeting their stated interests and priorities;
- a manageable size, so that it won't overload the organisation.

To cost a project properly, you need to include all the direct and indirect costs which can reasonably be attributed to the running of the project: an appropriate percentage of management salaries, the cost of occupying the building, using the phone, doing the photocopying and so on. Some funders say that they will not fund these core costs, but you will have to get them paid for somehow. (See chapter 6 for more on the issue of core costs.) If you are going to be responsible for raising funds, you need to have agreed with your management committee and relevant managers how you are going to go about presenting your work as fundable projects.

Six essential ingredients

Most donors, whether they are big trusts, major companies or individual members of the public, receive thousands of requests each year. How are you going to construct your case so that it stands out from the crowd? Before you start to fundraise, you need to ask yourself:

- Why would anyone want to support our work?
- What are the specific reasons why different types of donor (individuals, trusts, companies, government etc.) would want to support our work?
- What is so important about what we are planning to do?

Try out your answers to these key questions on a couple of friends who know nothing about your area of work. Are they convinced? Now you are ready to fill in the detail of your case with answers to the following questions.

- *Who are you?* In other words, are you reliable and respectable, with a strong track record of good work successfully completed?
- *What is the need that you intend to meet?* This should not simply be an emotive statement, but should include factual evidence about, for example, whether the situation is local or national; how many people it affects; why it is urgent.

- *What is the solution that you offer?* This is where you can describe what you intend to do, the results you expect to obtain and how these will be measured. You may want to use examples of how similar projects have worked.
- *Why should you do it?* This is where you establish your credibility. What other work have you done? Have you had good publicity for this? Do you involve volunteers and/or beneficiaries in your work? Have you got a track record in attracting funding?
- *How much do you need?* You need to have a clear idea of the total, who you intend to approach for the money, and how the total could be broken down for donors who want to contribute but could not possibly fund the whole thing.
- *What future do you have?* If you can show that you have thought ahead and attempted to achieve long-term stability, funders will be more inclined to support you.

Once you have the answers to these key questions, you will be able to use them in your fundraising, when you write an application to a trust or company (see chapter 15 for more on this), or when you put together a mailing to the public.

2.4 Organising your fundraising

Equipping a fundraising office

Some items of equipment are essential for a fundraiser; others are extremely useful. The main items are as follows.

1 *Telephone* This is absolutely essential. Ideally you need a line of your own, because of the volume and length of your calls, and to have it in a quiet place, so calls can be made in privacy. Fundraisers are often out of the office, so you need to ensure either that someone is there to answer your calls or that you have an answer machine. A mobile phone will enable you to make calls when you want and to be more accessible.

2 *Computer* A PC together with a basic software package such as Microsoft Office will help you produce high quality letters and proposals as well as storing your database of supporters and perhaps your budget and financial records. You will also need a good printer and as part of your start-up package you are likely to be offered a scanner, which can be useful for producing publicity leaflets etc.

3 *Photocopier* This will help you prepare large volumes of printed material for circulation to supporters. If you don't have access to a photocopier, try to make arrangements with your local copy shop and ask them to give you a good price.

4 *Fax* These are now quite cheap and allow for instant communication. You can get combined machines that also take care of small volumes of photocopying, or you can arrange to send and receive faxes by e-mail.

5 *E-mail and the internet* More and more information is sent by e-mail, and many funders have websites. Many PCs now come with a built in modem for instant internet access and there is a wide choice of service providers. You may want to have a second telephone line for fax and e-mail. All sorts of package deals are now available, from BT and various Internet Service Providers (ISPs).

6 *Annual reports and brochures* You have to produce an annual report by law. However, it is also an important fundraising document as many funders will want to see your report and accounts. They do not need to be expensively produced, but should be well prepared and presented. You may also need a small range of information leaflets for the public which include reply coupons to encourage a direct response. See chapter 15, section 15.3, for more on producing printed materials. Desk Top Publishing (DTP) software on your computer will help you produce simple leaflets and other printed materials rather than having to use a designer. However, beware of spending hours playing around with designs as an alternative to getting on with the hard fundraising graft!

7 *Books* Handbooks on fundraising, grants guides and technical information on tax are all very valuable. Directories of trusts and companies which list the major givers and provide information on their grants policies are essential. A CD ROM will be more expensive but will enable you to search more easily. See chapters 6 and 8 (*Resources and further information*) for suggestions. You may be able to consult directories and CD ROMs through your local CVS, RCC or public library.

8 *Cash collection facilities* You must have a bank account so you can pay in donations. If you expect to have large sums on deposit for any length of time you should have a high interest account. If you plan to do house to house or street collections you will need to have the appropriate envelopes or collecting boxes. See chapter 12 for more on this.

9 *Letterheads* Most organisations will need stationery such as letterheads, compliments slips and return envelopes. Letterheads need to include certain information (name and address, logo, legal status and charity registration number, etc.). The design of your letterhead is important; it is the first point of contact for many people. You can also spread your message through a strap-line explaining your mission or through an outright appeal.

10 *Display equipment* Fairs, exhibitions and shop windows can be a good way of gaining more interest in your work. You will need attractive equipment and good display material.

Setting up an office can be expensive. Some of the equipment you need you may be able to borrow from friendly organisations or supporters; others you might get cheap or secondhand. You can also try to get equipment donated (local companies often have surplus equipment or furniture), or ask local suppliers for a heavy discount. You could also buy through the NCVO discount scheme, if you are a member.

You might want to prepare a shopping list of your needs and present it to a major funder as an investment package. It is in their interests to get you set up as a fundraiser so as to reduce your dependency upon them.

Who should do the fundraising?

There are several options to consider.

1 The management committee

These people are legally responsible for ensuring that the organisation has sufficient funds to carry out its work and doesn't become insolvent. They should ensure that the fundraising is done effectively and on time, although they don't have to do it themselves. In smaller organisations, it is often the committee members who do most of the fundraising.

2 The chairperson

The chairperson occupies a special position of leadership. Part of the responsibility may be to deal with major donors, along with the director, and to attend meetings with foundations and businesses. In very small organisations, the chairperson may have to do all or most of the fundraising work.

3 A fundraising committee

Not all management committee members are good at fundraising, or even like doing it. So some organisations try to recruit committee members who have good fundraising skills and personal contacts. This is not always a good strategy. Any committee must include people with a range of skills, expertise, and standpoints, as it is responsible for the proper management and strategic direction of the organisation as well as ensuring that it has sufficient funds.

It might be better to form a separate fundraising or development committee. This group can be charged with overseeing the fundraising, and even undertaking much of the work, and will include some members of the management committee plus others who are interested in or valuable to the fundraising process.

4 The director

The director of the organisation is the senior staff member and is in a good position to do the fundraising – with an expert knowledge of the work being done and sufficient seniority to be an effective persuader. Fundraising can be a creative process. When dealing with donors, you will be testing out ideas and getting feedback, negotiating different forms of support and having to think creatively about turning people's goodwill into cash. The director should know how far he or she can go.

One problem is lack of time, which means that the director may not always give fundraising sufficient priority. A possible solution is to give the director administrative assistance so that the fundraising part of the job can be done well.

5 A member of staff

Larger organisations, or those where fundraising is given a high priority, may create a specific post of fundraiser. This should ensure that someone with the time and skill to do the job properly is responsible for fundraising.

However, all too often organisations appoint a fundraiser, and tell them to get on with the job, and then a couple of years later find that nothing has been achieved. If you decide to delegate the job of fundraising, both the director and the management committee need to keep control of the process – setting goals, monitoring progress, providing active support where needed and giving encouragement. It is also crucial to appoint someone who is capable of doing the job.

6 A volunteer

Another option is to find a part time (or even a full time) volunteer to do the fundraising or set up a fundraising group. Someone recently retired might find this an exciting challenge.

Volunteers are more often given responsibility for just one aspect of the fundraising, such as organising a fundraising reception or a gala film evening. This means that some of the fundraising work and responsibility can be handed over to someone else, but again you need to set targets and hold the volunteer accountable for their performance.

7 A fundraising consultant

Fundraising consultants or consultancy organisations are in business to help voluntary organisations with their fundraising – for a fee. Some specialise in major appeals, some in event organising, some in direct mail campaigns, some in corporate sponsorship, and some in working with smaller organisations to help them clarify their approach to fundraising and get started. Using a consultant can be expensive, but particularly where you are developing a major initiative, their experience and knowledge can add greatly to your fundraising efforts. It is very rare that you will hand over all your fundraising work to an external consultant.

When you need a fundraiser

Not every voluntary organisation needs a paid fundraiser. Grant-funded bodies may leave the fundraising to the senior worker or to committee members. Others will simply use volunteers. However, organisational growth or particular funding needs may make a paid fundraiser the best option.

A key issue is whether you can afford to employ a fundraiser, and what effect it will have on your administrative costs. Not many organisations are lucky enough to obtain sponsorship for their fundraiser, so you will have to meet their costs from the extra income that you are able to generate. On the other hand, can you afford not to? Without a fundraiser, you may not have the capacity to raise the resources you need – as nobody else is prepared to do the work or give fundraising sufficient priority. As a rough guide, to employ a junior fundraiser full-time will cost at least £25,000 including overheads. To justify this, you will need to generate around £100,000 a year in extra revenue – although it may take some time to achieve results on this scale.

Initially it may seem that all the fundraiser is doing is raising the costs of their own salary. However, you need to take a long-term view. It takes several years to develop the full potential of the fundraising effort put in. Any fundraising appointment should be seen as part of the organisation's longer term strategy.

Recruitment of a fundraiser

Once you have decided to recruit a fundraiser, you should consider the following:

1 Objectives

What are the objectives for the fundraising post? Is it to:

- develop alternative sources of funds to replace grants which are coming to an end?
- launch an expansion programme?
- run a major capital appeal?
- develop independent and local funding?
- create a large and active membership?
- develop corporate support?
- organise high profile events which will raise awareness as well as money?

You need to be clear about your objectives. This will help you write a job description and a person specification, so that you recruit someone with the experience and ability to do a good job. The objectives must be realistic. They should recognise your need for money and the opportunities that exist to raise it, without being impossible to achieve. There is always a learning process at the start when nothing much happens other than the fundraiser getting familiar with the work of the organisation, doing background research and developing contacts. But it is also important that results begin to flow.

2 Budget

There is no point appointing a fundraiser unless you also provide a budget for equipment, operational costs and promotional activity. Without such a budget the fundraiser will be unable to do a proper job. The box gives a list of headings that you will probably need to include.

Budget headings (employing a fundraiser)

Recruitment and training

Salary, National Insurance etc.

Computer + printer

Mobile phone

Stationery, photocopying

Share of office overheads

Travel

Subscriptions to professional organisations, magazines etc.

Purchase of directories / CD ROMs etc.

Design and print of leaflets

Mailing costs

---

3 Recruitment

Once you have decided your objectives and written a job description you will need to identify someone with the right:

- experience and expertise
- personal skills and qualities to do a good job
- ethical values and commitment to the cause.

The last two of these are really important. You can gain experience and expertise, but the personal skills and ethical stance come with the candidate. (The personal skills required in a fundraiser are discussed in some detail in section 2.2.)

There is always a chance that the appointment will not work out, that you have chosen the wrong person. It is advisable to include a six-month probationary period in the contract for a newly recruited fundraiser, as for most other key staff.

Where to recruit a fundraiser

- Circulate information about the job opportunity to your staff. This job might be something that a current member of your staff team might like to do.
- Circulate information about the job opportunity to your existing supporters and volunteers. They already have some commitment to the organisation. Someone might be just the right person for the job.
- Advertise in the local newspaper, the charity press, the *Guardian* on Monday, in marketing journals, or via the Institute of Fundraising. These will reach the sorts of people you are looking for.

4 Induction

As for any other appointment, there should be a satisfactory induction process, which might include:

- meeting the management committee
- meeting senior staff
- site visits to projects to see the organisation at work and discussions with project workers
- discussing and agreeing what the organisation stands for and how it should be presented to the public
- discussing which donors the organisation is not prepared to accept support from
- reviewing existing donor support, identifying problem areas and opportunities
- agreeing the fundraising strategy and the targets for the first year, and sketching out what might be achieved over the first three years
- being introduced to any key contacts.

Management and motivation of fundraisers

Fundraising is a demanding and often a lonely job. With all the difficulties inherent in raising money and a steady flow of rejections, it is easy to get downhearted. Proper management of the fundraiser's job means:

1 Keeping in touch with the work of the organisation

The fundraiser should be in regular touch with those doing the front-line work, visiting projects, talking to project workers and beneficiaries, getting a feel for the needs and the quality of the work, the issues, approach and ethos of the organisation. This will also help increase awareness of the fundraising process and the concerns and interests of your donors.

2 Setting targets and monitoring progress

Targets should be agreed with the fundraiser rather than imposed, and progress should be regularly monitored. It may not be the fundraiser's fault if targets are not being met. They may have been over-optimistic, or one large donation may have failed to materialise.

Try to learn from mistakes. You may want to create a small fundraising advisory group who will take a particular interest in the fundraising and where the fundraiser can discuss issues or refer problems.

Keep track of the time and effort put into each fundraising initiative. You can spend a lot of time chasing after marginal or unlikely sources, and too little developing those central to your future. Fundraising events can take up a lot of time for little financial return. Time is usually your most expensive item of cost, so use it effectively.

3 Giving fundraising due importance

Fundraising must be seen to be important, and the fundraiser needs support to do a good job. Fundraising which is just delegated and forgotten about, or starved of resources, will rarely work well. The director and the management committee must have confidence in the fundraising process and the fundraiser's abilities, and provide appropriate support and encouragement.

You must also recognise and celebrate fundraising success.

4 Access to information

The fundraiser will represent the organisation and answer on its behalf in a range of situations. They need to be able to speak authoritatively to any interested parties. Therefore, any fundraiser must be kept informed of what is going on, how the organisation is doing financially and what new initiatives are in the pipeline.

5 Training and meeting other fundraisers

Fundraising courses and conferences are run all over the country. These are good places for the fundraiser to brush up on skills, share ideas and experiences, and meet and network with others doing a similar job. Fundraisers should be encouraged to find out what and how other organisations are doing, and to get hold of annual reports and other promotional material from rival organisations.

6 Free time to think

Some of the most creative fundraising comes from thinking about what you are doing, chatting to people about your ideas, meeting people and talking about your work (with no immediate intention of asking for money). The pressure to raise money means this creative time is often lost. This needs to be built into the work schedule.

Getting outside help with your fundraising

Periodically you may need help with your fundraising, whether to tackle a campaign, discuss new fundraising schemes or devise a new fundraising plan. You may just want a few words of advice, some administrative support or you might want some technical assistance. Different tasks require different skills with different costs associated with them. You must be absolutely clear about what you want, especially when you are briefing potential consultants.

Networking

When dealing with smaller problems or ones that only you can resolve, informal networks can help. The main body that can help facilitate this is the Institute of Fundraising with its 3,000 members. There is a strong culture of one fundraiser helping another despite the highly competitive nature of much fundraising today. The best way of accessing the network is to join the Institute of Fundraising. Membership gives you access to its list of members, their phone numbers and your nearest regional group.

You can also attend training courses or conferences run by the Institute of Fundraising or by the Directory of Social Change, where you will meet people in similar situations to yourself.

Fundraising consultants

Many people now work as self-employed fundraising consultants (at least 500 members of the Institute of Fundraising are consultants). Consultants will say that their costs are small compared with the returns. However they would also admit that their costs are guaranteed while the returns are not. Costs tend to range from a low of £250 a day to highs in excess of £600 plus VAT.

There are also fundraising consultancy firms. They would argue that they have a greater capacity to work for you and a wider range of skills. They are generally more expensive so it is more sensible to use them for things like advertising, capital giving, direct mail, payroll giving, design, and video or print production.

Since there are plenty of possible consultants and consultancy firms around, it is not difficult to find names. There are four main areas to look initially.

- The Institute of Fundraising members handbook, *Who's Who in Fundraising*. This lists all current members and those that are independent consultants. It also has adverts for relevant services.

- The Association of Fundraising Consultants (AFC) This group contains both independent consultants and consultancy companies. It has its own code of practice.
- The National Council for Voluntary Organisations (NCVO) also keeps a list of consultants.
- The specialist press. Consultants often write articles to raise their profile or generate business. Others simply advertise. Have a look at *ThirdSector* and *Professional Fundraising* magazines.

Working with consultants

The use of consultants could be a major issue for your donors and supporters, who may positively dislike the idea that some of their donation will go to a paid consultant. You need to think very carefully before going down this particular road.

Once you have decided to go ahead, you must produce a clear brief against which you can compare quotes from different people (consultants expect to tender for business). Once you have identified your consultant, you must agree precise terms in a clearly-written contract. The Institute of Fundraising has a useful set of guidelines for charities wishing to appoint a consultant.

If you are paying someone not directly employed by you to sign appeal letters on your behalf, to visit donors or to make phone calls to donors, the Charities Act 1992 requires them to declare their status as a professional fundraiser and how they are being paid. There must also be a written agreement in a prescribed form between the charity and the professional fundraiser. A standard agreement can be obtained from the Institute of Fundraising, or see *The Fundraiser's Guide to the Law* for a model.

Payment by results

You may be tempted to pay commission rather than a flat fee to link cost with performance. This is problematic.

- Under the Charities Act 1992, if the consultant asks for money they have to make a declaration that they will receive a part of the donation as commission, which can affect the chances of getting support (although if they simply advise on strategy or write out the letter for you to sign, no declaration needs to be made).
- The Charity Commission is not keen on commission fundraising. They feel that the charity should employ someone based on their competence to do the job and the expectation that they will succeed, and pay the consultant on this basis. But this payment could include a success fee if certain targets are achieved.
- If you have not made a financial commitment, you have less incentive to manage the consultant effectively.

- The consultant might cherry pick – get those donations you were expecting anyway, and do little more.

If you can't afford a professional fundraiser, which is a common situation for small organisations, you could:

- look for sponsorship to cover the costs of the consultancy – show it as a cost-effective investment in the future of your organisation;
- seek a grant for an initial feasibility study – the Charities Aid Foundation makes grants for this;
- find someone to do the work for nothing – a long shot!
- do the work yourselves, but gather around you people with the required expertise to advise you.

How to select an adviser

Whoever you decide to choose, there are a number of steps to go through.

1 Be absolutely sure of the help you need. Is it just to devise the strategy, or do you need additional help with its implementation? Do you need someone to do a specific task done, or just advice?

2 Write a good brief and clear job description covering what needs to be done, the timetable, and the specific objectives.

3 Have a selection of people or companies to choose from – ensuring that you choose the best.

4 Agree the basis of payment. Is this acceptable? What control over success and failure will you retain? How will expenses be charged? How much notice is required to terminate the arrangement if you are dissatisfied?

5 Obtain and follow up references. If you do not get good – or indeed any – references, proceed only with the greatest caution.

Resources and further information

See also general lists at the end of the book.

Organisations

AFC (Association of Fundraising
  Consultants)
Harpenden
The Grove
Herts
AL5 1AH
www.afc.org.uk
Tel. 01582 762446
Fax 01582 461489

Institute of Fundraising
Central Office
Market Towers
1 Nine Elms Lane
London SW8 5NQ
www.institute-of-fundraising.org.uk
Tel. 020 7627 3436

NCVO (National Council of Voluntary Organisations)
www.ncvo.buy.co.uk is a website produced for the voluntary sector to enable purchasing over the internet at specially negotiated rates.

NCVO offers its members a growing range of discounts on products and services. For information, contact:
Business Development Manager
Tel. 020 7520 243
e-mail deals@ncvo-vol.org.uk

Publications

The following publications are available from the Directory of Social Change. Prices were correct at the time of writing, but may be subject to change.

The Fundraiser's Guide to the Law, Bates, Wells & Braithwaite and Centre for Voluntary Sector Development, DSC 2000, £16.95

Other publications

Fundraising for Social Change 3rd edition, Kim Klein, Chardon Press 1996, $25
Chardon Press
PO Box 11607
Berkeley
CA 94712
USA
e-mail chardon@aol.com

Professional Fundraising, subscription £45 (individuals), £60 (charities)
TM & D Press
41 North Road
London N7 9DP
www.professionalfundraising.co.uk
e-mail info@tmdpress.com
Tel. 020 7700 3479
Fax 020 7700 2049

ThirdSector, published 24 times a year, subscription £44
Lime Wharf
Vyner Street
London E2 9DJ
Tel. 020 8709 9050

DEVELOPING A FUNDRAISING STRATEGY

This chapter will help you produce a strategic plan for your fundraising. It covers the preliminary stages of analysing your position and gathering information, as well as the follow-up work of monitoring and measuring your results.

Details of organisations and publications referred to in this chapter are on p.56 .

3.1 Planning your approach

Your strategy is the backbone of your fundraising. Getting it right requires a good deal of attention at an early stage, and should involve people both inside and outside your organisation, especially if you have major fundraising ambitions.

Headings for a fundraising strategy paper

Review of the current position
- Current strengths and weaknesses
- Past fundraising experience
- Existing fundraising strengths and resources

Projection of fundraising needs

Overall funding strategy

Proposed new sources of income

Suggested methods to meet fundraising targets

Resources needed to do this

Strategy is about organising your ideas to produce a viable plan to take you forward beyond this year. If you just need £250 for equipment, all you need is a couple of successful coffee mornings or a few people taking part in a sponsored event. This doesn't really require a strategic plan. However, if you have a wider hopes or major existing commitments to fund, you will need to spend more time and be more creative in developing your fundraising strategy.

Your strategy will indicate where you want to get to (in a period of, say, five years) and how you aim to get there. It is an integral part of your organisation's business plan. Obviously, not everything will go according to plan and you will want to incorporate new ideas as you go along. You should therefore aim to update your plan every year, and produce a completely revised strategy every two or three years.

Outlining the needs

The starting point for any fundraising strategy is to define the needs of the organisation. This can be done at three levels.

1 Just to keep going

How much money do you need to continue at your current scale of operation? How much is already assured, and how much do you need to raise to meet spending requirements? These calculations usually take the form of annual and rolling budgets for the short and medium term (up to three or even five years ahead).

2 To expand to meet growing need

Most organisations believe that they are only scratching at the surface of the problem. If they had more resources, they could do much more to meet the need. Furthermore, the need may be growing or the problem getting worse. Ask yourselves the following questions:

- What is the current level of unmet need?
- What will happen if nothing is done?
- How are the needs growing and what changes do you foresee over the next few years?
- What should you be doing to respond to the challenges of the future?
- Who else is doing something to meet the needs?
- How does your plan fit in with what others are doing?
- Is your idea an effective way of addressing the needs given the limited resources that are likely to be available?
- Could or should you be providing solutions to the problem rather than simply addressing the needs?
- Are there ways of collaborating with others which could combine efforts and resources for greater impact?

Future plans should be discussed and developed. Is it just a question of expanding what you are doing? Or will you be developing new mechanisms for addressing the problem? If the need is not significant and your role not clear, then developing a good fundraising case can become extremely difficult.

3 The future development of the organisation's work

Organisations do not stay still. There is often a momentum to develop, and even to expand. Success with one project gives an organisation confidence; it also throws up new ideas and brings greater credibility with potential funders and partners.

What developments do you have planned? What new services or projects will you want to run? Will you want to export your work into other regions? Will you want to enter into major collaborations with funding partners to extend your work? Will you want to enter into partnerships with government authorities, working with them on a much wider scale to address the problem?

If you are a community development organisation, what about your relationship with the people you are helping? Are you empowering people to help themselves? If so, what happens to you when local people have the structures and skills to organise their own development? Will you extend and develop your work and maintain your development role? Or will you develop a withdrawal or exit strategy?

The future of your organisation starts with what you want to do. It is up to the chief executive to plan this, with input from other senior staff, from the fundraiser (if there is one in post) and from the organisation at large. Then it is up to whoever is doing the fundraising to get the resources to put the plans into action.

However, it is vital that you do not do things simply because you can get the money. You must be led by the work that you want to do, the needs that you want to meet, rather than the money that you think you can raise. If you are not, you will soon find that the organisation will lose its sense of direction and will be in serious danger of simply fizzling out.

Different approaches to fundraising strategy

Besides funding the work, you will also need to fund the organisation and its future. There are several factors to consider.

1 Capital developments

Capital developments, such as acquiring new buildings or IT systems, can have an impact on future fundraising needs in four ways. On the plus side:

- they can reduce operating costs
- they can generate income from fees and charges (for example from letting out space)
- they can generate a greater capacity to fundraise (for example when organising a major appeal, you will be building a mailing list of important contacts which you can approach later on for further support).

On the minus side:

- they may increase your revenue costs if they require extra people to run them.

2 Endowment

Many organisations want to develop an endowment – that is, a capital reserve which can be invested to produce a regular income for the organisa-tion. Some approach major donors for contributions to this fund; others set aside some of their income each year. They feel that this will give them greater financial security, remove some of the fundraising pressure or act as a reserve in times of unexpected difficulties. However, most trusts and com-panies prefer to fund your work directly rather than have their money tied up as an investment.

Examples of successful capital fundraising

- The Campaign for Oxford endowed several professorial chairs by raising enough money to generate the annual income needed to support a professor.
- Community Links, a community-based project in London, organised a major appeal to take over a town hall in Canning Town and turn it into a community centre. The building was seen as an asset which could continue to be exploited for community benefit.

It takes a lot of hard work to raise an endowment. Might it not be better to spend that time on exciting and successful work? This would make the organisation more attractive to funders and make future fundraising easier.

3 Reducing dependency and developing independent sources of funding

There is a fundamental difference between an organisation that receives all its money from one source, and an organisation which receives money from several or many sources, each contributing towards the total requirement. Over-reliance on one source can give the donor too much power over what the organisation should be doing and where it should be going. It creates a risk of failure – that the organisation will not be able to survive if the grant is cut back or withdrawn.

You need to decide whether your organisation's funding base is too narrow, and, if it is, how you can broaden it. You will need to think about all the possible sources of income, and decide which are the most sensible for your organisation to develop.

On the other hand, although it is good to have a broad base of support, there is a danger of taking this principle too far and having so many small-scale donors that all your fundraising energies go into servicing them without increasing the financial return.

4 Developing a membership and a supporter base

A strong membership or supporter base helps create financial independence by:

- creating a constituency of support (the numbers of people who support you add to your credibility as an organisation and give you lobbying power);
- building a local base for your organisation (your relationship with your local community will be different if the funding is drawn from it rather than obtained externally);
- creating opportunities for further fundraising. Each donor can be asked to give regularly and more generously; to recruit other donors; to volunteer their time and skills; to donate items of equipment, or even to leave a legacy. The more people who support you, the greater your fundraising opportunities.

Some key concepts

Before deciding who to approach there are some more general issues to think through.

Fundraising costs – an ideal ratio?

Research carried out by the Directory of Social Change in 1999 showed an enormous variation in fundraising costs amongst the major fundraising charities, from over 90% of income raised to less than 10%. While there may be good reasons behind this, and differences in reporting methods mean that it is not always possible to compare like with like, there is no doubt that to the public at large, fundraising costs matter. The public perception of fundraising costs is, possibly wrongly, 'the lower the better', but the key to maintaining public confidence in your organisation is absolute honesty and transparency. Be prepared to explain openly and fully the good reasons for your costs and your donors are more likely to stay with you.

- *Be cost conscious*. You need monitor carefully the money you spend. You should ask supporters only for what is strictly necessary, and use as much as possible on the work of the organisation. Keeping costs down is a factor in this.
- *Someone has to pay*. Many charities exist to provide a service to beneficiaries that is free or highly subsidised. This means that the amount raised determines the volume of work that can be undertaken. However, you may be able to charge for your services. You need to decide what is appropriate for you and your users. Alternatively, in the current contract culture, statutory bodies may be able to pay for the services you deliver. Either way, you must cost what you do carefully and accurately. Someone has to pay for it – your funders, your sponsors, your donors or your users.
- *Avoid risks*. The cash used for fundraising is ultimately intended for the beneficiaries of the charity. If it is used to generate extra funds for the charity, then fair enough. But you can't just squander it on a high risk venture. Fundraisers must minimise risk. You might need to pilot or test new fundraising ideas; you should identify the worst case scenario for a new fundraising event and insure against it (and even scrap it when it looks set to fail).
- *The long-term approach*. You can simply concentrate on getting cash now, or you can devote some of your fundraising resources to ensuring the longer-term viability of your organisation. For example, committed giving by individuals and appeals for legacies have high costs in the short-term, but their long-term value usually far outweighs that of casual giving.
- *The multiplier approach*. A good way to maximise fundraising results is to cascade. A sponsored run can bring your organisation to the attention of large numbers of people, since every runner will sign up sponsors, some of whom may subsequently become interested in the work of your organisation rather than in simply sponsoring their friend. The cascade effect can multiply the number of people supporting you and the amount you can raise.
- *Sustainability*. In the ideal world your organisation would be structured so as to minimise the need for permanent fundraising. Even if this is a mere pipe dream for you, there are a number of ways of making yourself more sustainable and therefore more secure:
  - develop a range of income generating activities
  - develop partnerships with larger bodies capable of giving larger sums of money – government for example
  - raise an endowment fund
  - recruit volunteers and get support donated in kind
  - develop income sources that continue over many years, such as membership

– only organise events that are repeatable, so that if they work, they can be done again and even better next time.

- *Time*. A key element within the strategy is to be realistic about how long things take. To go from £0 to £100,000 a year from grant-making trusts may require years of patient fundraising effort. To land your first major company sponsorship requires professionalism and good relationships that you may not yet have. Be realistic about how long things will take.

3.2 Analysing your position

Analysing your current position is a key starting point for any strategy. Not only will it help you answer some of the difficult questions you are often asked by funders, it will also help you see your work in new ways and to better understand your strengths and weaknesses. The first step is to look at the work which you are seeking to fund.

- What is the need that your work is addressing?
- Who are the ultimate beneficiaries of your work?
- What difference to the beneficiaries does your intervention make?
- Are there competing agencies, and how does their work fit with yours?
- What is distinctive about your approach?
- Is the need expected to increase or change over the next few years and how will you respond to this?
- What are your medium-term plans?
- Is the need you are addressing an on-going social need or is it occasional, seasonal or one off?

Projection of financial need

The next step is to make a financial projection of the resources you will need to undertake your planned programme of work over the medium term. This must take in all planned expenditure and all probable income. It should show you two things: the funding gap that needs to be met, and possible fall-back options if funding is not received. This is best illustrated by the example set out in the box overleaf.

Example of a funding projection for a small organisation

Source of income	Current year	Next year	2 years' time	3 years' time
Current local authority grant	10,000	10,000	5,000	5,000
Grant from charitable trust	2,500	2,500	nil	nil
Membership subscriptions	250	250	250	250
Total committed income	**12,750**	**12,750**	**5,250**	**5,250**
Reserve at start of year	500	2,050	2,050	1,550
Current operational costs	10,000	12,500	15,000	15,000
New project costs	1,200	3,500	5,000	5,000
Projected fundraising target	**nil**	**3,250**	**14,750**	**14,250**

The example shows that your funding position for the current year is good, and that you have a small target to meet next year which is a realistic goal for your fundraising. However in two years' time, as your major grants run out, you will need to find alternative funding, or develop new ideas for the organisation.

Analysis of your environment

There are various ways in which you can explore your fundraising environment. These exercises are better done with a small group of people and a brainstorming approach.

1 SWOT analysis

The first, and most commonly used tool available is a SWOT analysis. This involves trying to identify your organisation's:

Strengths
Weaknesses
Opportunities
Threats

Strengths and weaknesses are internal to your organisation – those things that you know to be true which either give you an advantage or hold you back. Opportunities and threats relate to the external world and how, both now and in future, they will impact on your work and funding opportunities.

An example of a SWOT analysis for a small organisation

	Positive	Negative
Internal factors	*Strengths* Established team Experienced management Good relations with local authority Good reputation	*Weaknesses* Limited contact with funders Existing grants running out No evaluation undertaken
External factors	*Opportunities* Public attention on your issue New company in the area	*Threats* Change in benefit regulations Local agency expanding aggressively

2 PEST analysis

To explore the external factors in more detail, a PEST (sometimes also known as STEP) analysis can be useful. It is similar to a SWOT analysis (see above), although you will be looking at the trends in society which are going to affect your fundraising and your work generally. This is done under the headings:

Political
Economic
Social
Technological

You are looking at the future and focusing on external changes which may affect you. For example:

- *Political*: what will a second term of New Labour mean for voluntary organisations? What will the continuing contracting out of public services mean?
- *Economic*: what effect will the next budget have on fundraising? How will increased public spending impact on voluntary organisations?
- *Social*: what will be the impact of the growth in the elderly population? What will be the results of the continuing fragmentation of the family?
- *Technological*: what does the internet mean for you and your users?

These and other factors will affect your organisation and your fundraising. There may be little you can do about some, but bear them all in mind as you develop your fundraising strategy.

PEST Analysis of a small employment charity for people with disabilities

Political: full implementation of the DDA may bring advantages

Economic: improvements in economy will bring more work opportunities

Social: car based society will continue to disadvantage those on low incomes and with mobility problems

Technological: it will be possible to do more work at home

If these are the main factors that were identified, you then have to consider what impact they will have.

---

3 Stakeholder analysis

Stakeholder analysis looks at all those groups who have an interest in your organisation and in its funding. For example, a refugee service concluded that it had a number of key stakeholders. They included:

- the local authority, who would otherwise have to provide support to refugee families;
- members of the organisation, who have joined because they feel strongly about the issues being tackled;
- refugee community organisations, who already provide direct support to new refugees;
- second generation refugees, who have stayed on in Britain and who wish to put something back to help other refugees.

This exercise should help you identify both who has a particular interest in supporting your work and why.

4 Audit of your existing fundraising

Before you set off, you need to know where you are starting from. Even the smallest and newest organisation will have some fundraising experience (or look at how similar groups got going). You need to know where you are currently getting funds from, where you might get more and whether you are especially vulnerable to any particular source disappearing or being cut back. Also, note any problems you have experienced with each of the sources and what any trends highlighted by this analysis may be revealing.

Listing your fundraising sources

Source of funds	Funds received			% of total
	previous year	last year	this year	
Central government				
Europe				
Local government				
Trusts				
Companies				
Membership				
Individual donations				
Fundraising events				
Legacies				
Charges and fees				

You can also include volunteer inputs and support in kind, if you wish. This gives a better picture of the total resources you are deploying.

5 Competitor analysis

You can glean a good deal of information from an intelligent look at your collaborators and competitors. The successful ones may have tried already to develop some of the fundraising sources you are considering and failed; or they may be succeeding with a source or technique that you have not yet considered.

It is pretty easy to find out where other organisations get their money from – read their annual report and accounts. It may be harder to find out about their fundraising methods. Try reading the trade press, talking with your colleagues in other organisations and asking them how they are doing. Or phone them and enquire about making a donation and see what happens.

Assessing the opportunities

It is always worth comparing your current funding with what else is on offer. These include:

- a grant from a central or regional government department
- a grant from a non-governmental agency (such as the Arts Council)
- a grant from a local authority or health authority
- a contract or service level agreement with one of the above to deliver a specified service
- a contract with another body (perhaps a commercial organisation or another voluntary agency) to deliver a service
- fees and charges from users

- support from individuals through membership or donations, and legacy income
- support from individuals raised through collections, fundraising events, entertainments or other fundraising activities
- grants from trusts, the National Lottery and other independent grant-making bodies
- support from companies (cash, kind, sponsorship, facilities, skills, secondments)
- support from individuals who donate their time as volunteers
- investment income and interest.

These are the main types of funding that are available. They are examined in more detail in Part 2 of this book. Not all will be appropriate to your organisation. You will need to select those that are right for your organisation's needs, and where you feel that you have the greatest chances of success. Here are some of the factors to take into account.

- *Past experience.* The results of your fundraising so far provide a good indication of both what to do and what not to do. Things that have gone well can be developed to do even better. Donors that have supported you can be encouraged to continue their support, perhaps at a higher level. New donors can be brought in to match the support you have got from existing donors. Invest effort and resources to develop those areas of fundraising that already appear to work for you.
- *Scale of need.* If you need to raise substantial funds, these can be raised either in large grants from a few sources, or in smaller donations from a large number of donors. You need to approach those fundraising sources that are capable of making a realistic contribution to your overall need.
- *The attractiveness of the cause.* Some causes seem able to sell themselves. People working with cuddly animals or children's cancer funds have causes that are extremely compelling, so fundraising seems much easier. An overview of which causes the public gives to appears on page 62. If your cause is not a popular one, you will have to work that much harder to make it seem important, to persuade donors to support it.
- *The style of your work.* Are you radical or conservative? Young or old? Innovative or steady? Every organisation will be able to identify institutions and individuals that share its vision and outlook. Equally there will be those that don't, and these will be much less likely to give their support.
- *The resources and skills available to you.* Do you have the people to mount a collection, the contacts to develop a big gift campaign, or the organisational ability to run a major event? It is always best to do what you are good at.

- *Your natural constituency of support.* Is this government? Trusts? Individuals? Who has a stake in the problem or need you are addressing? Can you get them to share in its solution by becoming an investor in your work?
- *The type of organisation you want to be.* A membership organisation is very different from one funded by government; a fundraising organisation is different from one that relies on the sale of its services. Your fundraising provides the money to enable you to do what you want to do. Your fundraising strategy will help you become the sort of organisation you want to be.
- *Short term and long term.* Some sources are essentially short term, whilst others can develop into long-term relationships and partnerships. If you are there for the long term, you will need long term sources of income. You will want to turn supporters into regular supporters, to organise a successful fundraising event annually and make it even better each year.

Assessing possible funding sources

Source	Past experience	Competitors' experience	Relevance to cause	Resources needed	Rating
Central government					
Local government					
Trusts					
Companies					
Big givers					
Members and supporters					
Events					

Clarifying the constraints

There will be limits on your fundraising, some stemming from the nature of your organisation, some which are internally generated, and others which are externally imposed. Many touch on areas which may also be your key opportunities.

- *Geography.* An important constraint is the geographical remit of your organisation. Some sources only give to organisations with a national focus; others only give locally. Some companies may give nationally through head office, but make smaller local grants through local plants or branches. Local people are concerned about their own local communities. However, if what you are doing locally is particularly innovative or interesting, it may catch the interest of national funders, both because they like being associated with excellence and because the project may provide answers to similar problems in other areas.

- *Appropriateness*. Some sources are inappropriate because what the donor represents is the complete opposite of what the charity stands for. The British Heart Foundation will take sponsorship from margarine producers but not butter producers; cancer charities will not accept support from tobacco companies. If they did so, they would create bad PR for themselves and problems with their other donors by endorsing a product which causes the problem. There may be other reasons for refusing a grant. For example, a campaigning organisation might not wish to be seen in the pocket of a vested interest or the government; and it might gain strength in its campaigning by being seen to be supported by a large membership. It is difficult to draw up a definitive set of rules on where you can and can't fundraise. But it is important to discuss and try to agree a policy on what you are not prepared to accept before you set about asking, rather than creating problems for yourself afterwards.

- *Resources*. The resources available to you determine what you can and can't do. If you are planning a public collection, do you have or can you get sufficient people to do it? Money is another key resource. Much fundraising involves investing now to achieve a result later. Some fundraising, such as a direct mail, an advertising campaign or even a large building appeal, may require a substantial immediate expenditure. Anyone soliciting legacies is unlikely to see their efforts rewarded for several years. You need to know how much your fundraising is going to cost and when the results will come in, and then decide if you can afford to do it. Some fundraisers see these constraints as a challenge – they will find the people or the money they need somehow!

- *Contacts*. Your contacts can lead you to sources of money. If you have a good contact in the business world, they can ask other business people in their networks for money. If you have celebrities waiting to get involved, you might use them as an anchor in a fundraising event. If you don't have good contacts think how you can develop better ones as a major resource for your fundraising.

- *What other organisations are doing*. Not many organisations can expect to get away with being just imitators of others. You need to be – and be seen to be – distinctive.

3.3 Gathering information

Too often charities assume that they know what their supporters and potential supporters think, what they are interested in and what they need to know about the charity. This is dangerous. You need to check your assumptions and find out what your supporters really think about your organisation and its activities. The more you can understand your donors and potential donors, the more you will be able to communicate effectively with them and to motivate them to give.

There are various types of research that you can carry out, and for a wide variety of purposes. In this section we look at researching your own donor base, finding out what the public thinks of you, and using research to seek out new supporters.

Donor research

Whatever the size of your organisation you want to know who your supporters are and what they think of you. You depend on their time or money to carry out your work. If they are becoming disenchanted with what you are doing or can no longer meet your expectations, you have a problem which you will need to address.

Knowing who your supporters are will also help you identify other sorts of people you might try to recruit as new supporters – and it could indicate categories of people who you have not yet been able to reach out to and enlist.

You should always chat informally to your supporters at events and open days, or indeed whenever you come into contact with them. This shows that you are interested in them and will help you find out what they are thinking.

You may want to do more formal research, such as a postal survey. If you have a mailing list or can enclose the questionnaire with a newsletter, this is relatively easy and cheap to do.

Obviously you want to find out your supporters' attitude to your organisation and its work. However, you may also want to get information which will help you communicate more effectively with them (this is easier to do if you know who they are) and get ideas on where else you might look to recruit people with a similar profile. So, you might also want to ask about their:

- age
- sex
- marital status
- number of children
- income band
- working status
- job
- newspaper readership
- voting habits

- religious membership
- trade union and other membership
- giving methods to the organisation
- frequency of giving
- preferred areas of support
- support for other charities
- volunteering (whether and how much time they give)
- legacy intentions (whether they have made a will and if it contains a charitable bequest).

These simple questions and others you might want to ask that relate more particularly to your work can form the bases of the questionnaire you send out. But be careful when interpreting the results. Is the information from those who responded representative of the whole (which includes those that didn't respond)? Responders are likely to be more keenly interested than the average supporter. Also, poor survey technique can lead to misleading results. For example, if your questionnaire is too long, only those who have the time and interest will respond, so your results could be biased in favour of older people or those not in full-time employment.

Surveying your own supporters is not expensive. You can easily put some effort into doing it yourself, especially if you pay attention to the question composition and getting the replies back. You need to make the survey seem important and it needs to be easy to respond to. Enclosing a reply paid envelope and offering an incentive to those responding, such as a free entry into a prize draw will both lift the response rate.

Public opinion research

Finding out what the public at large thinks is more difficult and expensive than a supporter survey. For some organisations it can be essential – for example, if you are trying to change the government's environmental policy, evidence of strong public feeling will add weight to your argument.

Postal surveys are not usually effective for this. A full public opinion survey using a specialist research company will be expensive – so you will need to assess whether the cost is worth it. Omnibus research may be appropriate: this is where a research company puts together questions from several organisations and sends interviewers out to ask all the questions in one survey. If you just want to know a few things, and the questions can be answered yes or no, this can be relatively cheap and quick. If you want to know how the public are likely to react to a proposed appeal or restyle of your organisation, then focus groups will be better (see below).

Interviews

Interviews take time, require professionals and are expensive. However, the findings can be invaluable. You can find out how you are seen, how you compare to others in the same field, who are prospective supporters, and what their attitudes are to the cause and work being done. The questionnaire will be drawn up for you and you should get well-balanced responses and reliable results (including the differences between supporters and non-supporters). If you depend upon high levels of current public awareness of your cause for your success, this type of research will tell you how well you are doing.

Focus groups

Focus groups are useful when you want to explore key issues (for example, new fundraising materials, an advertising strategy, a new name, or attitudes to important issues). It works by getting a number of people together for a period of discussion. It needs an experienced facilitator to help steer the conversation and record the results. The groups are formed in different locations to give balance and compare different types of supporter and public. Reports and transcripts are made available to the client.

Sources of data

There are various good sources of information. The National Archive or the public library is always a good starting point, as is the internet. Reports from the census will contain a wide range of research at a national and local level. Market research companies produce interesting reports about people's behaviour and buying habits (these may be available in business libraries). Your local reference library or university social studies department should be able to tell you about any local research that has been carried out and help you find out about relevant academic research. This information can be particularly important in highlighting the importance of social problems and issues.

Statistics

Not all research data is reliable. Proper samples are needed to get meaningful results. Samples can suffer from several forms of bias. One is associated with the nature of the sampling process. For example, does it cover all the areas of the country? Does it cover all age and income groups? Is the sample self-selecting? Have you only selected those who answered?

Equally important is sample size. There are statistical formulae to determine the sample size required to get a reliable conclusion 95% of the time. If you are doing your own survey, you might be able to find a university lecturer or graduate to help you as a volunteer to design your sampling procedures.

3.4 Developing a fundraising plan

Depending upon the choice of sources of funds, you will already have reduced the many options open to you for fundraising methods. The next stage of the process involves setting down the most plausible methods that will be available. Make a detailed list of sources (direct mail to individuals, events, legacies, applications to trusts, company sponsorship etc.). Then for each source, try to identify what you will need in the way of staff, volunteers, money, equipment, important contacts or specialist advice.

Investment

Most fundraising techniques require investment. For example, appeals to charitable trusts require a good deal of time to research the proposal, to write it up, to get others' views on it and to get the presentation right; you will also have to spend equivalent time identifying suitable trusts to approach and tailoring the application to each. Other fundraising may require you to print leaflets, buy collecting boxes or spend money before you get anything back. Before proceeding, you need to see whether you have the budget to do what you need – money to pay for what you will need to purchase, and the time you will need to put in. The box gives some approximate start-up costs for different methods. All are dependent upon the scale at which you do them and whether you are lavish or frugal in your purchasing.

Start up costs for successful fundraising methods

The ratio of fundraising start up costs to potential income is estimated as shown below.

1–5%	5–15%	15–40%
Donor mailings	House to house	Temporary shops
Appeals to trusts	Lotteries	Events
Payroll giving	Collection boxes	Radio/TV appeals

40–70%	70–100%	100%+
Permanent shops	Advertising	Cold mailing

Just as you need to invest in getting the fundraising going, so it will take time before you see the income. You need to organise collecting boxes and leaflets well before you can carry out a collection. Some charitable trusts, especially the smaller ones, do not meet more than quarterly, so it could be up to six months from the time you post the application to the time you hear whether you have succeeded.

Planning times for fundraising	
1 month	Advertising for support, postal appeals
2–6 months	Lotteries, events, appeals to trusts and companies, radio/TV appeals, National Lottery applications, house to house collections, Gift Aid campaigns
6–12 months	Government grants, payroll giving
1 year +	Legacies, Christmas cards

3.5 Measurement and control of fundraising

Your fundraising strategy is not cast in stone – even though you may feel that after all the effort in creating it, you never want to see the document again! It will need periodic updating to take account of changes both inside and outside your organisation.

The first step with a new or revised strategy must be to ensure that all the staff understand and agree with it. It will not be possible for everyone to be involved in producing the strategy document, so before you start work on it or before you present it to your committee, make sure that the issues are widely discussed. This process of consultation will help everyone feel more committed to the outcome.

You need to review your strategy periodically. This does not mean going through the whole analysis each year. However, you will learn more about what works and what does not, and there may be changes in the environment which challenge your basic assumptions. Aim to review that strategy each year and completely rewrite it every three to five years.

Monitoring strategy

Without a strategy and a detailed plan, it is hard to monitor how you are getting on. Monitoring is important:

- to check your overall returns
- to compare the effectiveness of different aspects of your fundraising
- to justify the level of investment that the charity is making
- to help assess the fundraiser's performance.

You will need to keep a particularly close eye on:

- costs incurred by each fundraising method
- cash received
- pledges of future support received
- offers of help and support in kind received.

Monitoring is easier in a small organisation but can be surprisingly difficult in many larger charities because their financial systems are not usually designed for the convenience of fundraisers. They usually outline total costs and the total income, rather than the results of each separate fundraising method so that it is not easy to compare the effectiveness of the different methods. A sample monitoring form is shown below.

Monthly monitoring sheet

Appeal type	Income this year	Income budget	Income this month	Direct costs	Profit ratio
Collections					
Postal appeal					
Sponsored event					
General income					
Office costs					
Total					

Detailed measurement of fundraising

You can measure the effectiveness of your fundraising in a number of ways, although not all measures are appropriate to all situations. The most common measures are the cost ratio and the profit.

The cost ratio is calculated by taking the direct income generated and dividing it by the total costs that can be attributed to that activity. This is then expressed as a ratio (for example, 5:1) or a percentage (for example, 20%). The main problem is that it does not tell you how much you have raised.

For example, you may discover that your public speaking to a wide range of local groups and appealing for support raised £2,380 and cost only £340 (a ratio of 7:1 or 14%). On the other hand, you raised £17,200 from trusts at an estimated cost of £6,500 (a ratio of 2.6:1 or 38%), so looks less successful. This is quite misleading.

1 You may have exhausted all the local speaking possibilities and so you cannot repeat your success, even if this has been your most cost-effective method of fundraising.

2 Although this was your most cost-effective method, it only generated £2,010, whereas you have generated £10,700 in grants from trusts.

The cost ratio is an important management tool for controlling costs, but on its own it is not a sufficient measure of fundraising success. There are other measures which you can use.

If you are using the phone to recruit collectors for your flag day or house to house collections, you need to know how efficient your phoning is. The first measure is the response rate to your request (divide the number of successes by the total number approached). This measure can similarly be used in postal appeals and payroll giving campaigns.

But knowing how many people will respond is not enough. You also need to know how they respond and how much have they given. It may be good to get 10 people in 100 saying yes; but if they only give £1 each, you will still be disappointed. The average donation is the measure of how much they give. You can then try to increase both the response rate and the average donation. For example, when you ask a supporter to renew their membership, why not suggest that they increase the level of their giving. When organising a sponsored event, you can ask people to sponsor by the minute rather than by the hour, and they are then likely to give more. If you ask a supporter to pay monthly contributions, you will receive more than if you ask for quarterly or annual contributions.

Another measure is the yield. This is the income received divided by the number of people approached. Thus, if you mail 1,000 people and receive £550 in donations, the yield would be 55p per donor mailed.

Finally you will need to have some way of measuring the impact of long-term or open-ended commitments. Your fundraising commitments have gained you a donor. You can measure the donation they have made. But many of them will go on to give further support, and the costs of getting this further support will be much lower than the costs of getting the first donation. A very few may even go on to make a major gift or leave you a legacy. This is valuable to you.

So another measure you can use is lifetime value. This is a useful measure because it helps you justify a higher level of initial expenditure on promotion and fundraising. For example, you mail 1,000 people and get 20 responses and a total of £550 in income. You predict that those 20 people on average will each make two further donations of the same amount. The total income you expect to receive from these donors is £1,650. The total cost is the cost of the initial mailing to 1,000 people plus the additional cost of further mailings to your 20 new supporters. From this you can calculate the lifetime value of these 20 donors and demonstrate that the costs of acquiring them were very reasonable.

Selecting appropriate measures to assess your fundraising is extremely important. It enables you to manage the process better – control costs and try to generate more income and more supporters, and to retain these supporters for longer periods. It enables you to see what works and what doesn't, to develop new and better fundraising techniques and to test out new ideas. It is important that you succeed in generating the money you have committed to raise and that you do this within budget. It is also important that you continue to improve your fundraising skills. The rest of this book is designed to help you do so.

Resources and further information

See also general lists at the end of the book.

Organisations

Office of National Statistics
(for census data)
Segensworth Road
Titchfield
Hampshire PO15 5RR
www.census.ac.uk
Tel. 01329 813800

Publications

The following publications are available from the Directory of Social Change. Prices were correct at the time of writing, but may be subject to change.

The Complete Guide to Business and Strategic Planning 2nd edition, Alan Lawrie, DSC 2001, £12.50

Other publications
Social trends
Regional trends

These and other Stationery Office publications can be ordered from:
Stationery Office Publications Centre
PO Box 276
London SW8 5DT
Tel. 020 7873 9090 (orders)
020 7873 0011 (enquiries)

PART
two

SOURCES OF FUNDS

4 INDIVIDUAL DONORS

Individuals are by far the biggest givers to charity: the top 500 fundraising charities received some £2.8 billion in voluntary income in 1998–99, much of which was donated by the general public. The methods used to fundraise from individuals are far more varied and complex than those used to obtain funds from companies, trusts or government.

This section covers how and why individuals give. In Part 3 you will find some of the techniques that can be used to encourage them to support voluntary organisations.

Details of organisations and publications referred to in this chapter are on p. 95.

4.1 About individual donors

Every potential individual donor to an organisation has their own character-istics, motivations and preferred way of giving. You, as fundraiser, must be clear about which individuals you want to approach for a particular type of gift, and how you plan to attract the support of that group of people.

Potential donors to your organisation, excluding those who have already supported you, could include:

- those with personal experience of your cause as well as those with none. For example, a parent of a disabled child will have a different perspective on disability than a member of the public but both may be just as inclined to give;
- young and older people. People may have different interests at different stages in their lives. Over recent years young people have shown a partic-ular concern with the environment, AIDS, drug-related issues and homelessness; whereas the profile of donors to medical causes (such as cancer research and treatment or a hospice) or animal charities, is usually older. However, this does not mean that older donors would not be keen to give to 'young' causes or vice versa;
- people with large incomes as well as those who are less well off;

- individuals connected with institutions; these include philanthropic groups of local business people, for example Rotary Clubs; churches and other religious groups; schools and colleges; trade unions and employers, and through them employees;
- people in specific cities or regions, as well as the UK population as a whole;
- the family and friends of existing supporters. People are more likely to give if asked by a relative or someone they know, who already has an interest in the organisation.

The clearer you can be about who your organisation's potential supporters are, the more successful you will be in reaching them. Start with your existing supporters; for example, a survey could help to find out what sort of people have supported your organisation in the past and why; or if you have a database of your supporters, you could start your analysis there.

Why people give

As mentioned in chapter 2, people support organisations for many different reasons. However, the more your fundraising message ties in with an individual's personal motivation the more successful that approach will be.

The following are some of the reasons why people give to charity.

- *Concern* is a strong motivator for many donors. They may be worried about the environment, horrified at the sexual harassment of children or want to improve the plight of starving refugees. Making a donation provides them with an opportunity to do something positive for a cause they believe in.
- *Duty* is another strong motivator, particularly for older donors. Many religions promote the concept of charity, with some recommending that their members allocate a certain share of their income each year for this.
- *Guilt* can motivate people to give. But unlike duty, if people give on impulse out of a sense of guilt, this is less likely to lead to a long-term relationship.
- *Personal experience*. People who have direct or family experience of cancer, heart disease or another illness might be especially motivated to give to this type of cause. Likewise, those with children at school will want to support their child's school or anything that helps their child's education.
- *Personal benefit*. Some people like the status or recognition that comes when their generosity is publicised. They may also like to be associated with prominent people involved with an organisation.
- *Being asked*. A primary reason for people *not* giving is that they have not been asked.

- *Peer pressure.* When people know that their friends and colleagues have given, or when these people are asking them to give, it can be hard to refuse.
- *Tax benefits* are unlikely to be a prime motivator for giving, but can be an important factor in encouraging people to make certain types of donation and to give more generously (see section 4.6 *Tax effective giving*).

It is important to understand why supporters generally, and especially why the specific individual you intend to approach, might want to give to your particular organisation. You can then tailor the message to make it more relevant and interesting to them.

You also need to understand why people don't give. They may not be interested in your organisation and what it stands for. Or they may have given to something similar recently. Other demotivating factors might be that your cause has had some bad publicity, that it appears to have high administration costs, there is a concern the money is not getting to the intended beneficiaries, or that you have not looked after your donors particularly well in the past.

Making contact

A suggested five point plan to follow when starting to approach individuals is outlined below.

1 Identify your potential supporters, those people whose background and motivations make them likely to want to support your cause.
2 Create the right message to appeal to them, which:
    – builds on their motivation;
    – starts from their understanding of the cause;
    – takes account of their natural hesitations or reasons they might have for not giving.
3 Direct that message to those people in the right way. For example, if senior business people are your audience, they can be reached by a variety of means: through the business press; Rotary Clubs, Chambers of Commerce and other associations of business people; personalised letters; or by asking business people who already support you to ask their colleagues and peers directly.
4 Make it easy for them to make their donation. Any materials that aim to get people to support your cause should include a clear means by which they can respond (whether by mail, phone, fax, e-mail or through a website), and clear contact details. To increase the likelihood of someone making a donation you could also consider the following:

- A freepost facility. A donation should not be lost because the potential donor did not have a stamp! However, almost all organisations now suggest that if a stamp is used this will save the charity money.
- A dedicated telephone line for credit card donations and enquiries, with a named person on promotional literature and at the end of the line. This makes the facility more personal and shows a concern for customer care. You might also consider a freephone facility.
- A CharityCard donation facility for Charities Aid Foundation clients, which include approximately 100,000 individual donors and about 2,000 companies. Around 2,000 charities now welcome the use of the CharityCard and are listed with their telephone numbers in a CAF directory and on the CAF website (www.allaboutgiving.org).
- A secure website, so that donations can be made online. See chapter 14, section 14.6, for more on using the internet for fundraising.

5 Support your fundraising with good PR, as people are more likely to give to your organisation if they have heard about its work and the importance of the cause. Public Relations is a key ingredient of successful fundraising, so if your organisation does not have a Press Officer, you will need to spend some time promoting the organisation and publicising its work yourself. See chapter 15, section 15.4, for more on Public Relations and dealing with the media.

Most popular causes

Figures for CAF's top 500 fundraising charities for 1997–98 showed that the most popular causes, using voluntary income as the measure, were, in descending order of priority:

international agencies
cancer charities
animal protection
children's causes
physically disabled people

'In terms of absolute amounts, AIDS attracted the least amount of support, and other important social needs such as mentally ill people, young people and hearing impaired and deaf people were very near the bottom end of the range in terms of financial support. ... If average charity incomes are compared, it can be seen that among the areas where there were the greatest increases in average voluntary income were arts and recreation, Israeli causes, young people, mentally ill people, the environment, and AIDS.'

[*Dimensions 2000*, volume 2, *CAF's top 500 fundraising charities*]

Five things to remember when fundraising from individuals

1   If possible, state clearly and precisely how much money is needed.

2   Express the need in human terms, giving graphic images of the issue being tackled and how the organisation helps people. Avoid abstract statistics describing the global importance of the problem unless a particular point needs to be emphasised. The more people can understand and identify with a problem, the more they will feel they are helping real people, and the more successful the appeal will be.

3   Ask for exactly what you want. Prospective donors will not necessarily know the size or nature of the donation expected of them. It is also useful to suggest a range of values, so the donor can choose their own level of giving. If relevant, a 'shopping list' might be used showing what different amounts can achieve; this is sometimes called a list of tangible items.

Example of a shopping list

£25 pays for the cost of fax messages in a life-saving 'Urgent Action Campaign' for a prisoner being tortured or facing death.

£50 covers the cost of printing 5,000 postcards for our supporters to send to governments demanding that they investigate a 'disappearance'.

£400 is the average cost of taking up the case of just one prisoner.

£2,500 pays for an Amnesty delegation to negotiate with a government or carry out research.

[Amnesty International UK leaflet in a mailing pack to recruit new members and donors]

---

4   Repeat the message that your organisation needs their help, and that with their support something can be achieved. Repetition reinforces the message so try to:
    - tell them what the appeal is about;
    - then tell them again in more detail;
    - finally recap what they have been told.

5   Target the appeal carefully, making the message as personal and relevant to the donor as possible. When approaching existing supporters, refer to their previous generous support and what has been achieved with it; or if approaching local people, focus on the local benefits of your organisation's work. The more targeted the message, the more successful it will be.

Building a supporter base

It is far easier to build on a base of existing supporters than to start from scratch. An existing donor is ten times more likely to support your organisation again than someone who has never given. However, if you have few or no current donors there are various methods you can use to acquire them.

1 Promotional or fundraising leaflets

Produce a leaflet giving details about your cause and illustrating your need for funds. These do not have to be expensive. Sometimes the simplest leaflet is most effective – for example, an A4 sheet, printed in two colours and folded to make a four-page leaflet with photographs of the organisation at work, and a reply coupon so potential supporters can express interest. You might also give people options for how they would like to get involved, for example by giving money, becoming a member, or volunteering their time. See chapter 15, section 15.3, for more on producing leaflets.

2 A membership or supporter scheme

Developing a scheme of this type can bring people closer to your organisation and keep them in touch with news and success stories. It can also provide a legitimate reason for communicating on a regular basis.

3 Supporter get supporter

Ask existing supporters to help by recruiting a friend, a colleague or a family member.

4 Mailing lists and reciprocal mailings

Look for another organisation, commercial or voluntary, whose customer or supporter profile is similar to yours and send an appeal to their list – for example, a health charity could send a leaflet and a short covering letter to doctors and other health workers. Once an organisation has built up its supporter base it is possible to carry out reciprocal mailings with others, where each organisation mails its supporters with the other organisation's literature. See chapter 14, section 14.2, for more on direct mail.

5 Local newspaper, radio and TV coverage

A paper, radio or TV station might be interested in running a feature about a local charity. To make this opportunity as effective as possible, you should make sure that your contact details are included so anyone who is interested is able to get in touch. See chapter 14, section 14.5, and chapter 15, section 15.4, for more on using the media.

6 House-to-house collecting or door-to-door canvassing

If your organisation is not well known, one way of rectifying this is to approach people face to face. This can be particularly effective for a local cause. If you are considering this type of fundraising you should consult the relevant Institute of Fundraising Codes of Practice on House to House Collections and Personal Solicitation (see Appendix 1). See chapter 12 for more on collections and face to face fundraising.

7 Events

Potential supporters may be attracted to an event where they have the opportunity to visit an exclusive venue, hear a well-known speaker or participate in an entertaining evening. Once there they might well be receptive to hearing more about the cause that the event is to benefit. See chapter 12, section 12.2, for more on organising events.

Once a donor has been recruited the aim is to keep them involved so that they continue to give.

4.2 Major donors

Some of your donors may have the potential to do much more for you than others. They might identify themselves by making a significantly larger donation than the amount you asked for, or you might find out that they have greater potential through researching your supporter base. You could then decide to set up a particular fundraising programme for these people.

Firstly you should make a decision about the point at which you will begin to treat people as major donors, since this will be different for different organisations. For a small charity a major donation from an individual might be £250 or even less; for a larger organisation with a developed strategy for encouraging big gifts, their major donor programme may only start with those giving several thousand pounds.

To help you make this decision look at your current range of donations by value. You will probably find that there is a clear cut-off point above which donations become scarcer. Once you have identified these people, you need to decide whether they will get similar communications to your other donors but with higher levels of gift asked for, or a totally different type of letter concentrating on more ambitious ways in which they can help you. Either way, you should aim to make them feel more involved rather than simply sending a standard donor appeal.

You might organise special events and visits for them or get them involved in your fundraising itself – see chapter 13 *Capital and big gift campaigns*, and chapter 16 *Fundraising with volunteers*.

Major donor programmes

If you feel that there are sufficient numbers of people who are or might become major donors, you could set up some sort of club to encourage them to increase their commitment to you. You could get your existing key donors to advise you on who else you might approach, or get them to approach their friends, colleagues and networks themselves to ask for support. You need to make sure that this is going to be cost effective for you, as these people are likely to take more of your time to look after than your other supporters. Also they may require particular types of benefits in return for their support, such as meetings with your chief executive or director, crediting in your literature (such as your annual report) and having some influence on the future of the organisation.

Examples of donor development schemes

Here are two examples of arts organisations offering special programmes for their supporters to develop commitment and bigger gifts.

- In 1999 Shared Experience Theatre Company set up their Friends scheme and mailed their supporters asking them to become Luvvies (£35), Darlings (£80) or Absolute Sweethearts – fun titles providing serious support to one of this country's most innovative companies. Each level offers increasing benefits, priority booking, acknowledgements, and invitations to special events, leading up to the title of an Absolute Sweetheart for donations of £1,000 or more.
- The National Theatre has a four-tier programme called Supporting Cast, starting with a minimum gift of £350 to become a Member and going right up to Life Benefactors, giving £30,000. As with the Shared Experience scheme, each level builds on the benefits of the one below culminating with an invitation to the chairman and director's annual lunch and use of the theatre's VIP room.

4.3 One-off donations and appeals

Individuals can support you in a wide variety of ways, for example with cash gifts of various types, or gifts in kind, or by buying raffle tickets, attending events or volunteering their time. The next sections look at the main methods by which you can encourage people to donate money.

Asking existing or prospective supporters for a one-off donation to support a cause has been a core method of raising funds for many organisations for some time. This can be done on a large scale by approaching hundreds (or thousands) of individuals through direct mail, or more directly face to face with individuals or small groups of people, particularly when asking for a high value gift.

One-off donation appeals are often used to encourage new donors to support you. Once that first donation is made you might go back and ask for another or offer other methods by which you can be supported, for example, by making a committed gift (see section 4.5 *Committed giving* below). You will find that some people who have supported you with a single donation will be happy to become more committed, some will want to keep giving on an occasional basis and some will never give again.

4.4 Legacies

Legacies are an enormously important source of charitable funds: they generated £807 million in 1998–99 for the top 500 charities. Legacy fundraising can often seem a mysterious activity which generates large sums of money with apparently little effort for the fundraiser. In fact, some of the largest legacy earning charities have carefully planned strategies for developing this income. Like other forms of fundraising, what you get out depends on what you put in.

Types of legacy

There are several types of legacy. Each is of value in different circumstances.

- *Pecuniary legacy*. This is the most straightforward type of legacy where a specified amount is given, for example, 'I leave £500 to Cancer Research Campaign'. The main drawback is that over time the value of the legacy is eroded by inflation.
- *Residuary legacy*. Where either the whole or a proportion of the residue of an estate is given, after all pecuniary legacies and specific bequests have been made. These legacies are on average ten times larger than a pecuniary legacy. Residuary legacies will keep up with inflation better as the main item of any worth is likely to be a property. Many people simply do not know their net worth, and would be surprised if they knew the value of their charitable bequest. With the decline in the birth-rate, the increase in life expectancy and property ownership, there will be an increase in the number of people with significant assets who may not have family to bequeath their estate to. This is a real opportunity for charities.
- *Specific bequest*. Where a donor leaves a specific item which can either be kept or sold by the beneficiary.
- *Long stop legacy*. These stipulate that if all the other provisions of the legacy fail, for example if all the named residuary beneficiaries have died, or if there are conditions attached which cannot be met, then the estate reverts to a charity. In these cases, it is unlikely that the charity will receive anything; but if it does, it will be a substantial sum.

- *Reversionary or life interest.* Where an elderly relative needs to be cared for, a life interest clause is often used such as, 'My house is given to the XYZ Charity with a life interest to my uncle Charles'. This gives the relative the right to live in the house during their lifetime, but on their death the right to the property reverts to the charity. This can be a useful way of carrying out a responsibility to the supporter's family while at the same time ensuring a valuable legacy to charity.

There are two other terms linked to legacies you should be aware of.

- *Codicil.* A codicil is an addition to a will, containing supplementary instructions, and is drawn up and witnessed in exactly the same way as a will. It is a simple way in which people can add instructions to their will without having the whole thing redrafted. For example they could draw up a codicil to add a £1,000 legacy to your charity.
- *Deed of Variation.* This is a way of changing a will after the person who made the will has died. This can only be done if all the beneficiaries of a will agree. Thus, if the deceased was a very keen supporter of the environment, then the family could instruct the executors (who are responsible for administering the will) to make a £500 bequest to an environmental charity. This has to be done through a legally drawn up Deed of Variation. Any amount given in this way to charity is exempt from Inheritance Tax.

Types of legacy received by charity

	% of total	average value
pecuniary legacies	52%	£3,000
residuary legacies	48%	£34,000
[Smee and Ford, 1998]		

Promotion and target audiences

The essence of legacy fundraising is that promotional effort is made now for a reward some years later. There will usually be a time-lag of between three to five years before you will begin to see any financial benefit. Strangely this is the average period between a last will being made and when a person dies.

There are a number of ways to promote legacies.

- Meeting donors face to face, often in their own homes, to discuss the benefits of legacy giving and the work of your charity.
- Direct marketing campaigns (for example by mail and telephone) to supporters may seem less personal, but may be the most practical way of getting an initial legacy message across. However, if you plan to target the general public this will require a very clear set of objectives, a sensitive

package and good administrative back up. One technique that has been used extensively by charities in the past is to offer a free booklet of advice on drawing up a will.

- Meeting solicitors face to face. Solicitors draw up wills and may be asked for advice on charitable bequests. In the early 1970s Oxfam set up a team of volunteers primarily to visit solicitors, but also to visit Oxfam's larger donors to discuss will-making. This could also be done by using paid staff which gives greater control over the process.

  Some charities organise meetings or seminars targeted at professionals to which they invite a number of their own supporters. This gives an opportunity to discuss will-making.

- Advertising in the press. This needs to be well targeted, coded and analysed and should carry a challenging message. However, even taking all this into account, the response is often negligible.

- Advertising in specialist legal journals and directories, which are targeted at solicitors and other legal professionals. This will ensure that they are aware of you and have your correct details to hand.

Obviously, for anyone to receive a legacy, a person has to make a will (they are referred to as the 'testator' or 'legator') and they then have to die. The will that includes a bequest to your charity has to be their last will. They may make several wills during their lifetime, and vary their charitable bequests as their interests and financial situation change. Therefore charities which attract predominantly older supporters are more likely to receive legacy income in the immediate term. Given that women live longer than men and, if they marry, tend to marry older men, a female supporter is more likely than a male supporter to have no direct family to leave her money to.

Before developing a legacy campaign it is important to:

- decide whether you are the sort of charity that might expect to receive legacy income;
- find out who has left you legacies in the past and if they supported you during their lifetime.

There are several questions to answer in respect of targeting. Whether to go for existing supporters, which is where you are most likely to find support, or whether to target the general public with a bias towards elderly women living in the south east, which is where substantial testators are most likely to be found, or whether to target legal advisers, such as solicitors, who help in the drawing up of a will. Research, however, has shown that many solicitors are not keen to make specific suggestions to their clients regarding charitable legacies or mention the possible inclusion of these types of bequest.

One aim of having a supporter base is to build up a good understanding amongst its members of how they might help you. If some form of regular committed giving is a natural successor to occasional one off gifts, then a legacy may be a step up from regular giving. In the process of communicating with donors over time you will build relationships which will enable you to discuss legacies – which can be considered a sensitive issue.

You might adopt an indirect approach with regular mentions in a newsletter, or write directly to them about making a will. One major charity mailed 100,000 of their existing supporters inviting them to request information on will making and indicate their interest in making a legacy. The resulting 3,500 enquiries may represent a huge success or little more than polite interest; only time will tell. However the additional alternative option of sending a donation if supporters were unable to leave a legacy, yielded £100,000 in immediate income.

One of the main stumbling blocks for charities is getting people to make their wills in the first place, but there are ethical issues linked to offering to write wills for your supporters, even when you have a legally qualified solicitor working for your organisation. If you want to suggest solicitors to your supporters, then it is best to give the details of at least three and allow them to make their own choice. A consortium of development charities run a biennial campaign with solicitors called Willaid which offers will making for a fixed donation to the consortium. The charities benefit from the donations which are equally distributed and may also receive legacies as a result, and the solicitors involved benefit by being associated with the promotion, and if they are appointed as executors they can levy normal professional fees. You could organise your own will making promotion working with local firms of solicitors or schedule your legacy promotion at the same time as Willaid, when public awareness of charitable legacies may well be higher.

Who gives legacies?

Women	69%
Men	31%
By age	
18–59	4%
60–69	9%
70–79	23%
80–89	41%
90–94	16%
95–99	6%
100+	1%

[Smee & Ford, 1998]

The message

There are three main types of legacy message used by charities.

1 Make a will (and leave a legacy to us). This approach leans on the fact that a high proportion of people die without having made a will (intestate), and the State then distributes their estate according to pre-set rules. Thus if the testator wishes to have any control over how their money is to be distributed and to minimise Inheritance Tax liability they must make a will. According to a Charities Aid Foundation survey, 64% of the population have not made a will.

2 'Remember us by adding a legacy or codicil to your existing will.' This approach must necessarily be directed at those 36% who have made a will. Will making can be a complicated process, especially when there are significant assets and family interests to consider. The value of this approach is that it gets to people who know what you are talking about and who could do something quite quickly – namely, add a codicil to their existing will.

Analysis of wills in UK

Total wills with estates over £5,000	219,893
Wills with charitable legacies	29,900
Total charitable legacies in these wills	85,950

Split by charitable area as follows:

Health and social welfare	23.9%
Animal welfare	16.0%
Physically disabled	9.1%
Medical research	8.1%
Cancer research	8.0%
Services and marine charities (including RNLI)	6.3%
Religious	6.0%
Child welfare	5.7%
Conservation/Heritage (including National Trust)	3.6%
Aged welfare	3.5%
Overseas aid	3.4%
Educational	1.8%
Mental disability	1.2%
Arts	0.8%
Others	2.6%

[Smee & Ford, 1998]

3 'Make a pledge to support us when you make or update your will.' This approach has several advantages. It allows you legitimately to keep the supporter on file and to keep in touch about the subject, whilst also allowing you to get a very direct measurement of the effectiveness of your promotion. Your aim is to get people thinking of leaving you a legacy to send you a pledge form.

'In Memoriam' gifts

An 'In Memoriam' gift commemorates a person who has died. These donations are usually made by the friends and family in memory of the deceased, for example by placing small ads in the personal columns of the newspapers inviting friends and family to send donations to a favoured charity rather than to send flowers. Funeral directors can be useful intermediaries for you here, displaying your literature in their reception area.

Legacy materials

When starting to promote legacy giving it is useful to produce some literature illustrating your organisation's need for legacies. Key points to make are:

- the importance of your charity's work and the need for continued support in the future;
- the importance of legacies as a source of income for your charity;
- the tax exemptions for charitable bequests;
- the legally correct forms of words, though you should always stress the importance of using a solicitor to draw up any will.

This information can either be mailed out to group of supporters or be used as an information pack for people enquiring about this method of giving.

Legacy administration

Getting people to leave a legacy is only the first step. You will want to keep in regular touch with those who have pledged to support you or told you that they have mentioned you in their will. If they make a new will, you want them to continue to support you or, possibly, increase the level of their support. Also there may be a good deal of administration to be handled once the legator has died. The process can at times be extremely protracted especially when you are sharing the residue with others, or when the will is contested. It is important to be prepared to carry out an effective chasing up function as well as being able to deal sympathetically with bereaved families.

The Smee and Ford service

Smee and Ford, a firm of legal agents, provides two services on a commercial basis which are useful to any charity receiving legacy income. The 'Will Notification Service' informs the charity when it has been mentioned in a will which has gone through probate (cleared by the Inland Revenue for distribution), so that the charity can notify the executors of its interest and press for an early distribution. The 'Discretionary Will Service' notifies charities of situations where money is left for charitable purposes to be distributed at the discretion of the executors, rather than to a particular charity. Here the charity can write to the executors and present their case for some of these funds.

Investment in the promotion of legacies

One of the issues often confronted by fundraisers is deciding how much to invest in legacy fundraising since, as mentioned earlier, it can take time to see any return and is often difficult to link actual legacy income to expenditure on promotion. However if you do nothing, you are unlikely to see any consistent development in your legacy income.

One idea is to use a percentage (say 10%) of your current legacy income for promotion. Another is to set a target for the number of pledges that you will receive each year. As time goes on you will find out both how many pledges turn into legacies and how much it costs to get a pledge. Coding your response form will give you an idea of the returns from each promotion.

4.5 Committed giving

Committed or regular giving is one of the most valuable and consistent ways your donors can support you and will provide one of the best financial returns for any direct marketing activity. Getting people to give their first donation can be expensive, and may not cover costs through the immediate income produced, but it is often the first step in building up a base of supporters. The follow up mailings are what generate the real revenue – people who have already given, often known as 'warm donors', respond much better to any appeal than people who have never given ('cold donor prospects').

Getting your donors to commit to regular giving creates a continuing income stream, broadens your fundraising base and enhances your organisation's sustainability. Also you can apply income from regular givers to those parts of your work which are hardest to raise money for.

To encourage people to make committed gifts you need to:

- stimulate their concern for the cause and interest in your work;
- help them recognise the importance of long-term support – your work may take time to yield results and you depend on them continuing to give;
- make it easy for them to give regularly; one way is to set up some form of membership or friends scheme with pre-set levels of giving;
- ensure that, where possible, donations are paid tax-effectively – which has been made even easier following the tax reforms in 2000;
- reasssure them regularly about the continuing value of their committed support.

This list will provide you with an agenda to develop your direct mail and donor acquisition programme, and to turn a new donor into a committed and enthusiastic long-term supporter.

Mechanisms for committed giving

There are three main ways in which committed giving can be developed:

- regular, usually monthly, payments which can be made tax efficient under the Gift Aid scheme (see section 4.6 *Tax effective giving*);
- a membership scheme. This will not always be tax-effective as there are restrictions on the level of benefit that can be received by the donor. Some schemes are concerned primarily with generating income, others aim for high membership numbers to enhance the credibility and campaigning ability of the organisation;
- payroll giving, which is also a tax-effective way of giving.

The specific mechanisms available for the actual transmission of money are:

- a banker's order, or standing order, where the payments are sent from the donor's bank to you;
- a direct debit which reverses the control of the transaction; you, the charity, claim the payments from the bank when they fall due;
- cash or cheque payments, though these are not so efficient to administer as you will usually need to remind donors when to send their payment.

Promotion

Not every donor will want to enter into a long-term commitment with you, but you should give all of them the opportunity to do so. Your strategy will depend on your answers to the following questions:

- What are the interests and motivations of your supporters?
- How much income do you need to raise, and how much are your donors prepared to give?

- How will you encourage your existing supporters to increase their commitment?
- Are there any other potential committed supporters that you can identify?
- What opportunities do you have for reporting back to your committed givers, so as to maintain their enthusiasm and support?
- What else can you do to get them to feel more involved in the work of the organisation and the cause it is addressing?

Do not take your committed givers for granted. Keep in regular touch and tell them what you are doing. Always recognise their commitment so that they understand that you are contacting them because of their regular donation, especially when there is an obviously good reason for an appeal, such as an emergency.

You can report back to your committed givers regularly through a newsletter, magazine or personalised letter from you or your chief executive. Committed givers tend to want to see their donations going to the cause rather being used on expensive communications so it is good to keep expenditure here to a minimum. Some charities hold events where donors can meet senior staff or see the organisation in action. This not only provides a good opportunity to thank them, but also enables the most committed to become even more involved, get more information and meet other supporters.

Promoting committed giving

The following are some of the promotional techniques you can use.

Approaching active givers
Analyse the response to your appeals. A number of your donors will have given more than once. These are your priority targets for committed giving. Contact them to point out the advantages of giving regularly and offer to send the appropriate forms. If there are only a few prospective targets, then contact them in person or by telephone.

Promoting committed giving more widely to your donor base
One strategy is to undertake an annual appeal to promote regular giving and encourage payment by standing order or direct debit. This may alienate those not able to give regularly. Another strategy is to mention the value of committed giving in each mailing, and allow people the opportunity to give in this way.

Regular upgrading of donation value
Once you have donors giving on a regular basis you might think about asking them to increase the value of their donation. It is easier to do this administratively if you have set up their donations via direct debit rather than a standing order, as the latter will require filling out a new form.

Using a sponsorship programme
Here the donor is linked to a specific project, community, family or person over a period of time. Action Aid have run a very successful child sponsorship scheme for many years with the donor receiving regular news of the subject of their sponsorship. Such an approach works well in fundraising terms, but has to be handled with care. Problems can arise where the donor really wants to help just one individual person (most projects provide support for the whole community), or where the donor builds up an expectation of a relationship with, for example, a sponsored child.

Recruiting large numbers of supporters with a low value regular gift by direct debit
Some organisations such as Oxfam use this very successfully. Then once donors are giving monthly donations of £2 or £3, there is the opportunity to go back to them and ask them to increase the value of their donation.

'Welcome Mailings'
These are sent following an initial gift to an organisation from newly recruited donors. There is a two fold purpose to these mailings: to welcome new donors and tell them more about the cause they have given to, and to ask them for more and regular support, often suggesting a regular monthly gift through their bank.

'Member-get-Member' or 'Supporter-get-Supporter'
This is simply an invitation to an existing member or supporter to nominate or recruit another. Various incentives (such as a free entry prize draw or some form of gift) can be used which are offered either to the original member or to the new one. This relies on the personal enthusiasm of existing members and their ability to persuade their friends and colleagues, but the technique generally works extremely well.

Membership schemes

Many voluntary organisations have membership schemes. Some are aimed primarily at people who are interested in getting more involved – helping the organisation campaign, attending cultural events, volunteering their time, but also giving money (for example, the Rambler's Association scheme). Membership schemes of this type may have their annual subscription levels set deliberately low to encourage as many people as possible to join, therefore increasing the organisation's influence. Then there are those schemes that have a fundraising purpose – the primary aim being to generate income for the organisation.

Benefits of membership

1 Membership offers a convenient peg upon which to hang the request for committed and long-term support.
2 Membership can enhance your campaigning ability. Organisations like Amnesty International and Friends of the Earth invite people to become members to harness their support for the cause.
3 Membership can open up the organisation to democratic control through annual meetings, giving the members some feeling that they control the direction of the movement.
4 Your membership list is also a good place to look for donations. These people have demonstrated their commitment to the cause and so qualify as perfect prospects for obtaining further financial commitment.
5 Membership can easily be structured to invite different levels of contribution (to reflect people's commitment, ability to pay, etc.).

Why people become members

There are a number of reasons why people will sign up as members of your organisation.

- *Personal benefit:* the member joins principally because of the benefits they believe they will gain. Examples of this are the RSPB and the National Trust which give discounted entry into their reserves or properties to members.
- *Support:* the member joins to express support for the work of the charity. In this case membership is organised to encourage members to subscribe at preferred rates as a way of making their contributions on a continuing basis.
- *Campaigning:* members are signing up to show their support for particular policies or causes.
- *Influence:* members join many local organisations simply to be able to influence their affairs. This will be done through regular meetings and AGMs.
- *'Clubs':* the member joins a club – such as the Friends of the Royal Academy – to signal their support for the work and also receive benefits from membership. Subscriptions may be higher in this case and there may be expectations of involvement in activities and events.

Membership and regular giving

The value of membership subscription income depends on:

- the number of members – the more you have, the better. Once you have established a scheme, your aim should be to find ways of recruiting new members economically;
- the annual subscription level. This will depend on your objectives – to make money or to involve as many people as possible. Some organisations give the member a choice of annual subscription levels;
- the cost of running the scheme. This includes the cost of member acquisition, collecting membership fees and communication costs (such as sending newsletters and annual reports). You need to analyse costs very carefully to establish the real net value of the scheme;
- the value of any additional income that is generated from further appeals to members.

It is most common to ask people to give on a monthly, quarterly or annual basis. You might even suggest a certain level of donation, and ask the donor to select the frequency. The value of encouraging regular giving for you is something that can be tested quite easily in a mailing. Usually requests for monthly or quarterly giving will be no less effective than an annual payment, and will produce much higher average annual donations.

Categories of membership

One of the key issues in this area is the way in which membership and committed giving is priced and styled. Membership fees have to take into account the possibility of attracting large numbers of people who are prepared to be identified with your organisation. They also need to allow concessions to people on low income and encourage higher levels of support from wealthy supporters, benefactors and corporate members. In fact you may decide to set up different schemes for people able to make larger donations.

Many organisations have several categories of membership with different levels of annual subscription. Other categories of membership can be created such as a sponsor or a patron. One organisation has three categories – 'Friends', 'Good Friends' and 'Best of Friends', another has 'Gold', 'Platinum' and 'Silver' membership. The fundraiser's challenge is to lift members from one category to the next.

Life membership is an opportunity to get a single large payment in one go, as well as enabling a member to be seen as an important benefactor of the organisation. But life means life, unless you state otherwise, and you are committed to servicing the membership for the duration without any expectation of an annual income. Therefore the price needs to reflect this.

Administration

The administration of membership demands a high degree of organisation, especially if you wish to maximise the benefits of your fundraising efforts. There are several issues to consider.

1 How do you get members to renew their subscriptions?

The best system is where the member has to do nothing – the membership continues until cancelled, and the subscription is paid by standing order or direct debit.

If there is a fixed-term commitment and this comes to an end, you will want to ensure that as many people renew as possible. The usual way to do this is by sending reminder letters, either a few months before the expiry, giving them time to renew, or to coincide with the expiry, to remind them that renewal is due. A follow up reminder after expiry, telling them that their membership will lapse if they do not renew, or a further follow up some months later – a final reminder – might also be appropriate. You may want to test different sequences to see which works best for you.

The telephone is also a valuable tool for renewal. You will need to decide at what point in the renewal cycle you use the phone – before the renewal date, at renewal or afterwards. The phone is also a good medium for asking a donor to increase the value of their donation, remind those who have just not got round to renewing to do so and can also gather useful information about why members may not be renewing.

Membership renewal can be done on one fixed date each year (for example with annual membership running from 1 January to 31 December). However you have the problem of what to do with members who join during the year – especially those who join later in the year and feel that they have already paid their subscription. An alternative is that each member's membership expires exactly twelve months after the annual subscription was paid. This requires more efficient organisation, as you will be dealing with renewals on a rolling basis throughout the year.

If you have a large membership you will need a reliable computer database to help you handle renewals. A key issue is the ability of the system to identify renewal points so that you can mail not only on the point of renewal but also before and after to stimulate the highest possible renewal rate.

2 Raising the subscription rate

Changing the annual subscription rate can be a very laborious process, because members have to be informed of the change and any standing order will need to be cancelled and replaced with a new one for the appropriate amount. As a result, some organisations review their subscriptions quite infrequently (perhaps once every three or four years) and take a conservative view of the need to increase rates. This means that membership fees can often lag well behind inflation – not so important during periods of low inflation.

One way around this problem is to ask for subscriptions to be paid by direct debit. You will still need to inform them in advance of any rise in the subscription, giving them a chance to cancel if they do not want to pay the higher amount, and you have to agree to reimburse any sums debited from the member's bank account in the event of a dispute.

3 Making membership payments tax efficient

Under the Gift Aid scheme, any payment can be made tax effectively provided the donor is a UK taxpayer and have declared (by ticking a box or filling out a form) that they wish the charity to reclaim the tax paid on their donations. The benefits received by the member are limited to 25% for a donation or subscription up to £100, £25 between £101 and £1,000, 2.5% above £1,000 with an overall maximum of £250. So if you want to make membership payments tax efficient you will need to check with the Inland Revenue to make sure they accept that the membership benefits you offer are within these limits.

If your primary aim is to generate funds, it makes sense for you to make your scheme tax effective and encourage as many members to pay in this way as possible. In addition, if the member is a higher rate taxpayer, they will benefit from Higher Rate Relief.

4 VAT liability on membership subscriptions

When more than an annual report and a right to vote at the AGM are offered to a member in return for their subscription, Customs and Excise will treat the subscription payment as being partly a payment for a service, and some or all of it may be taxable (for those organisations who are registered for VAT, or where the taxable subscription income takes them over the VAT registration threshold). Many organisations are keen to offer benefits to encourage people to subscribe. If you are unsure about the tax implications, you should consult Customs and Excise before finalising your membership scheme. More information can be found in *A Practical Guide to VAT*.

5 Maintaining donor records

Your committed givers and members will be giving money to you regularly and possibly supporting you in a number of other ways. You need to keep track of their support to identify people who might give you extra help when you need it, or to invite to special events such as receptions, or simply to personalise your appeals to them. All this information needs to be on one record not only in order to develop a full picture of each donor's support but also to avoid any duplication of mailings. If you are not yet ready to invest in one of the big tailor-made databases like Raiser's Edge, the 'How to' guide *Building a Fundraising Database Using your PC* will provide you with a step-by-step introduction to setting up a simple database using Microsoft Office. You should of course ensure that you comply with the requirements of the Data Protection Act (see Appendix 2).

Payroll giving

Giving at work has been around for some time in Britain. Originally it involved large numbers of factory workers giving a few pence per week and signing an authorisation to have the amount deducted from their wages each pay day. In 1987, the Government created a new scheme for tax-deductible payroll giving as part of its policy of encouraging charitable giving. It was seen as an opportunity for charities to mobilise support from the millions of people in employment and gave what had been a very marginal form of giving a completely new lease of life.

The scheme has not delivered anything like what was expected of it and still does not generate huge amounts of money for charity. However, it is an established way of giving and provides charities with a mechanism for regular committed income.

Inland Revenue figures for 2001–2002 show that a total of £72.5 million was given from 500,000 donors – an average donation of £74 in the year. Also, on average, payroll donors give for around nine years, a substantial time for a regular gift. There are 9,000 employers registered to operate payroll giving schemes with five million employees having access to the scheme.

How payroll giving works

The donor wishing to make a donation like this has to be an employee on the permanent payroll of an employer who subscribes to a payroll giving scheme. A company pensioner who is also on the company payroll can also give through the scheme. The donor signs a form authorising the employer to make deductions each pay day from their wages or pensions to donate to a selected charity or charities. The donor can alter the beneficiaries or increase or reduce the monthly amount or even cancel the arrangement at any time. The donation is allowed against the employee's income when calculating his or her tax liability, but it does not affect the amount of National Insurance contribution that has to be paid, which is calculated on the employee's gross income.

The employer then passes the money to an agency charity together with the employee's instructions for distributing the money. The job of the agency charity is to receive the money from the employer and distribute it to the charities selected by the donor. Agency charities are licensed by the Inland Revenue to operate a payroll giving scheme. There are certain operating requirements for an agency charity: the administration charges must be kept within 4%, the money must be passed to the beneficiary charities within 90 days, and a donor must be able to support any charity in the UK using the scheme. There are a number of approved Payroll Giving agencies, details of which can be found on the Inland Revenue website.

The upper limit on how much an individual can donate annually through payroll giving was abolished in 2000. Furthermore, from 6 April 2000 until 5 April 2003 the Government will pay a 10% supplement on all donations made under this scheme to encourage more people to give in this way.

Example

At 22% Income Tax rate (2000–2001 tax rates), a monthly donation works like this:

employee gives	£10	charity receives	£10
tax saving	£2.20	minus agency administrative charge 4%	£9.60
cost to the employee* £7.80		plus 10% supplement	£10.50

*For a higher rate taxpayer, with a tax saving of £4, the cost to the employee is reduced to £6.

Payroll giving in British Telecommunications (BT)

BT began offering payroll giving to its people in 1987, and further committed itself to the scheme in 1988, by offering matched funding up to a ceiling of £1 million each year.

BT offers employees complete freedom of choice over their selection of charities, and also pays the administration charge raised by the professional fundraising organisation which manages the scheme on BT's behalf. This ensures that every penny of each individual's contribution is received in full by their chosen charity.

Introducing this scheme across BT was a large undertaking, but it has been immensely appreciated. The take-up rate amongst employees has increased by nearly 20% every year, and now over one in ten employees use the scheme. The scheme's flexibility is also very much appreciated, with many people making their contributions to smaller charities that reflect their local concerns. The overall contribution is huge: during the 1999–2000 financial year, around 13,000 BT people donated more than £1.5 million to over 2,200 charities.

Together with the company's addition of a further £1 million of matched funding, this is one of the largest payroll giving schemes in the UK.

Promoting payroll giving

There are several different ways of promoting payroll giving to benefit your charity:

- circulate details of the scheme to those of your supporters who are not already making regular donations. Remember that only some of them will be in employment and working for an employer who is running a payroll giving scheme, and if they are not, they will not be able to give in this way;
- ask your existing payroll supporters to canvas support from their work colleagues, and provide them with the necessary promotional materials to do this;
- contact companies operating payroll giving schemes, and ask them to allow you meet and talk to their employees;
- use a commercial promoter or professional fundraising organisation (PFO), to put your cause alongside others. This will usually involve a charge for each recruited gift;
- join a consortium which then employs a commercial promoter to reach employees;
- use leaflets inserted in company magazines to recruit employees direct.

How to get started

There are a number of important decisions to make when considering whether to develop payroll giving.

- Is it worth it? There are opportunities, but it is not a major source of charitable giving and it takes time and effort to get going. If you do decide to investigate further, then the first step would be to identify all the major employers in your area (public and private sector) and find out whether they have a payroll giving scheme.
- Do you do it yourself using your own staff, or engage a PFO?
- Do you promote your charity on its own, or become part of a consortium?
- You will need to prepare promotional materials, including an explanatory leaflet for employees, which can include a deduction form for them to hand into their payroll department, and a poster to put up at the workplace.
- How will you fund the development costs, bearing in mind the long lead time involved before you actually begin to receive a flow of income?

How Compton Hospice encourages payroll giving

Terminally ill patients receiving treatment from the Compton Hospice are benefiting from £110,000 raised each year through payroll giving. The money is raised by a fundraiser on their staff, who identifies successful local firms and those active in the community. They always approach the senior person in the company, writing first to arrange a meeting at which they will request an opportunity to canvas staff face-to-face. Posters are put up in advance, and a small exhibition is arranged. They ask for a minimum of £1 per week. The resulting average annual donation is £23 per donor net of costs and only 14% of donors are lost each year.

Approaching employers directly

Some employers will be happy to recommend a charity or charities to their employees (for example, where a company adopts a 'charity of the year', or to supplement a donation or sponsorship that the company has undertaken). Other employers prefer to leave it to the employees to decide what to support, and may not want to give a particular charity the opportunity to canvas support in their organisation. A lot of UK employers, particularly smaller and medium-sized companies, still do not offer payroll giving facilities to their employees, nor are they likely to know much about the scheme. In such cases, you have to persuade the company to establish a payroll giving scheme first.

When approaching a company, you will want to do the following.

- Research what the company does, who makes the decisions, whether they undertake any charitable giving and, as mentioned earlier, whether they operate a payroll giving scheme.
- Approach the person who has the authority to allow you to set up a meeting to discuss your plans. For smaller companies, this will be the managing director.
- Discuss with that person how you might promote payroll giving to their staff.
- Arrange your payroll giving promotion in the company.

The best way to promote payroll giving is face-to-face. Indirect methods such as leaflets and posters on their own are less effective. You need to agree with the employer precisely what access you will be allowed to their staff. It is unlikely that you will be able to go round the offices or shopfloor and ask employees individually. It is more common that you will be talking to groups of people in their lunch break or at a pre-arranged meeting, or you may be able to set up a stand about payroll giving and your organisation in a common area of the building such as the entrance foyer.

Professional Fundraising Organisations (PFOs) for payroll giving

There are now a number of PFOs which specialise in promoting payroll giving to employees. The most usual procedure is:

- you enter into a contract with the PFO;
- they put information about your charity alongside that of other charities they represent;
- they go into the workplace to promote payroll giving taking along information about the charities they represent;
- they then charge you for each donor who signs up to support your charity.

There is now an organisation of payroll giving promoters and consultants, the Association of Payroll Giving Professional Fundraising Organisations (APGPFO), to help ensure standards.

Consortia

For smaller charities, the use of commercial promoters is problematic, since the charity will have very little public profile. When a prospective donor is faced with a list of charities, those which are unknown are the least likely to be supported. This is where a consortium approach can be helpful. These are set up by groups of charities specially to promote payroll giving. A consortium can include charities working for the same sort of cause (for example, there is a consortia of small children's charities called Childlife), or can be made up of a range of local charities. Donors are encouraged to support the consortium (which is usually constituted as a charity in its own right), and the proceeds are shared between consortium members, either equally or according to some formula agreed at the outset. Consortia have two important advantages:

- the costs are shared. This is a form of fundraising where many of the charities involved do not have any previous experience, so operating in this way can be less risky;
- the consortium is benefiting a range of charities. This can make it easier to gain access to a workplace, because the employer may not want to be seen as favouring one charity over another.

A charity wanting to get involved in payroll giving, but not wanting to go it alone, could attempt to join an existing consortium, or join with others to set up a new consortium. The consortium should have a catchy name, and comprise a compatible group of similar charities who are happy to collaborate.

4.6 Tax effective giving

Gift Aid

The rules regarding tax effective giving changed markedly on 6 April, 2000, with the government's 'Getting Britain Giving' Campaign. The situation has become technically much simpler. The main change for individual donors is that all tax effective payments, whether made by regular donation or with a one off gift must now be done under the Gift Aid scheme, and there is no minimum level (previously it had been £250 for a one off gift) for the size of donation. Therefore, in theory, any payment made to a charity by a tax-payer is eligible for tax relief as long as:

- the donor fills out a Gift Aid declaration (which replaces the existing Gift Aid certificate) which is then kept by the charity. This need only be a simple sentence included in the donation form that the donor signs and returns with the donation;
- the charity maintains an 'audit trail' linking the payment to the donor – the charity needs to record each donation separately and be able to prove to the Inland Revenue how much each donor has given.

You can get further advice from Inland Revenue (Charities) or visit the Inland Revenue website.

Example of a Gift Aid statement

❏ Please tick here if you would like XYZ Charity to reclaim the tax you have paid on this and all future donations you make.*

*In order for XYZ Charity to reclaim the tax you have paid on your donations, you must have paid Income or Capital Gains Tax (in the UK) equal to the tax that will be reclaimed (currently 28p for each £1 you give).

The Gift Aid declaration can state that it covers all donations from the date of the current gift onwards (and going back to April 2000), so one declaration can cover all future claims, although the donor can cancel this at any time. The level of benefits the donor can receive are limited to 25% for a donation or subscription up to £100, £25 between £101 and £1,000, 2.5% above £1,000, with an overall maximum of £250.

So, in theory, you can add 28% (on 2000–01 tax rates) to the income from, for example, a sponsored run if:

- all your sponsors are tax payers
- they all complete or have completed a Gift Aid declaration
- you can prove that they have made the payment.

Once you have proper record keeping in place, the system is now so simple that you can reclaim tax on almost any donation, whatever the size, as long as the donor is a taxpayer. The government has claimed that the changes will be worth £1 billion a year extra to charities once the system is operating effectively.

Tax-effective giving: who gets what?

For a basic rate taxpayer, paying tax at 22% (2000–01 rate)

A donor pays you £10.

This amount is net of income tax at the basic rate.

To earn this the donor will have to have earned a gross sum of £12.82.

To calculate this amount: $\dfrac{100}{100\text{-}22}$ or $\dfrac{100}{100\text{-}R}$ where R = rate of Income tax

The donor pays 22% tax on £12.82, which is £2.82, in order to earn £10.

You are able to reclaim this £2.82 from the Inland Revenue. And this increases the value of the donation by 28.2% (at a 22% tax rate).

For a higher rate taxpayer paying tax at 40%

You reclaim £2.82, as above.

But the donor has paid 40% tax on the £12.82 of income.

This amounts to £5.13.

The donor is able to reclaim £2.31 from the Inland Revenue in Higher Rate Relief (which can be done by a PAYE adjustment or when making an annual tax return).

The Giving Campaign has developed a new brand identity called 'giftaid it' to raise awareness of the benefits of Gift Aid among donors and to encourage them to use it when they give money to charity. A toolkit for charities shows how the brand can be applied to promote and maximise Gift Aid donations in many fundraising situations. The brand is freely available for charities to use and the toolkit, including the brand artworks, can be obtained from The Giving Campaign.

Deeds of Covenant, which used to be an important mechanism for charities asking for regular gifts, no longer count for a separate tax relief. So now if someone signs a Deed of Covenant to make regular payments to your charity you can only reclaim the tax if they also complete a Gift Aid declaration, as above, or if the wording on the covenant form includes a Gift Aid Declaration. As a transitional measure, any Deed of Covenant in force before 6 April 2000 is unaffected, although any payments outside the terms of the deed or after the deed has expired must be covered by a Gift Aid declaration. A covenant had the advantage that it was a legal agreement binding the donor to make regular payments for a stated period, a minimum of four years. However in practice it was virtually impossible to enforce in the event of non-payment.

Payroll giving (see above) is another tax effective form of gift, but here the donor receives all the tax benefit, and there is no additional tax that the charity can reclaim.

CAF accounts

A final method of giving tax effectively is where the donor uses the services of the Charities Aid Foundation (CAF). Here they pay a sum to CAF as a charitable donation and tax is reclaimed on this. The total amount, made up of the value of the donation and the tax reclaimed less an administrative charge of 2% and a compulsory donation to the National Council for Voluntary Organisations (which set up the scheme) of 3%, is kept in an account for the donor. The donor can then make charitable donations from the account either using vouchers which they give to the charity as they would a cheque, or by quoting their CharityCard number, or by asking CAF to make regular direct payments to a charity from the account. In the first two instances the charity claims the sum given from CAF. Since the tax has already been reclaimed in respect of this donation, no further tax can be reclaimed by the charity.

Gifts of shares to charity

From April 2000, individuals (and companies) are also able to get tax relief on gifts of certain shares and securities to charity when calculating their income for tax purposes. The tax relief will apply where the whole of the beneficial interest in any qualifying shares or securities is disposed of to charity either by way of a gift or by way of a sale at an undervalue. The following categories of shares and securities can be donated using the new relief:

- shares and securities listed or dealt with on a recognised stock exchange, whether in the UK or elsewhere, including those traded on the Alternative Investment Market;
- units in an authorised unit trust;
- shares in an open-ended investment company;
- holdings in certain foreign collective investment schemes.

To check whether the shares or securities qualify for the scheme, contact Inland Revenue (Charities) for advice.

Where an individual makes use of this relief, they are able to deduct the 'relevant amount' from their total income for tax purposes. The relevant amount is either the full market value of the shares (where the transfer is a gift), or the difference between the market value and the actual cash received (where the transfer is a sale at an undervalue). This figure is then adjusted by adding to it any incidental costs of disposing of the shares – for example brokers' fees.

Tax relief can be claimed at the donor's top rate of tax via their self-assessment tax return and for Capital Gains Tax transfer is deemed to have taken place at cost (so no CGT is payable) unless the shares are sold at an undervalue, where the sale price is taken as being the transfer price.

From April 2002, the same tax relief has been available for donors who give land and buildings to charity.

Example

A donor paying tax at the Higher Rate of 40% gives shares valued at £25,000 to a charity. The shares originally cost £10,000. From the donor's point of view the disposal is deemed to have taken place at £10,000 and therefore the gift does not act as a gain or a loss for Capital Gains Tax (CGT) purposes. If the donor were to sell the shares for their current value (£25,000), there would be a capital gain of £15,000 which would be taxed at 40% (£6,000). The net amount received on the sale would only be £14,000. For tax purposes the donor's annual taxable income will be reduced by £25,000 (the value of the shares donated). At the 40% rate this reduces their liability by £10,000. The donor saves £10,000 in Income Tax and £6,000 in CGT as compared with selling the shares. The effective net cost of the gift to the donor is therefore only £9,000.

4.7 Looking after your supporters

Your donors and supporters are a key part of your fundraising future. They have demonstrated their commitment to you through giving, and you should try to retain this commitment and strengthen their ties to your organisation. This is often referred to as donor or supporter care, or the latest term, Customer Relationship Marketing. This section concentrates on two aspects of developing your supporter relationships – thanking them, and increasing their involvement.

Thanking your donors

Being thanked makes donors feel good about their giving, and tells them that their donation has been received and is being put to good use. Thanking your donors gives you the opportunity to find out the depth of their interest, and perhaps some of the reasons why they support you. It can also enable you to tell them more about your work and your future plans. And all this will help you to get further support from them.

Your best prospects for a donation are those people who have already given to you, so when and how you thank them can be crucial. There are several ways of saying thank you.

1 By mail

Some charities reply to all donations, while others reply only to certain types or levels. It can be expensive to thank people for every donation whether large or small especially if there are a lot of them, but there are important advantages in thanking donors at some point, even if you do not do it every time. If you are worried about saving administrative costs, you might ask donors to tell you if they do not want a reply.

When you do say thank you, try to do it immediately, say within three days of receipt of the donation. Try and make the letter as personal as you can, recognising how long the person has been supporting you and their level of giving. It might be useful to develop a set of generic letters which you can then adapt as necessary. Some organisations get their chairperson or director to sign the letter. This is not necessary except for very large donations. Your smaller and regular donors may be more interested in getting to know you (the fundraiser) or a donation administrator, who they will be able to contact if they have a query or want further information.

2 By telephone

If you want to respond quickly and personally particularly for larger donations, the telephone is ideal. As soon as you receive an exceptional gift, ring the donor and thank them personally.

3 By e-mail

If you have e-mail and know a supporter's address this can be a very immediate way of thanking which also has the advantage of appearing very cost effective. It is sensible to request a donor to provide their telephone and e-mail details alongside their address.

4 Face to face

Personally visiting important donors is a time-consuming business. However, it can be an extremely worthwhile. The visit should be made by an appropriate person. Depending on the level of donor, this might be the fundraiser, a member of the management committee or fundraising committee, or a trained volunteer. Donors may be wary about the object of such visits until they have actually received one. A simple chat to tell the donor more about your work and to thank them for their gift will often naturally lead on to discussing other ways they can help without your having to introduce the subject yourself or ask directly.

5 Through an event

If a face to face visit is not possible, another way of meeting and thanking supporters is by setting up an event, such as a reception or open day. A senior person from the organisation might attend and give a short talk; then staff, committee members or other volunteers can be on hand to talk to those who have been invited to the event. This requires careful planning and briefing of your staff, committees and volunteers to ensure that everyone is spoken to.

You might hold the event at your office. People are often interested in seeing how an organisation works, even when all there is to see are desks and filing cabinets. Or you could organise a site visit to see a project at work and enable the donors to meet some of the beneficiaries and the local community.

6 With a gift

Some fundraisers offer some sort of incentive or token in return for gifts of a certain size or type. This might be something heavily promoted by the charity to encourage a particular response, or a token of thanks used to build commitment and help spread the message to others. For example, a special Christmas card from your president; a certificate for a pledged legacy; or a wildlife print. Though giving is often a private matter, some supporters welcome opportunities to discuss their favourite cause with their friends. A thank you token or certificate which they can display in their home can help them do this.

7 By public acknowledgement

You can also thank people through a public announcement – such as an advertisement in a newspaper, a mention in your newsletter, magazine or annual report.

Think carefully about your annual report. Not only can you credit your donors, but this also sends signals to others that you need donations and will publicly acknowledge any support you receive. Indicating the level of gifts creates a certain peer group pressure for others to give at similar levels. Perhaps more importantly it gives credibility – 'If they have given, then it must be a good organisation'. As an organisation grows, the number of donors may get too large to list everyone; but the major donors should still appear. See chapter 15, section 15.3, for more on annual reports.

Taking paid advertising to thank donors might be expensive but can be worthwhile if there are other messages to communicate (for example that the cause has widespread or prestigious support). Remember to get the donor's permission before you do this and also check how they wish to be credited, as some will not expect to see their names publicly in print.

Involving supporters in a campaign

In 1999 the NSPCC launched a national campaign to put a stop to child abuse, the Full Stop Campaign. This initiative not only involved a fundraising target but also aimed to increase non-financial involvement among existing supporters and the general public. The campaign used both direct marketing and broader awareness raising methods such as television advertising – some involving celebrities – and billboard posters to encourage support. Also a pin was produced, the wearing of which showed support for the campaign.

Increasing donor involvement

The more your donors and supporters understand your cause, the issues and policies, your problems and failures, the more likely they may be to make a greater financial commitment to your organisation. There are a number of ways of giving donors a fuller picture of what you are doing that will help build their commitment and support.

Regular mailings

Mailings to supporters are crucial for keeping them in touch whether these are purely to communicate information, or to ask for further donations. You can use them to report back on your progress and, by implication, how you have used their money. You might highlight successes and achievements, including any major grants received, and set out future plans.

Obviously, you want your supporters to read what you have sent; you may also want them to respond. Both are difficult in a world where people are constantly receiving unsolicited information from all manner of sources. In order to make your letter stand out you might use a device such as a questionnaire or link your mailing with a particular campaign your organisation is running. A questionnaire can tell you what your supporters think (and who they are), and you can use their views to make important campaigning points. For example, Shelter has used surveys to build connections between the organisation and its supporters, such as asking them to contribute their views on what the government's housing policy should encompass.

Sending a questionnaire to supporters in a regular appeal mailing can increase response rates. Some people will be motivated by the appeal and some will be motivated by the request to provide information. You can also use questionnaires to ask donors how they want to be involved or how they want you to communicate with them. You can include a postcard in your mailing asking supporters to return this to, for example, a government minister, either directly or through your office, and thereby engage them in your campaigning. This is something that Amnesty International UK has done for particular campaigns.

Other involvement techniques

Other ways of increasing involvement include the following.

- *Lectures and talks*. An event where your supporters can hear experts discuss a particular issue gives them the chance to understand more fully the cause you are addressing, and makes them feel that their contribution is important and useful. You can also highlight a new initiative that needs support. However, the essential purpose of such a meeting is not to raise money, but to build interest and involvement, thereby providing a solid platform for future fundraising.
- *Involving donors in your fundraising*. On the principle that the best person to ask is someone who has already given, you might try to find ways of inviting donors to accompany you to fundraising meetings, particularly where you know they are enthusiastic. If they can convey something of what motivated them to get involved, it can encourage others; equally importantly, it will cement their relationship with you.
- *Friends groups*. By 'enrolling' donors as members of a friends group or a supporters club (either free or for a subscription) and sending them a regular newsletter which focuses as much on the donors and what they are doing for the organisation as on the work of the organisation, you can create a sense of belonging. You can then organise special events for these key supporters and also develop special appeals where you ask your existing supporters to raise a sum of money for a specific purpose. By giving them the responsibility for doing this and a target to achieve, this will encourage them to give generously. For example, the Friends of Covent Garden are sometimes asked to sponsor a new opera production.
- *Campaigning*. Many voluntary organisations campaign. The campaigning is usually spearheaded by the paid staff, but can often be reinforced by members and volunteers. Those who become involved in advocating a cause will develop a much deeper commitment to it and may become your best supporters in the long term.

Fundraisers should never allow fundraising to become divorced from the advocacy work. It is important to ensure that there are a number of different ways for people to support an organisation: giving money, volunteering, fundraising, and campaigning. Some people will only be able to do one of these. However many may want to do more – and by becoming more involved, this will strengthen their concern and commitment to you.

Challenges for the fundraiser

1 To get the donor to give again.
2 To get the donor to give regularly and frequently, ultimately on a committed basis.
3 To get the donor to increase their level of giving.
4 To get the donor to give in several different ways.
5 To encourage the donor to leave a legacy.

Recruiting volunteers from your donors

It is sometimes assumed that volunteers and donors are two separate categories of supporters which should not be mixed. Many charities feel that they should not ask their donors to volunteer, nor their volunteers to give money. This assumes that people compartmentalise their concern and their response, which is plainly not true.

All those who are giving their time should also be given the opportunity to give money. You may feel that they should be protected from such requests, but some may be happy to give. Unless you ask them, you may miss out on their support. (See chapter 16 *Fundraising with volunteers*.) Donors can also be invited to become volunteers. Most will not have the time available or wish to, but some will – and they will continue as donors too. Even if they do not wish to volunteer, their support may be all the stronger when they are made aware that other people are volunteering their time.

Resources and further information

See also general lists at the end of the book.

Organisations

Association of Payroll Giving Professional Fundraising Organisations (APGPFO)
4 West St Helen Street
Abingdon
Oxon OX14 5BL

Charities Aid Foundation
(for Give As You Earn, CAF accounts and CharityCard)
King's Hill
West Malling
Kent ME19 4TA
www.cafonline.org
www.allaboutgiving.org
Tel. 01732 520000

Charities Trust (for Work Aid)
PO Box 15
Liverpool L23 0UU
Tel. 0151 949 1900
Help desk 0151 949 0044

Customs & Excise
(for VAT matters)
www.hmce.gov.uk
Find your local office in the telephone
directory under Customs and Excise
Vat Business Advice Centres.

Inland Revenue
(for tax matters)
Inland Revenue (Charities)
St John's House
Bootle
Merseyside L69 9BB
Tel. 0845 3020203
www.inlandrevenue.gov.uk
All enquiries from Scottish charities:
Tel. 0131 777 4040

Smee and Ford
2nd Floor
St George's House
195–203 Waterloo Road
London SE1 8UX
Tel. 020 7928 4050

The Giving Campaign
6th Floor
Haymarket House
1A Oxendon Street
London SW1Y 4EE
Tel. 020 7930 3154
Fax 020 7925 0985
www.givingcampaign.org.uk
e-mail admin@givingcampaign.org.uk

Publications

The following publications are available from the Directory of Social Change.
Prices were correct at the time of writing, but may be subject to change.

Building a Fundraising Database Using your PC 2nd edition, Peter Flory,
DSC/CAF 2001, £12.95

Dimensions 2000, Volume 2 CAF's top 500 fundraising charities, CAF 2000, £12

Effective Customer Care, Amanda Knight, DSC 1999, £10.95

Legacy Fundraising 2nd edition, ed. Sebastian Wilberforce, DSC/CAF/Institute of
Fundraising 2001, £19.95

Looking after your Donors, Karen Gilchrist, DSC/CAF 2000, £10.95

A Practical Guide to VAT 2nd edition, Kate Sayer, DSC 2001, £12.95

Other publications

Institute of Fundraising Code of Practice on House to House Collections

Institute of Fundraising Code of Practice on Legacy Fundraising

Institute of Fundraising Code of Practice on Payroll Giving

Institute of Fundraising Code of Practice on Personal Solicitation for Committed
Gifts

5 COMMUNITY FUNDRAISING

This chapter looks at three ways of fundraising at a local level:

- forming a local group specifically for fundraising
- using local clubs and societies to mobilise support for your project
- fundraising through schools, where you can get the support of young people.

Details of organisations and publications referred to in this chapter are on p. 111.

5.1 Fundraising through local groups

Whether you are an established national organisation or a small local group just starting out, raising money locally through events and collections can be an important source of income. However, this requires time and effort.

There are two main approaches: using paid staff to do the fundraising, or recruiting a group of volunteers. Wherever possible it is best to work through volunteers. The staff member's job is then to recruit and support those volunteers. The point of doing this is that the fundraising effort is taken on by the local group, leaving you free to concentrate on other tasks. It is often not cost-effective for a paid member of staff to spend time organising craft fairs, dinner dances or coffee mornings, although paid staff should be responsible for particularly important events – especially where there are large sums of money involved. The more you raise money yourself, the more you will have to do in the following years in order to maintain your levels of income, and therefore the less time you will have to develop volunteers, so it is best to recruit your volunteers early.

The local group can be given responsibility for raising money in a specified area or for a particular activity (a special ball, for example). You can establish local fundraising groups in different towns and cities, or in different areas of the same city. They will work largely independently, but you will need to provide proper management and support. The more groups you establish, the more money you should raise. It can take a long time (up to 18 months or longer sometimes) to get a group established and raising money successfully, but the investment can be worth it. The volunteers you recruit, if properly supported, may stay involved with your organisation for many years.

Getting started

To establish a local fundraising group, you need to:

- be clear where you want a group and what you want the group to do
- find people who are willing to put in the time to raise money for you, and in particular
- find someone to lead the group (as the chair)
- establish the group with a constitution or set of guidelines, which defines how it will work and its relationship with the organisation it is raising money for
- help the group identify appropriate (and ideally repeatable) fundraising activities
- supervise and support the group in its fundraising work
- and THANK THEM!

The following example illustrates how you might set about forming a local fundraising group. The key is to follow up on every idea or contact, to ask persuasively – and to get the volunteers doing something.

Getting a local fundraising group going

I wanted to form a new fundraising group in the town. It was a fairly affluent dormitory town of about 10,000 people – a day-trip holiday resort. The Society used to have a fundraising group there a few years ago but it had grown old together and disbanded and no one could help anymore.

I contacted the local MP, who had expressed some interest in our work some years before but who had done nothing. He suggested that I contact a number of his political colleagues in the area and was happy for me to say that he had suggested it. I contacted them all. Only one person showed any interest. He made it clear he did not want any long term involvement – but would host a meeting for us if we wanted to invite people to an information-type evening.

I looked through the records of any donations or enquiries that had been made in recent years and came across a request for information from two mature students living in the town. I called them to see if they would be interested in coming to a meeting and they thought they would be. I took up the offer of the evening and discussed with the host who else we might invite. We sent out about thirty invitations and received eight acceptances, including the two mature students.

Only the two mature students turned up on the evening. They felt embarrassed by the non-attendance of the other people and said they would help. I suggested that they could organise a coffee morning/evening and invite their friends and neighbours. They did so, and about 40 people attended. I was there to talk to people and see if anyone else was interested – four were. I asked if the original two would think about organising another morning/evening and this time suggested involving the four other people. They were happy to – and we had the beginnings of a new fundraising group.

The next event came and went with another four or five people wanting to help. This exercise was repeated twice more – we had new people join and the original people began to withdraw. After 15 months we had a lively group of 22 young women eager to help and enjoying themselves in the process.

[Harry Brown, NSPCC]

Recruiting the right people is another key to success. In particular you need to look for key people to chair/lead the committee or take overall responsibility for a particular area of fundraising. Identify the skills and resources that people will need for the job – time available, use of their home, contacts, ideas, initiative, enthusiasm, and so on. Allow plenty of time to find the people you need. Try to find out what motivates them. Do they want to meet new people? Do they need public acknowledgement? Do they want to make a name for themselves? Do they enjoy 'achieving' things? You can also ask the people you contact to suggest other people. Ask if they would be willing to make the approach or introduce you. If you are setting up a local branch of a national organisation, start with existing supporters who live in the area. They will be already interested in the cause, so may be keen (or may be persuaded) to help. As the group begins to organise fundraising events (and starts to be successful), you will find that there will be more interest in what you are doing and more people will be come forward to volunteer their time. At any stage in the process, good publicity in the local press or on local radio can bring further support.

Recruiting for a County Committee

The steps you need to take are as follows.

- Recruit a researcher
- Train the researcher
- Identify key individuals
- Meet key individuals
- Seek contacts from key individuals
- Obtain the commitment from the 'leader' or leading people
- Organise inaugural meeting (try to get one of the interested people to host the meeting)

Joining a committee is an opportunity to make a contribution to the welfare of the community in an interesting and enjoyable way, which leads to personal satisfaction.

It is an opportunity to acquire a personal profile and influence in an acceptable way, to meet other business contacts and be seen as the supporter of a national charity.

People of the calibre of those invited to join a county committee have very limited free time, but are in a position to select and actively support fundraising events that fit into their lifestyles.

Funds raised through the efforts of the county committee will be spent in the county on projects based in places where it might be difficult to raise money locally.

There is satisfaction to be gained from becoming part of a (national) charity with the occasional opportunity to meet and talk with the decision makers in the organisation.

Constituting the local group

You need people – and you need something for them to do. You also need a constitution, or a set of guidelines, which defines how the group will operate and clarifies their relationship with the charity they are raising money for. If you are setting up lots of local groups, you can draw up a model constitution. The local group can be simply a sub-committee or branch of the charity, with no separate legal identity of its own. Or it can be a separate organisation in its own right, constituted independently as a charity, with the object of supporting the charity it has been set up to raise money for.

A separate legal structure will be more expensive to operate, but it will give full responsibility and control to the local group – they will be completely accountable for what is raised and what the money is spent on. A structure with branches gives the parent charity direct control – and trustee responsibility for how the money is raised and spent. The most appropriate structure depends on a number of factors, including the length of time the committee has been in operation, the amount of money it is raising, the number of local groups around the country raising money for you, and the parent charity's own constitution and byelaws. *The Voluntary Sector Legal Handbook* covers this area in more detail.

Make sure that the group operates in the interests of the parent charity and does nothing to bring it into disrepute. If the group is independently constituted, this can be done through a licence agreement, which authorises the use of the charity's name and logo provided that certain standards are met and values adhered to. The Charities Act provisions on unauthorised fundraising provides some safeguards against independent groups of people who decide to raise money for you without your permission.

Constitution of a Local Committee

The following are some of the headings for the constitution of a local fundraising committee. These responsibilities are not to be taken lightly.

- The committee and the charity
- Support to be provided by the charity
- Responsibilities of committee members
- Name
- Location
- Bank account / banking arrangements / transfer of funds raised
- Objects of the committee
- Structure including: patronage, election of officers, responsibility of officers, terms of office
- Meetings and operation: quorum for meetings, frequency of meetings, voting, resignations, termination of memberships, annual general meetings
- Remuneration of members, expenses policy
- Alteration of constitution

Local fundraising activities

There are an enormous range of fundraising activities that a local fundraising group can undertake. Here are a few that work well:

- coffee mornings and other 'socials'
- bridge tournaments and other games such as whist or chess
- sponsored walks, jogs, cycle rides, fun runs – and anything else that can be sponsored
- heritage walks and cultural evenings for tourists
- craft fairs and sales of work
- fashion shows
- film premières
- concerts and other cultural events
- dinner dances and balls
- discos for young people
- picnics and outings for families, if possible at interesting locations
- auctions of donated goods and 'promises auctions' (where a promise to do something useful or interesting is auctioned)
- sports events and tournaments
- New Year's Eve parties, and events on other festive occasions
  (Organising fundraising events is covered in chapter 12.)
- getting supporters and businesses to advertise in calendars and diaries, brochures and annual reports
  (Getting companies to advertise is covered in chapter 8.)

- sales of greetings cards
  (Selling goods is covered in chapter 11.)
- public and house-to-house collections
  (Public and house-to-house collections are covered in chapter 12)
- raffles, lotteries and sweepstakes (which are regulated under the Lotteries Act)
  (Lotteries and raffles are covered in chapter 12.)
- competitions with an entry fee to participants (which are not regulated)

Supporting and managing a local group

It is important to make sure any local group actually does the work, does it well, operates in accordance with the values and aims of the charity it is raising money for, and does not call unreasonably upon staff time. You will need to manage and support the group if you are to to get the most out of it. Here are some ideas for how to do this.

- Provide the group with some form of induction, so that they understand the importance of the work being done by the charity, see the staff at work and meet and talk to staff and beneficiaries. They will then know what they are raising the money for and it will give them the enthusiasm they need to convince those they are asking. Make sure you provide them with appropriate literature about the work of the organisation.
- Help steer the group towards those fundraising methods which are most likely to work. Your experience will help, and you can also research what other local fundraising groups are doing. You may have a number of tried and tested ideas and be able to give them all the information they need to put them into practice.
- Give the group a budget (they will need to spend some money to raise money) and talk to them about fundraising targets to achieve. Don't expect too much too soon. It is best to start slowly, and to allow more time than they think will be necessary. If they are too optimistic at the outset, there will be a sense of failure when targets are not achieved.
- Continue to show your personal interest in what they are doing. Monitor their progress and be on hand with advice if they have difficulties. At every opportunity, acknowledge your appreciation of their hard work, find ways of celebrating their success, and thank them.

Your relationship with your group leader is critical to the success of the group. The leader will act as your key contact and their enthusiasm is vital to maintaining the overall energy and commitment of the group. A good leader will also help to ensure that a long-standing group does not slip into a rut where new ideas and people are blocked and will get the group working as a team.

The characteristics of a good fundraising leader

1 The leader must be an efficient and capable **organiser**.
2 Leaders must be able to **plan** an event in every detail.
3 Leaders must be able to **communicate** with their helpers. They should enjoy working with people and should be able to **lead** without causing offence.
4 A leader must be able to **motivate** others and inspire them with enthusiasm and zeal.
5 Leaders must be good judges of people. They must get to know their committee and helpers well and be able to **recognise and use the talents and abilities of individual members of the group**. They must also be able to understand each person's strengths and weaknesses in order to be able to **direct** and **guide** them in a way that they can accept and enjoy.

[Sterrett, *Complete Guide to Fundraising*]

5.2 Local clubs and societies

There are a wide range of local groups and associations which can be extremely valuable for your fundraising. They can provide you with money, influence and human resources. There are many different organisations which can fulfil this role, but this section will concentrate on:

- Trade Unions
- membership bodies
- local groups
- churches and other religious bodies.

These are unlikely to be major donors, even where there are clear links between their interests and your work. However, they can be invaluable for their contacts and their ability to mobilise large numbers of people to volunteer, attend events, organise collections and give you access to their friends and colleagues. They can help raise your profile.

Trade Union giving is an extension of their political stance and will link with some campaign or sectional interest. For example, in the 1970s and 1980s, many unions made donations to the voluntary organisations combating apartheid. Giving can be in the form of gifts in kind, advertising in brochures or journals, appeals to or collections from the membership, or a small cash grant from union funds. A good starting point is a personal contact at a local union branch.

Membership bodies such as the Women's Institutes (in rural areas) and Townswomen's Guilds (in urban areas), Young Farmers, Round Tables and Rotarians (and other similar bodies for men or women), Masonic Lodges (if you have an active supporter who is a freemason) can all be helpful. Usually these organisations don't make large grants themselves, but they can encourage their membership to support a particular appeal and you might spot a potential key supporter amongst them.

Local groups such as Scouts, Cubs, Girl Guides, Brownies, sports clubs and dance schools can all help. You may be running a sponsored walk or a fun run, or a fete or a fair, and require people to staff the event. Such organisations can be a useful source of people, perhaps in return for a small grant to their own funds.

A wide range of church and religious bodies give to charity. Many local congregations decide to allocate an annual collection to a particular cause – not all are religious in nature, and can be in addition to traditional collections such as Christian Aid Week. Groups within congregations often meet to explore particular themes and this will lead them, for example, to become interested in homelessness or poverty. At a diocesan and national level, the Churches have boards of social responsibility (or their equivalent) whose role is to mobilise support for social action. Other religions and denominations too will operate in a similar way.

Each type of organisation is different; you will need to find out what they can do for you. Try to get invited to speak at a function. If you do, take plenty of literature with you that explains your organisation and the sort of help you are looking for. You could ask if you could appeal for support there and then. Or they might write about your appeal in their next newsletter. Or you might ask for permission to write to the membership afterwards. A few organisations have been able to develop significant support in this way. It is easier if there are one or two enthusiastic volunteers that you can use as speakers.

Support you can expect

Depending upon the organisation you are approaching, you could look for:

- a cash donation
- a gift of equipment for a local project
- mobilising the involvement of volunteers for your project or for a fundraising event
- encouraging donations from their members or getting them to organise a collection for you
- running a fundraising event
- an invitation to speak at meetings or to appeal to their membership
- an endorsement for your work
- an introduction to key individuals who might be willing to support you and get involved in your work.

Groups to consider approaching

Trade unions and professional bodies

- The TUC
- National trade unions
- Local branches of trade unions
- Professional associations
- Employer groups and business associations

Membership organisations

- Rotary
- Lions
- Round Table
- Soroptimists
- Inner Wheel
- Women's Institutes
- Mothers' Union
- Ladies' Circle
- Rotoract

Other local bodies

- Student rag committees
- College student unions
- Scouts and guides
- Young Farmers' clubs
- Police
- Fire brigade

Religious bodies

- Churches (Church of England, Catholic, Methodist, Baptist, Pentecostal and other denominations).
- Other faiths (Hindu temples, Moslem mosques, Sikh gurdwaras, Jewish synagogues)
- Boards of social responsibility for particular faiths and denominations

Getting started

1 Consider what support you are looking for. Is it cash support from the organisation or its members? Is it people's time to help you as volunteers? Is it their ability to mobilise support for you from friends and contacts? Is it their access to individuals with influence? Is it their facilities you wish to make use of? Or is it an endorsement of your work?

2   Review your records to see if they have supported you in the past, and what other similar organisations and networks have given you support.

3   Check with your own committees and supporters to see if they are members of any relevant organisations. This can provide a first point of contact.

4   Draw up a short list of possible organisations who you believe have the interest and the resources or membership to support you.

5   Make contact at the appropriate level and try to establish what might be of interest to them.

6   Follow this up with a specific proposal; make this something that they could reasonably do for you.

5.3 Working with schools and young people

Some basic principles

There are four reasons for wanting to involve young people.

- You will be generating money for your work, although this will not always be a substantial amount. Young people are likely to have time rather than money, but they do have the ability to raise money for you.
- You will be involving young people in your cause, giving them a better understanding of the issues involved and the work you are doing. They may need the help your organisation provides at some time. You may even find ways of encouraging them to volunteer.
- You will be laying an important base for future support. If people get involved in supporting charity when they are young, this can influence what they do and choose to support in later life.
- You will be reaching adults through children. Raising money through young people inevitably includes their parents and parents' friends in a way that you otherwise might not be able to.

How you approach young people and what you ask them to do will depend on two factors: the institution you are approaching them through and their age. You can reach young people through the following.

- *Educational institutions*: these include not only primary and secondary schools (and middle schools where these still exist), but also FE and sixth form colleges, as well as universities, for the increasing number of young people who go on to higher education.
- *Youth clubs*, where there is more freedom to undertake creative activity.
- *Out-of-school projects*, which include out-of-school learning projects funded by the New Opportunities Fund as well as projects for young people with special needs.

- *Formal volunteering programmes*, including those funded under the Millennium Volunteers programme, which encourage young people to develop their own ideas and solutions in response to problems and needs.
- *New Deal employment projects* and projects funded through the *Connexions Service*, which aim to create further opportunities for learning and skills development for young people.

You also need to design your approach differently for different age groups.

- Up to 11 years old, where children can be reached through primary schools, ideas need to be simple and have good educational content. At Key Stage 2 (age 8–11), young people are beginning to use their own initiative to do things.
- From 11 to 16 (Key Stages 3 and 4), young people will have Citizenship Education as part of their official curriculum from September 2002, and they will be encouraged to do active projects in the community. You should be aware that below the age of 16, there are legal issues involved for your charity if you organise projects for young people off school or youth club premises without a teacher or youth leader being present.
- Post 16, through to university and beyond, young people can be expected to organise activities independently, for example through a charity committee or by organising one-off events such as a disco or fun run in aid of a charity of their choice. The National Federation of Youth Action Agencies encourages young people's involvement out of school. At university, Student Volunteering UK promotes student volunteering.

There are three issues to take into account: the interests and concerns of the young people themselves; what they are capable of doing; and their educational needs. If you can design an approach which deals with all three, then you will find that there is enormous potential.

Legal and ethical issues

If you are planning to raise money from young people, you should remember that you are dealing with a vulnerable and impressionable group. You need to approach them with care and be sensitive to their interests and their needs. You should not put undue pressure on them or their parents and families. Instead, try to get them to understand your work, the reasons for it and why it is important. There are several issues to consider.

- Legal constraints. Young people under the age of 18 are not able to enter into legal agreements, and should not be expected or invited to make contributions of any contractual nature.
- Educational considerations. The role of a school is to educate young people and prepare them for their future life. Though charity and charity

appeals certainly confront them with issues from the outside world, exploring these may best be done through classroom work rather than some fundraising event. The school must be the judge of what is appropriate, and many have tough stipulations on whether and how to work with charity appeals. This is well covered in the ICFM code of practice on fundraising in schools.

- The pressure that children apply implicitly or explicitly on their parents to give money or participate in an event ('pesterpower' as it is known in advertising). Most fundraising by younger children involves getting parents and close relatives or neighbours to contribute. Parents may react negatively to the number of times and the purposes they are asked to give to through their children, and may even try to prevent their children from taking part.

- Safety concerns. Children should not be encouraged to solicit support of any sort from people outside quite a narrow circle of family and neighbours for personal safety reasons. There are also legal and safety issues relating to young people under 16 when they are taken outside school premises.

Making the approach

To obtain access to young people through a school, you will need the permission and support of the headteacher (or the support of a committed class teacher, who will then get the agreement of the headteacher). You can make the approach directly, or a committed supporter or volunteer who is a parent or a teacher could do this for you.

Most heads receive a large number of approaches from charities (some of the larger charities have departments which concentrate on this form of fundraising), and they will want to ration the number of activities taking place in the school. It is unlikely that you will be able to involve a school more than once a year, so you will need to contact as many schools as possible if you are to get a reasonable number involved in raising money for you. You need to be conscious of the time it takes to approach schools (ten visits to schools of 30 children or one visit to a school of 300 children) and the effect that has on your own work – costs, income, hours available to work etc. Personal visits are the best way of making the approach. If this is not practical, a telephone call is better than a circular letter, which is likely to find its way into the bin.

Some fundraising ideas for schools and young people

Some of these will work best with younger children, others will be fine right up to the sixth form:

Cake and biscuit stall

Carol singing

Disco

Fancy dress or 'no uniform' day (teachers too!)

Litter picking

Picnic

Promises auction (babysitting, ironing, gardening, bike servicing etc.)

Raffle

Recycling

Sponsored event: walk, silence, swim etc.

Summer fete with activities including:

    face painting

    name the teddy

    lucky dip

    puppet making

    treasure map

    book stall

No school is going to invite you in if the only thing you plan to do is raise money. A useful guide is to make your activities:

- firstly fun;
- secondly educational;
- and only thirdly fundraising.

The usual starting point is to offer to give a talk about your organisation, the work it is doing, and the issues or problems that it is dealing with. This will usually be to a school assembly or to a relevant year group. Now that citizenship is due to become a compulsory element of the curriculum at Key Stages 3 and 4 from 2002, you may find secondary schools more willing. You will need to make your presentation as attractive and interesting as possible because this introduces the next step – the invitation to fundraise for you. This will either be taken up by the school or by a particular class if it fits into their educational programme.

For primary schools you will need a very clear set of fundraising ideas. The NSPCC, for example, has a series of worksheet games for different age groups, where younger children (5–7 year olds) find and colour shapes in a seaside picture, and older ones (7–13 year olds) take part in a sponsored spell. The tasks are designed to fit the National Curriculum and are accompanied by Teachers' Guidelines, which not only provide notes on using the activities but also give helpful advice on what to do if a teacher suspects that a child has been abused. The fundraising element is that the children raise money for the NSPCC by getting sponsorship from family and friends for completing the activities, and the reward for the children themselves is that they earn prizes such as stickers, badges and door tags.

Examples of materials for schools from the NSPCC.

Sponsored competitions are popular as they offer opportunities for learning, and sponsored events such as walks or swims offer an element of physical challenge which may be attractive. For secondary schools, the students themselves are in a better position to decide how funds should be raised and then to organise the process.

Fundraising by and for schools

According to *School Fundraising in England* schools raise about £35 million for charity each year. About £15 million of this is raised by state primary schools; £14 million by state secondary schools and the rest largely by independent secondary schools. The competitive pressure is increasing, with more and more charities competing to raise money from a fixed number of schools.

But there is also a whole new sector of organisations seeking to raise money from young people and their parents – the schools themselves. Schools have realised that often the only way to expand or improve the quality of their education or to provide for extras is to raise money themselves. Schools are currently raising over £400 million a year for their own needs on top of the main school budgets and at the time of writing it is unclear how far new government funding will ease the pressure. It is natural for the school to have first call on the generosity of both the children and their parents. Mostly this fundraising activity is carried out by Parent Teacher Associations, which comprise a group of active and already committed parents. Raising funds for the school itself can be carried out in a whole range of ways, many of them covered in this book: fetes, discos, sales, quiz evenings, Christmas cards, entertainments, and 100 clubs have all proved popular and effective.

Publications for schools

A number of the larger charities produce publications for children. These fall into two categories.

- School packs of teaching materials specially designed for use in the classroom (where they must be linked to the curriculum). Sometimes the pack is sponsored by a company whose interests overlap with the subject of the pack. The NSPCC, for example, had sponsorship from Microsoft for the activity worksheets described earlier in this chapter.
- Simple information aimed at young people, which is sent in response to enquiries or as a thank you for a donation. This could include a book or a pamphlet, a newsletter and an information sheet. You might even consider setting up a junior supporters 'club' to nurture the interests of young people. These undoubtedly build a strong loyalty to the organisations concerned and are an important ingredient of a successful fundraising programme.

National competitions

National and larger local charities might consider an award scheme for young people – such as an essay competition, an art competition, or an ideas competition. You will need to offer prizes, which can be to the young people or to the school – or perhaps to both. The prizes might be in cash, books, bursaries, or travel opportunities and they will usually represent around 10%–25% of the total cost of running the scheme. You also have to pay for publicity, printed material, judging, the awards ceremony, and all the administration involved. However, you may be able to get sponsorship as competitions are attractive to companies, who are looking for ways to reach young people and get good publicity from having supported an exciting award scheme. For local and city-wide competitions, you may be able to get the local newspaper to become a media sponsor, providing you with free publicity at all stages of the competition, rather than cash support.

Resources and further information

See also general lists at the end of the book.

Organisations

National Federation for Youth Action Agencies (NFYAA)
Northern Office
26 High Market Place
Kirkbymoorside
North Yorkshire YO62 6BQ
www.youth-action.org.uk
Tel. 01751 430116
Fax 01751 430122
e-mail ragar@compuserve.com

Publications

The following publications are available from the Directory of Social Change. Prices were correct at the time of writing, but may be subject to change.

Charity Matters (a resource pack for secondary schools), Tony Thorpe, DSC 1999, £5

Organising Local Events, Sarah Passingham, DSC 1995, £5

Raising Money for Good Causes, Jane Sutherland and Mike Eastwood, DSC 1998, £5.99

Tried and Tested Ideas for Raising Money Locally 3rd edition, Sarah Passingham, DSC, available autumn 2003 (check our website for information), c. £14.95

School Fundraising in England, Nicola Eastwood and Anne Mountfield, DSC 2000, £9.95 or download for free from www.dsc.org.uk

Schools Funding Guide, Nicola Eastwood, Anne Mountfield and Louise Walker, DSC 2001, £16.95

Voluntary Sector Legal Handbook 2nd edition, Sandy Adirondack and James Sinclair Taylor, DSC 2001, £42 (voluntary organisations) £60 (others)

Other publications

Complete Guide to Fundraising, PF Sterrett and PW Sterrett, Management Books 2001, £12.99

Institute of Fundraising Code of Practice on Fundraising in Schools

6 TRUSTS AND FOUNDATIONS

Grant-making trusts, sometimes known as foundations, are independent grant-making bodies. They get their income from investments or through their own fundraising. They are set up specifically to give money away for charitable purposes and for community benefit. There are currently nearly 9,000 of them, giving nearly £2 billion a year. They are a must for most fundraisers – for well-established national and local charities, but also for new and smaller community-based projects. This chapter gives the basic information you need to start fundraising from trusts.

Details of organisations and publications referred to in this chapter are on p. 127.

6.1 About trusts

Trusts come in all shapes and sizes, founded for a variety of reasons, with different social and political perspectives, and with different approaches to their grant-making. Most trusts will not be interested in funding you, but there will be plenty who are. You need to research carefully which trusts are worth approaching, what aspects of your work they will be interested in, the size of their current grants budget, and the range of their grants.

Most trusts say that they receive far more applications that they can possibly support – but not enough good ones. Many are circular letters produced on a word processor, sent to a large number of trusts without being tailored to the trust's particular interests and priorities. These are generally rejected on sight. The key to success is to make sure that each application you send is relevant to the particular trust and that you ask for an appropriate amount. See chapter 15, section 15.1, for advice on writing applications.

Many trusts see their key role as being to support innovation – new ideas, new ways of doing things, new needs, new organisations. They will be wary of anything which could be interpreted as simply compensating for cuts in statutory funding or of continuing to fund the core costs of your organisation over a period of time. Many organisations owe their existence to progressive trusts who were prepared to shoulder whatever risk there may have been during its early stages. The downside of this, of course, is that in order to obtain funding beyond the initial start-up period (usually a maximum of three years), organisations are compelled to repackage their work into 'new' projects, even if they are still addressing the same long-term need.

Successful fundraising from trusts involves identifying suitable trusts, finding out as much as you can about them, trying to get them interested in your work even before you approach them for money, finding an aspect of your work that they will want to support, and persuading them to say yes. What could be easier than that?

How a trust works

A trust has the following structure:

THE DONOR or FOUNDER
who provides the money

▼

A CONSTITUTION or TRUST DEED
which sets out how the funds are to be managed and distributed

▼

THE TRUSTEES
who ensure that the funds are properly invested and managed, and grants
are made according to the terms of the trust deed

▼

ADMINISTRATIVE STAFF
Many of the larger trusts employ staff to manage the affairs of the trust, to
deal with applicants and to assess applications (some use external assessors); the staff are accountable to the trustees, who retain the ultimate
responsibility for the trust's decisions. However, the majority of trusts have
no paid administrative staff at all.

▼

THE APPLICANT
who applies for a grant from the trust (that's you!)

The diversity of trusts

- The largest trust by far (after the National Lottery Community Fund) is the Wellcome Trust. It gives mainly to medical and scientific research, and so it is not relevant to the majority of fundraisers. Trusts like the Tudor Trust and the Garfield Weston Foundation have much broader remits – both give over £20 million a year in grants across a wide range of charitable purposes. At the other end of the scale are tiny (usually local) bodies with just a few hundred pounds a year to distribute.
- Trusts may have an international remit, such as the Aga Khan Foundation, which funds in Africa and South Asia, and Comic Relief, which works predominantly in Africa. Trusts may give nationally, such as the Joseph Rowntree Foundation or the Lloyds TSB Foundation. Or they may operate regionally or locally. Some local trusts are very large and if you are fortunate enough to work within their beneficial area, they may be your best source of funds. Not all areas of the UK are as well provided for as others in terms of local trusts, so the luck of geography can play a significant part in successful fundraising.
- Some trusts support a wide range of activities, while others specialise in providing funding for a particular type of work. Part of the knack of tailoring an application lies in identifying an area of work that a trust will support and highlighting that aspect in your proposal.
- Some trusts will give grants to individuals. Others only fund organisations. Many limit their support to registered charities.

6.2 Understanding how trusts work

There are various key factors that influence how each trust operates, and you need to develop an understanding of these in order to increase your chances of success.

1 Where trusts get their money from

Most trusts are established with a capital sum provided by a founder during his or her lifetime or in their will. This could be cash, shares in a company or even land. The founder could be a successful business person – such as Paul Hamlyn or David Sainsbury, who have both set up major foundations – but there are also many trusts set up by individuals with much more modest sums.

Some trusts are set up by public subscription. The various royal Jubilee Trusts are examples, as are the Winston Churchill Memorial Trust and the Diana, Princess of Wales Memorial Fund, both of which were set up in memory of famous individuals.

Some trusts have no permanent funds, but rely on continuing fundraising to provide them with money for distribution. The largest of these are the BBC's Children in Need and Comic Relief, both of which raise money through a major television appeal. The Network Foundation is a much smaller trust which brings together a group of like-minded socially responsible individuals who pool their charitable giving to support projects promoting peace and a better world.

Some trusts are set up by companies as a vehicle for their charitable giving. Depending on the way this is done, some are truly independent, whilst others are obliged to follow company policy in their grant-making (in which case you should probably approach them in the way that you would approach a company – see chapter 8).

How a trust is founded can have a significant impact on its grantmaking. Although the trust's declared area of interest may simply be recorded as 'General charitable purposes', the founder's wishes, sometimes set out in a letter attached to the founding trust deed, will guide the trustees in their grantmaking. The founder and his or her family may often play a leading role in the affairs of the trust as trustees, supporting concerns and projects which particularly interest them. This is perfectly legitimate; trusts are in one sense 'private bodies' set up for 'public benefit'. They are not, however, private in the sense of being permitted to keep information about their assets and grant-giving to themselves. Like other charities, all charitable trusts must be registered with the Charity Commission and file their annual accounts according to the requirements of the Statement of Recommended Practice (SORP). Over time, the founder's influence can diminish as outside trustees are appointed, which has happened with the Joseph Rowntree and Nuffield Foundations.

Examples of major trusts established by successful business people

- Esmée Fairbairn Foundation (Ian Fairbairn, M & G Group, unit trusts)
- The Gatsby Charitable Trust (David Sainsbury, J Sainsbury, supermarkets)
- The Paul Hamlyn Foundation (Paul Hamlyn, publishing)
- The Mackintosh Foundation (Cameron Mackintosh, musical theatre)
- The Wates Foundation (the Wates family, house builders)
- The Garfield Weston Foundation (Garfield Weston, Associated British Foods)
- The Westminster Foundation (Duke of Westminster, landowner)
- The Wolfson Foundation (Sir Isaac Wolfson, retailing)

2 The trust's objects and policies

The trust deed (or governing or founding document) sets out the objects or purposes of the trust, defining what can and cannot be supported. Objects can be very broad, defined only as general charitable or educational purposes, or quite specific: one of the principal objects of the Childwick Trust, for example, is to support charities for people connected with mining in South Africa; and the Great Britain Sasakawa Foundation exists to support links between Great Britain and Japan.

The trustees can also decide on a policy and priorities for their grantmaking (so long as this falls within the objects of the trust). So a trust set up for the advancement of education might decide to give all its money for literacy and numeracy (as the Shine Foundation is doing), or as bursaries to young people aged 16 to 18 in order to encourage them to stay on at school, or to primary schools to buy computers. You need to check to see whether your application falls within the trust's current grant policy and priorities. It is also worth looking at what grants it has given in the recent past, since this may help you to identify the trustees' preferences – although these can change from year to year, and just because a trust gave to a lunch club for the elderly last year, it may not intend supporting similar schemes this year. It is also possible to misinterpret why a particular grant was given; funding for a church choir may have been given because the trust supports music, or it may simply support church-related activities or an activity closely connected with a trustee, in which case, there is little point in applying for money for your community brass band. Not all areas of giving are equally supported and trusts determine their own priorities for giving, which may not relate to current needs or issues in society. Research by the Charities Aid Foundation, however (see *Dimensions 2000 Patterns of Independent Grantmaking*), has shown that around a third of trust grants – and a quarter of the total money – is given for social care.

3 The beneficial area

Many trusts are restricted in where they can give support. Some trusts can give throughout the UK, or even throughout the world. Many can only give locally. For example, the City Parochial Foundation can only give grants for the benefit of the people of London, and the Cripplegate Foundation for those who live or work in two wards of South Islington. If you are lucky enough to operate within the beneficial area of a large trust (and the City Parochial can give over £5 million a year!), then your chances of success are greater than if you are based in an area which is less well-provided for.

Community trusts

Community trusts work in specific geographical area to provide grants for local charitable activity. The idea is relatively new. They operate in two main ways:

- by building an endowment of capital raised from companies, trusts and rich individuals in their area, and through legacies. The income from this is then used to make grants. Some also organise fundraising events to generate further income for their grant-making;
- they work with other donors to help them distribute their money more effectively. Donors can direct their funds to a favoured cause or within a specified geographical area. Themed funds can address a particular issue, such as crime prevention, and projects can be supported with donations from several sources.

Community trusts are being promoted, supported and trained by Community Foundation Network. This is how they describe their role:

'Community Foundation Network is a membership organisation which exists to promote, develop and support community foundations throughout the United Kingdom. Community foundations help build and strengthen the capacity of local communities through: constructive local grantmaking for voluntary and community activity; building endowment to create permanent community capital; encouraging local philanthropy; being a vehicle for donors' charitable interests; and acting as a catalyst in local initiatives. They are committed to being sturdy, flexible and responsive organisations at the heart of their communities for generations to come. They understand the importance of involving donors and providing them with a professional service to maximise the effectiveness of their donations through long-term endowment building and well directed grantmaking.

Community foundations are now well-established in many areas and are starting in a number of new parts of the country – developments already cover around 80% of the UK. Community Foundation Network is committed to maximising both the growth of sound community foundations and the scope for building local, regional and national partnerships which include them.'

Community trusts are growing in importance, and at an impressive rate. In 1999–2000 the 29 fully operational community trusts gave a total of £22 million – a 16% increase on the previous year's funding. A further 27 fledgling trusts were also developing. They can be key funders of local work, and may also give advice on raising money from other local trusts. You may even be able to use their support as a lever to obtain further funding; a national trust is likely to react more positively to your application if you can demonstrate that you have already successfully raised money locally.

Read the guidelines before applying

Most of the larger trusts publish guidelines to what they will and will not fund. It is important to read these before applying to see whether what you are proposing fits within their policies and does not fall within their exclusions. For example, the Bridge House Estates Trust Fund was established by the Corporation of London to distribute money surplus to what is required for maintaining Blackfriars, Southwark, London and Tower Bridges. The overall object of the trust is 'Welfare in London', but if you examine its guidelines more closely, you will see that its policy is to concentrate its giving in the following five main areas, in Greater London:

1 transport and access for older and disabled people;
2 environmental conservation;
3 children and young people;
4 the provision of technical assistance to voluntary organisations;
5 assistance to older people to stay within the community.

The exclusions are:

- political parties
- political lobbying
- non-charitable activities
- statutory or corporate bodies where the body involved is under a statutory or legal duty to incur the expenditure.
- grants which do not benefit the inhabitants of Greater London
- individuals
- grant-making bodies to make grants on its behalf
- schools, universities and other educational establishments, except where they are undertaking ancillary charitable activities specifically directed towards one of the agreed priority areas
- medical or academic research
- churches or other religious bodies where the monies will be used for construction, repair and maintenance of religious buildings or for other religious purposes
- hospitals.

4 Large and small trusts

Larger trusts are managed professionally and tend to have a clerk, secretary or director (the title varies), who is in executive charge of the grants programme, together with some administrative support. Some very large trusts have a team of specialist or regional grants officers. The director will report to a board of trustees. The trustees remain responsible for policy and grant decisions, but base their decisions on the recommendations of their staff. Most of the larger trusts have well thought through policies for what they are interested in supporting. Applications are assessed according to these and there is no point in applying if you cannot demonstrate that your project or organisation fits within the guidelines.

Smaller trusts are often run by the family or the individual who set them up. They may be administered by a firm of lawyers or accountants who will prepare the accounts, and sometimes provide an address for correspondence. They usually cannot afford to employ professional staff to assess grant applications. Many simply support the interests of the founder or family that established the trust. Some will not even consider applications received from charities they have no contact or connection with – so good contacts with their trustees or some form of personal or local connection is often vital.

5 How grant decisions are made

Most trusts respond to the requests they receive for support, rather than seeking out projects they would like to support. So the first stage in the grant-making process is receiving a proposal from an applicant. What happens next depends on the size of the trust. Larger trusts will have a procedure for assessing applications, which could include:

- the trust director or a specialist grants officer assessing the application and making a recommendation;
- a site visit or a meeting with the applicant;
- engaging a consultant to investigate and report (which would only be done for very large applications).

A report with recommendations is prepared for the trustees, with the final decision being made at the next trustees' meeting. Some of the very large trusts allow their staff discretion to decide smaller grants without reference to the trustees.

Smaller trusts tend to do everything through the trustees. They read all the applications they receive, reject clearly inappropriate ones and discuss together which they will support based on the information in your application.

6.3 Some important considerations

1 Charitable status of the applicant

Almost all trusts can only support charitable work. A handful of trusts have been set up specifically to support non-charitable work, the main ones being the Barrow Cadbury Trust and the Joseph Rowntree Reform Trust, both of which are associated with larger charitable trusts. The Network Foundation also has a non-charitable arm.

This requirement to support charitable work does not mean that trusts can only give to registered charities, but they must support work for public benefit. Many trusts, however, have a policy of only giving to registered charities. Newly established organisations which have not yet obtained charitable status, or those which have decided not to register as charities, will not be able to obtain a grant directly from such trusts, although you can arrange for another charity to receive the grant on your behalf (some community trusts and local Councils of Voluntary Service are prepared to do this).

There are also trusts which have been set up to support individuals in need or to give grants for educational purposes (see *A Guide to Grants for Individuals in Need* and *The Educational Grants Directory*). Some trusts also provide bursaries to individuals – for example the Prince's Trust supports young people, the Winston Churchill Memorial Trust provides bursaries for people to undertake study visits, and unLTD provides awards for people who wish to create change in their communities. Many trusts which make grants to organisations specifically exclude grants to individuals.

2 National or local projects

Many large trusts have a national or international remit. They support national projects, important local projects, or projects of national significance (such as pioneering local work which has implications for the way things are done in other parts of the country).

Some national trusts also make purely local grants. Many have a particular interest in supporting projects close to where they are based. Some also have defined areas of the country where they give their local support (on the basis that it is more effective to concentrate their resources on a particular area, and that it is difficult to assess applications from all parts of the country). For example, the Wates Foundation supports projects in South London, the Baring Foundation supports local projects in Merseyside and Cornwall, and 29th May Charity supports projects in the West Midlands. Such trusts usually also want to focus on need, so any local project should try to make a convincing case that local needs are particularly pressing – comparative local data, possibly from census figures, can be useful.

Some trusts have been established specifically to make grants in a local area, so if yours is a local project, you should start by finding out what trusts are active in your area. Trusts are, unfortunately, distributed unevenly around the country. The majority are based in the London and the south east. Some other areas are also quite well served. For example, although there are few trusts in Manchester or in Wales, there are thriving trust networks in Scotland, Liverpool, and Birmingham. If you come from an area with few local trusts, you will naturally find it harder to get trust support for a local project, although there are moves to encourage trusts which *can* give nationally to look further afield. You could try making a case to a national trust based not just on need but on the lack of available trust funding to meet that need.

3 One-off or continuing support

Most trusts either make one-off grants or give regular support for only a limited period (usually no more than three years, although a few trusts fund for longer than this), as they want to keep themselves free to respond to new requests. Many have a maximum grant limit. Trusts also want to feel that, unless you are proposing to eradicate a problem altogether, the work will continue once their support has ended. You therefore need to be clear about the long-term goals and funding strategy of the project and the organisation. Where the proposal is for a building or to buy some equipment, you need to show how the facility will be used and how the running costs will be met. Where the grant is towards running costs, you should show what will happen when it runs out. The phrase 'exit strategy' is increasingly being used to describe this.

Whatever kind of grant you get, if you are able to show that you have used the money effectively, the trust may well be willing to support another aspect of your work once the current funding runs out – although some trusts don't give a second grant to an organisation until at least a year has elapsed since the first grant terminated.

4 Grants or loans

Most trusts simply make cash grants. Some may make interest-free or low-interest loans, but you must be able to repay the loan and this can only happen if there is some return expected from the project. The Charities Aid Foundation and the Triodos Bank have set up social investment funds specifically to make loans to charities. Contact them for more information.

5 Trust preferences

Every trust has a different approach. Some prefer to give start up or 'seed' money; others prefer the development of more established projects. Some favour capital projects, others revenue. Some prefer safer, more conservative work, whilst others are radical and pioneering. Some want to make a large number of small grants, whilst others concentrate on a few major projects.

What trusts like to fund

Trusts like to fund particular aspects of an organisation's work (projects) that they can identify with and feel that they are having some impact on. They also like to back innovation, responding to new needs or meeting existing needs in new ways. Here are a number of project ideas that a local advice service might put forward to a trust.

- The training of volunteers to provide welfare rights advice.
- A nutrition advisory service using peer group advisers to provide advice to families with young children.
- A conference or research report on school bullying, which would get an issue of enormous concern further out into the open, with the opportunity to discuss some positive and practical approaches for dealing with the problem.
- A Desk Top Publishing system to produce and print leaflets on a wide range of topics for distribution throughout the community.

All these are likely to be much more attractive than simply applying for money towards the costs of running the organisation. The trick is to find things that you are already doing or want to do which are likely to appeal to a donor, and then to include in the budget a reasonable contribution towards the running costs of the organisation.

Almost all trusts prefer to support specific projects and initiatives rather than to make a contribution to general costs. Terminology such as 'core costs' and 'overheads' has historically been used inconsistently by both fundraisers and funders, but a useful set of new terms has been proposed by ACEVO (Association of Chief Executives of Voluntary Organisations) (see *Funding our future: core costs revisited*), which may help you to clarify what a trust is prepared to consider:

- **development funding**, through which the internal infrastructure costs of an organisation are met for a time in order for it to grow and develop;
- **strategic funding**, through which the funder recognises the need for an organisation to exist and is prepared to contribute over an agreed period of time;

- **full project funding**, in which all reasonable associated costs are met as part of a funding package.

An acceptance in particular of the term 'full project funding' by trusts will be enormously helpful in enabling organisations to apply for sufficient funding to cover the real costs of a project.

To summarise, in order to have the best chance of success, make sure that your application matches:

- the trust's policies and priorities. There is no point sending an application to a trust which has no interest in that sort of work;
- their scale of grant-making. There is no point approaching a tiny trust for a large grant, or a major one for a small item of expenditure;
- their ethos and approach. You will have the greatest success with those trusts that share your outlook and values.

6.4 Getting started with trusts

Published information about trusts

The Directory of Social Change publishes a range of grant directories on trust giving for fundraisers, including its own *Guides to the Major Trusts* and *Guides to Local Trusts*, and the Charities Aid Foundation's *Directory of Grant Making Trusts*. The CAF directory covers more trusts, and reports what the trusts themselves say about their policies and grants, whereas the DSC guides include the results of independent research and analysis of what the trusts actually do in practice. They also go into greater detail, particularly for the larger trusts, where most of the money is. All the information from both the CAF and DSC databases of trusts is also available on a single, comprehensive CD ROM, which although it is more expensive makes the process of searching a lot easier and quicker. Or you can subscribe to the website version of the database, www.trustfunding.org.uk. Another useful database is maintained by an organisation called Funderfinder. If you are short of funds, the directories and CD ROMs may be available to consult at your local CVS or RCC, or you can visit the DSC library.

Don't forget the internet, which potentially gives you access to vast amounts of information – if only you can find it! Some trusts, such as the Baring Foundation, have their own website. Umbrella organisations such as the Association of Charitable Foundations (ACF) have sites, often with useful links.

Finding the right trusts: a step by step approach

1 First of all, find out what links you have had with trusts previously, and whether they have been successful. For those that have failed, try to find out why. Those that have supported you once are often likely to want to support you again – especially if you have done a really good job with their money.

2 Those that have turned you down are also likely prospects for future support. You have already identified them as being potentially interested in your work – but as yet, you have failed to convince them of the value of supporting you. Try to find something really interesting for them to support, and present a better case next time.

3 Go through the directories of grant-making trusts to identify and match possible funders with aspects of your organisation's work. Divide the trusts in two ways:
   a) those that seem most likely to give to you

      those that might just be interested

      those that it is not worth contacting
   b) larger trusts which could make a reasonable sized grant

      smaller trusts where you could only expect to receive a small amount.

Your final list may only contain 20–30 trusts, but this is likely to be much more successful than a scattershot approach. Concentrate your efforts on approaching those that are most likely to support you. Find out whether the trusts on the list produce an annual report or guidelines for applicants. If they do, then get hold of these. Thoroughly research your application from the available information. Find out whether any of your trustees, volunteers or staff members have good links or personal contacts with any of the trusts you are planning to approach. Personal contact can be important – try to use it to get a good word put in on your behalf or ask them how to frame your application. Trusts are unlikely to give a large grant to organisations they have never heard of. If you are looking for large sums, it may be better to apply for something small now, spend it well, then go back for something more substantial. Or maybe work in partnership with a larger, longer established and better known organisation. Their partnership with you will vouch for your credibility.

6.5 Making contact

Getting in touch with trusts is a process with several stages:

1 General PR to make people aware of your organisation and its work, so that when you approach a trust, they have heard of you and understand the importance of your work. You can send copies of your annual report or relevant publications well before you intend to raise money; get coverage of your work and achievements in the press, and send photocopies of

articles to people who might be interested; or participate in radio or TV discussions, or in specialist conferences (as a speaker or asking questions from the floor).

2 A phone call to establish contact. Ask whether there is a best time in the trust's year to apply, whether the trust can support your type of work, and the procedure for applying for a grant. You may be able to get a clearer picture of the sort of work that the foundation is likely to want to support. Find out the deadline for applications. Many trusts meet quarterly; but smaller trusts may only meet annually, or may not respond at all to applications from people and organisations not known to them. Sometimes the trust will suggest that you delay your application until the next meeting, as there are just too many requests this time for your proposal to stand any chance of success.

3 A written application setting out your request. Find out first whether there is an application form or whether a particular format is required. Make sure that you attach a copy of your latest accounts, together with your annual report (if you have one) or some other description of your organisation and its work (see chapter 15, section 15.1, for advice on writing a fundraising application).

4 Ask for an appropriate amount. Use your research to find out typical levels of grant that the trust makes and tailor your request accordingly. Some trusts make larger grants to larger national charities, and smaller grants to smaller or more local projects.

5 A trust will often back the ideas and energy of a key individual in your organisation. If you have such individuals, emphasise their strengths in your proposal, include a CV, and try to get that individual to meet the trust.

6 For a large proposal where you are unlikely to get all the money from one trust, think carefully about what to ask for. You could invite trusts to match the giving of another trust, or to money raised from elsewhere. For example, if you are seeking support for a community venture, getting the local council to pay for the staff and premises and asking the trust to cover the project costs can be an attractive way for both to give their support. Or you might try to get four trusts each to contribute a quarter of the project costs, where the total you require is beyond the reach of any one of them.

7 You might then telephone to see whether your application has arrived, and to ask whether any further information is required. You might try to get the staff or trustees to visit you. It will considerably enhance your chances if someone has visited the project. Make sure that everything is working well, that the premises look well kept and well used, and that they meet some of your users who can speak enthusiastically about your work and the help you have given them.

8 If you have contact with a particular trustee, try to discuss your proposal with them and enlist their support before the matter comes up for discussion.

9 Remember to say thank you if your application has been successful. Note all the conditions attached to the grant and the reporting requirements – and make sure that you comply with these.

10 Keep in regular touch, and let them know how the project is going, and tell them about anything that has been particularly successful. This helps build a relationship with them, which may lead to further support.

11 Keep a record of all the approaches you make, both letters and phone calls, and of the response you receive. This will be helpful when you approach them next time.

12 If you find you have raised more money than you need as a result of approaching several trusts, be truthful and go back to them with alternative suggestions. Offer to extend the project or improve it, rather than have to repay the money. They will almost always agree.

What trusts are looking for

1 Can you define the problem clearly?

2 How will you make a difference? And does it work?

3 Can you show what difference will be made?

4 How long will you need before you can demonstrate an impact?

5 How do you see the problem and your approach to it fitting in with the trust's priorities?

6 What skills will be needed for the project? Can you demonstrate that you have them? If not, how will you get them?

7 Have you supplied details of your training and past experience, if this is relevant?

8 What is innovative about the project? And how far can the innovative aspects be replicated in other situations?

9 If the project isn't innovative, why does the application merit a grant?

10 How do you propose to evaluate and disseminate any practical experience, outcomes and lessons learned from the project?

11 Do you have a clear management structure?

12 Does the application come from or clearly have the support of the senior people in the organisation – both the senior staff and the Management Board?

13 Have you supplied your latest annual accounts? And do they give a picture of a well run, effective organisation?

14 What are the major sources of income for your work at the moment, and will these continue into the future? If not, what are you planning to do to secure your organisation's future?

15 Is your budget realistic? Many applications undercost their projects.

16 What proportion of the total you require is being requested from the trust?

17 Where do you propose to obtain the balance? Have you already made other applications? Have any been successful? Are any pending, and when will the outcome be known?

18 What if you can't raise the whole of the budget you have proposed? Will you be able to work on less? Will you have to adjust your plans? Will you go ahead?

19 What will happen when the trust's grant runs out? Is there a strategy for obtaining continuing funding? Or will the project become self-sufficient or terminate at that point?

20 When do you need the funds? Most trusts have a decision process which takes several months to receive, evaluate and decide on the application. Many applicants apply far too late.

These 20 questions have been adapted from a leaflet given to applicants by the Joseph Rowntree Charitable Trust. They are the sorts of questions you will need to address in your written application (see chapter 15) and in any subsequent discussions with a grants assessor.

Resources and further information

See also general lists at the end of the book.

Organisations

Association of Charitable Foundations (ACF)
2 Plough Yard
Shoreditch High Street
London EC2A 3LP
www.acf.org.uk
Tel: 020 7422 8600
This is a network for trusts, which produces a newsletter, runs an annual conference for members, and organises special interest groups to keep members informed on particular areas of charitable work. Its website provides links to its members' sites and their funding information.

Community Foundation Network
2 Plough Yard
Shoreditch High Street
London EC2A 3LP
Tel. 020 7422 8611
e-mail network@communityfoundations. org.uk

FunderFinder
65 Raglan Road
Leeds LS2 9DZ
www.funderfinder.org.uk
Tel. 0113 243 3008
Maintains a database on disk to match your project proposals with funding opportunities. Your national association or your local Council of Voluntary Service may have a copy you can use.

Publications

The following publications are available from the Directory of Social Change. Prices were correct at the time of writing, but may be subject to change.

The main grants directories are:

The Directory of Grant Making Trusts, CAF 2003, £80

The Grant-making Trusts CD ROM (all the trusts from the CAF and DSC databases on one CD ROM), developed by FunderFinder for DSC 2003, £115 + VAT

www.trustfunding.org.uk: this subscription website allows you to access the same range of information as on the CD-ROM, but updated throughout the year. Annual subscription £115 + VAT (charities and voluntary organisations) £160 +VAT (statutory and commercial)

Guide to the Major Trusts, Vol 1: the top 300 trusts (making grants annually of over £400,000), DSC 2003, £20.95

Guide to the Major Trusts, Vol 2: the next 700 trusts (making grants annually of over £60,000), DSC 2003, £20.95

Guide to the Major Trusts, Vol 3: a further 500 UK-wide trusts and trusts in Northern Ireland, DSC 2002, £17.95

A Guide to Local Trusts: four volumes covering local trusts in the North of England, the Midlands, the South of England, and Greater London, DSC 2002, £17.95 each

A Guide to Scottish Trusts: provides comprehensive coverage of trust giving in Scotland, DSC 2002, £16.95

The Welsh Funding Guide: provides comprehensive coverage of trust and other giving in Wales, DSC (available autumn 2003), c. 16.95

Directories of trusts that will fund individuals:

The Educational Grants Directory, DSC 2002, £20.95

A Guide to Grants for Individuals in Need, DSC 2002, £20.95

Specialist funding guides include:

Arts Funding Guide 6th edition DSC 2002, £18.95

Directory of American Grantmakers, Chapel & York 2002, £45

Environmental Funding Guide, DSC 1998, £12.50

International Development Directory, DSC 2001, £16.95

South Asian Funding in the UK, Karina Holly and Zerbanoo Gifford, DSC 1999, £9.95

Sports Funding Guide 2nd edition, DSC 1999, £16.95

Youth Funding Guide 2nd edition, DSC 2002, £16.95

The following handbooks may also be useful:

Avoiding the wastepaper basket 2nd edition, a practical guide for applying to grant-making trusts, Tim Cook, LVSC 1998, £5.50

Fundraising from Grant-making Trusts and Foundations, Karen Gilchrist, DSC/CAF 2000, £10.95

Find the Funds, Christopher Carnie, DSC/CAF 2000, £12.95

Writing Better Fundraising Applications 3rd edition, Michael Norton and Mike Eastwood, DSC 2002, £14.95

The following journal will keep you up-to-date with the trust world:

Funding for Change, ed. Susan Forrrester, DSC, published four times a year, subscription £40 (voluntary and community organisations) £50 (statutory and commercial organisations), Issue 1 available April 2003

Research into trust funding appears in:

Dimensions 2000, Volume 3, Patterns of independent grantmaking, CAF 2000, £25

Funding our future: core costs revisted ACEVO 2001, £22.50

7 THE NATIONAL LOTTERY

The National Lottery is now the largest single source of funds for voluntary organisations, and for arts, sports and heritage projects. By the end of the first seven year licence in 2001, some £14 billion had been raised for 'good causes'. The Lottery is of such size and importance that many organisations are now gearing a substantial part of their fundraising effort towards getting support from the various Distribution Boards. This chapter gives an overview of how these operate.

Details of organisations and publications referred to in this chapter are on p. 147.

7.1 About the National Lottery

The National Lottery, launched in 1994, has rapidly established itself as a key funder of voluntary activity. There were early worries about its impact – competition with existing charity fundraising, and in particular long-standing charity lotteries; the encouragement of gambling; and the transfer of money from the poor to the rich. While these have not entirely disappeared, the major concern expressed in 2000 was that any delay in awarding the next operating licence could lead to a significant loss of funding to the sector.

Many voluntary organisations have applied for Lottery grants – many have succeeded. However, it takes time and effort to put together a good application, and the assessment process is a rigorous and demanding one.

7.2 How the National Lottery operates

The National Lottery is operated under licence until 2009 by Camelot plc. They run weekly lottery games (the main game is run twice weekly, on Wednesdays and Saturdays) and sell scratch cards for instant prizes. For the new licence period (2002–2009) the costs of running the Lottery and selling the tickets (including any operating profit) will be kept to 3.5% of the total take (see chart). After the prize money, the tax due to the Treasury and these operating expenses, 28.5% of the total take is passed to the National Lottery Distribution Fund for distribution to good causes.

Distribution of each £1 of Lottery income from 2002

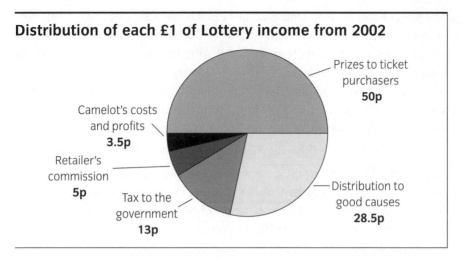

Prizes to ticket purchasers
50p

Camelot's costs and profits
3.5p

Retailer's commission
5p

Tax to the government
13p

Distribution to good causes
28.5p

The Distribution Fund passes the money to the five Distribution Boards. The five boards are:

- The Community Fund (formerly known as the National Lottery Charities Board)
- The Arts Councils in England, Scotland, Wales and Northern Ireland
- The Sports Councils in the same four countries
- The Heritage Lottery Fund
- The New Opportunities Fund

A sixth Distribution Board, The Millennium Commission, received Lottery funds up to 2001 for Millennium projects. From 2002, the New Opportunities Fund, which supports specific government-determined programmes, receives a third of all Lottery funds, with the remaining four boards receiving 16.7% each (see chart).

Distribution of funds to the National Lottery Distribution Boards – from 2001

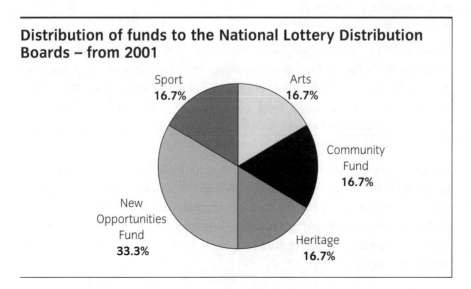

Sport
16.7%

Arts
16.7%

Community Fund
16.7%

New Opportunities Fund
33.3%

Heritage
16.7%

The priorities of the New Opportunities Fund have been openly set by the government. The other Distribution Boards are nominally independent, but they are distributing public funds and their distribution policies (and even specific grants) are subject to influence from the Secretary of State. Their grant making is under close public and media scrutiny, and there has been much criticism and debate. This has centred not only on certain recipients of grants but also on the short-term nature of revenue funding (three years only) and the excessive concentration on capital projects in the areas of arts, sport and heritage.

The National Lottery operator does not have any influence on the distribution of the funds, although Camelot has set up its own foundation (which operates in exactly the same way as those of other prominent companies), which in 1998–99 gave £3.1 million in community contributions, concentrating on combating disadvantage (see *A Guide to UK Company Giving*).

7.3 The Community Fund

The Distribution Board which most voluntary organisations think of first is the Community Fund: the new name from 2001 for the former National Lottery Charities Board (NLCB). It aims to 'help meet the needs of those at greatest disadvantage in society, and to improve the quality of life in the community'. Unlike the other Distribution Boards, it has not required any matched funding to be provided from other sources and is prepared to give grants to cover salaries and running costs. Grants can be for up to three years. Unlike the other Boards, the relief of poverty is central to its grant-making.

There are various grants programmes, of which the two main ones in 2000 were:

- Community involvement
- Poverty and disadvantage

These were merged in a single programme in April 2001, in order to avoid the possible confusion for some groups about which programme to apply to. They make grants for charitable projects of all kinds, either one-off or for up to three years, for amounts from £5,000 up to more than £1 million; the majority of grants are between £20,000 and £400,000, although it is rare for local projects to receive a grant at the higher end of the scale.

Under the community involvement programme the Board has funded projects which enable people to become involved in activities which improve the quality of life of the whole community. In particular, it has given support to projects aiming to support community organisations and activities, to promote volunteering and community action, and to develop voluntary and community groups.

Under the poverty and disadvantage programme, the Board's aim has been to improve the quality of life of people and communities who are disadvantaged by poverty or who are at risk of poverty. They are particularly interested in helping people on low incomes or living in disadvantaged areas, and in preventing or minimising future poverty.

The other programmes are:

- International grants: awards for UK charities working overseas (or on development education in the UK). This is an annual programme with fixed closing dates. Grants generally range from £20,000 to £400,000, but can be spread over as long as five years. The programme funds projects which address the causes of poverty and inequality and make a significant improvement to the quality of life of some of the most vulnerable people in the world.
- Health and social research: this is likely to become a permanent programme in 2001–2002.

Small grants of under £5,000 are dealt with under the Awards for All programme (see section 7.9 below).

The Community Fund has 13 grant-making committees:

- UK committee for UK-wide projects. This committee also deals with International and Research grants.
- Four country committees, for England, Wales, Scotland and Northern Ireland. The England committee deals with projects that cross more than one English region.
- Nine Regional Awards Committees (RACs), one in each of the English regions.

Each committee is backed by its own office and staff, who administer the entire grant-making process.

Submission and assessment of applications

Applications have to be made on a standard form, and each application then goes through a rigorous process of scoring and ranking.

In brief, the process is as follows.

- The applicant completes the form and meets all the requirements. Besides answering all the questions, you must submit annual accounts and a copy of your organisation's constitution, provide a business plan for large projects (over £200,000, or £100,000 for the International programme), and have three signatures, which must include a trustee and a third party referee.

- Stage 1 assessment by a Community Fund assessor. Inadequately completed applications and applications from ineligible organisations are rejected at this stage.
- Full assessment by a Community Fund assessor.
- Consideration by the appropriate panel (UK-wide, England, one of the nine regions of England, Scotland, Northern Ireland, Wales).

The application form runs to around 30 pages, but nonetheless is a model of its type. Considerable effort has gone into making it easy to understand and complete, and it comes with a detailed guide which sets out the criteria against which the application will be assessed, and gives advice on completing the form and what is required. In future, it will also be possible to apply online or to download the form from the Community Fund website in order to complete it electronically. At the time of writing, in a further move towards simplifying the process for smaller organisations, a shorter and easier application form was due to be introduced for sums under £60,000.

Full assessment is usually carried out either through a face-to-face meeting with the assessor, or over the phone for smaller applications. This can be quite an intensive session (phone calls have been known to go on for three hours), and it is important that the right people are present to ensure that a correct presentation of the organisation and the proposal is given. Assessors are mostly Community Fund staff.

Your application is scored numerically against a set of criteria (see box). This is quite a rigid process, with little scope for rating something highly because it seems imaginative or 'a good thing'. It is as important to have a project which genuinely meets all the criteria as it is to complete the application form skilfully. For example, there are extra points for having disabled or non-white trustees; and user involvement in management and decision making is rated highly. Some of these are factors that you can do something about before making your application; others will influence how you design your project. But being aware of the assessment criteria will ensure that you present a good case well and do not slip down the score sheet for the wrong reasons. Training is available from the Directory of Social Change on how to complete high scoring applications.

Any project with a budget in excess of £200,000 (£100,000 for the International grants programme), whether or not the amount being applied for from the Community Fund is below or above this figure, has to supply a business plan with the completed application form and will receive extra scrutiny.

The assessment criteria

All applications are considered under the following criteria:

About your organisation

1 The organisation is well managed and financially sound.
2 If awarded a grant, the organisation would be able to manage the project.
3 The organisation reflects the diversity of the community it serves, and takes account of the community's needs in all its work.

About your project

1 The project responds to a clearly-defined need and is in line with Board's mission statement.
2 The project is additional to statutory services.
3 The project has clearly defined objectives and a thorough and reasonable project plan.
4 The project budget is accurate and reasonable, and is matched by realistic income projections.
5 There is a sensible plan to secure new funding if the project is expected to continue after the end of the grant.
6 The project will be monitored and evaluated against its objectives, and the project plan reviewed accordingly.
7 Beneficiaries are involved in all aspects of the project, and have full access to it.

The project is also assessed on the extent to which it meets the criteria of the particular grants programme under which the application is being submitted.

Grants are available not just to charities, but also to any organisation with benevolent objectives – although the vast majority of grants awarded by the Community Fund have been to charities. Recipients can include associations, societies, cooperatives or non-profit companies. Grants will not be made to an educational institution (schools, FE colleges, universities, etc.), local councils, NHS trusts or appeals on their behalf. Applications may not be made directly by professional fund-raisers (as defined by the Charities Act – broadly fundraising consultants), though they can assist in the preparation of applications.

Unlike the other Distribution Boards, matched funding for a Community Fund grant is not a requirement. However, Community Fund money does qualify as matched funding for other grants – for example, from the European Social Fund.

Unfortunately, Community Fund grants are only available for three years. Although you can apply to 'develop' the work at the end of this period, the budget for such applications is capped at 25% of the total available. In other words, the Community Fund strongly prefers financing new projects rather than previously funded ones. This can create serious difficulties if you have to set up a project from scratch, get the work underway, and get it fully funded, all within three years.

Furthermore, the Community Fund will not contribute to existing overhead costs (i.e. rent, rates, management and administration). It will only pay for the extra costs incurred by the project it is funding. Again, this can cause real problems – your management and property costs have to be covered with funding from somewhere.

Types of grant

There are a number of restrictions relating to the size and types of grants you can get from the Community Fund. You can apply for:

- one, two or three-year funding
- some or all of the project's costs
- revenue costs (including core costs, as long as they are not being paid for by anyone else)
- capital costs
- matching funds for European Union grants.

You cannot normally apply for:

- endowments
- loans or loan payments
- retrospective funding
- making up deficits
- promoting particular religious beliefs
- sports, art or heritage projects (as these are the responsibility of other Lottery boards)

No grants will be awarded which replace (or may replace) lost statutory funding, nor where the money will subsidise statutory provision, nor where it will make up a deficit on a service otherwise funded by the state.

Dealing with an assessment – 10 tips from a Community Fund assessor

1   Remember that not all assessors have experience of your kind of work. Do not assume too much knowledge of what you are trying to do and how you are proposing to do it.

2   Have all your documentation to hand. If an assessor rings and you do not feel prepared with the necessary information, ask for another more convenient time when you will be better organised. Ask what information they will be looking for so that you can everything to hand. An assessment phone call usually takes about an hour (some have taken up to three hours). It will save you time and stress, and make the assessor's job easier, if you are organised and prepared.

3   If you are having an assessment visit, make sure that the person meeting the assessor and answering the questions knows the details of the application.

4   Remember that assessors are human. There's no need to go overboard but make sure they feel welcome. Cocktails and canapés are too much, but coffee and biscuits will be welcome.

5   Be open and honest. Don't be over the top or try to cover over the cracks. If your organisation is perfect, why do you need the money anyway?

6   See the assessment as a discussion not an interrogation.

7   Use friendly, jargon-free language. Be straightforward in your answers.

8   If your proposal is for a mini-bus or a building or a salary, you may need to supply copies of your supporting documentation to the assessor if they don't have them.

9   Keep a record of what information you have been asked to provide. This will help you after the assessment make sure that you have fulfilled your side of things. At key points in the conversation, ask the assessor to reflect back his or her understanding of what has been said. This will avoid misunderstandings.

10 At the end of the assessment, do not be afraid to ask questions about anything you are unsure of. It should be a two-way process, and this is your chance to get some first-hand knowledge of when you can expect to hear, what happens next, or anything else that is needed.

Answering the assessor's questions

Assessors can, and sometimes do, seem to ask about anything and everything. In practice, they want to know the following:

- Is the organisation financially sound and well managed? For example, does it produce annual accounts which show a reasonable surplus? Does it pay its bills on time? Does it have a reasonable amount of money in the bank? Does the management committee meet regularly and review what is going on? Does the organisation have a good track record in delivering the kinds of services it is applying for?

- Is the project properly planned and organised, and will it be staffed appropriately? Is there a project plan? Does it seem sensible? Has it got measurable targets? Are they realistic? Are the management structures clear?

- Is the budget accurate and does it offer value for money? Are all costs covered, including overheads? Do they seem appropriate for the work that is being done? Can you show that this is money being very well spent?

- Will the project be monitored and evaluated in a meaningful way? Are there clear targets for the project? Will there be regular progress reviews? What will happen if targets are not met?

- What will happen when the Lottery money runs out? Will the project simply stop? If you want it to continue, how is it going to be funded? There is some discussion now as to whether continuation funding might be offered to projects that have been supported by the Community Fund once the original funding has run out.

- Is the organisation committed to equal opportunities? A statement on a piece of paper is not enough. You have to show that you are genuinely representative of your community at management committee level, among the project leaders, volunteers and users. If you are not, what are you doing about it? (The argument that 'I don't think we have those kinds of people here' does not carry much weight.) How many people with disabilities are involved in your activities? What access do you offer to people with special needs?

- How does the project encourage the people who benefit to be involved in the planning and running of the project? You need to show that you have actively consulted potential users or beneficiaries in the planning of the project and how they will be part of the management, monitoring and evaluation of what is happening (for example, by setting up a project steering committee which will include users).

- Does the organisation have the necessary financial and management experience to cope with the added workload and responsibility associated with a Community Fund grant?

- Have you researched the work of other voluntary groups in your locality, and are certain that your project will not duplicate existing services?

- Are you doing what the government should be doing? Are you applying to the Community Fund to make up for lost local authority funding? If so, you won't get a grant.

Getting started

Phone for an application pack. These are available in English and Welsh, in printed and audio form. The guide to each particular round is also available in Braille and large print, in a variety of minority languages, and in a special edition for people with learning difficulties. You will also in future be able to apply via the website.

Read through the guidelines, paying particular attention to the assessment criteria. Decide on the project you want to do and how it fits Community Fund themes and priorities. On key questions, such as the level of need, the degree of benefit, the extent of user involvement, your equal opportunities approach, and the detailed breakdown of the budget, make detailed notes giving information in more detail than is required for the application form. This can then be referred to during the assessment process when particular questions are asked.

Send off the application form in the envelope provided, retaining a copy for yourself. Then wait to be contacted for the assessment process. You will hear whether your application has been submitted properly and can go forward for assessment. Once the assessment has taken place, you just have to sit and wait for the letter informing you as to whether the application has succeeded or failed.

7.4 Arts grants

Arts grants are handled by the four national Arts Councils – for England, Scotland, Wales and Northern Ireland. The Arts Council for England has delegated a limited amount of responsibility to the Regional Arts Boards, and Lottery funds are now integrated with direct government funding. Most of the money is for capital expenditure, albeit defined in a broad way (see below). In March 2001 the Arts Council of England announced plans to unite with the ten regional arts boards to create a single funding and development organisation for all the arts in all parts of England. The new arrangements were due to come into effect from April 2002.

Almost any type of organisation may apply for a grant – there are a very few exclusions. The lower and upper limits for grants depend on which Arts Council is being applied to. The largest grant awarded so far is the £78.5 million for the Royal Opera House redevelopment in Covent Garden. Matched or partnership funding is required and will vary depending upon the size of the grant.

Capital programmes

The key requirements are that projects should:

- be for capital expenditure, defined as building work (new developments and refurbishment); the purchase of equipment or instruments or vehicles; the commissioning of works of art. All forms of art are included – from circus to video;
- offer the widest possible public benefit (including maximum access for disabled people);
- have long-term financial viability;
- involve high quality in design and construction;
- demonstrate a high quality of planned artistic activity and contribution by artists;
- be of relevance to other plans for the arts;
- meet a demand which is not currently being met;
- demonstrate proper planning for education and marketing activity.

Most of the money awarded in the first years was for large-scale projects based disproportionately in central London. Although there may be an intention to redress the balance, there are now inadequate funds available to fully undo the earlier pattern: a high percentage of the money is still used for a handful of large grants, and the same areas (East Anglia and the East Midlands) continue to be the least successful. It remains to be seen whether the new strategy put forward in the consultation paper *Making a Difference* will be fully implemented, so that the promise implied in its title is fulfilled. If so, priority will be given to projects that:

- are in areas that have had few or low awards so far
- are for types of arts activity that have had low awards
- contribute to national or regional strategies
- are in areas of social deprivation
- address social exclusion
- are to refurbish existing facilities (as opposed to 'new build').

Other areas of concern which are still to be addressed include:

- that there will not be sufficient income to run the capital projects once they are built;
- that the large amounts of capital grants will create pressure on trusts and companies to provide matching funding, thus reducing further the money available for other activities;
- that long-term revenue needs will be met through increased admission and other usage charges;
- that the system favours those areas where the local authority is rich enough to be able to match fund big projects;

- that although there was a commitment by government that the arts funding available through the Arts Councils as grant-in-aid from government would not be affected by the arrival of Lottery funds, government funding for the arts might decline in real terms.

Other programmes have also been introduced by the regional arts councils. The Arts Council of England, for instance, has started a National Touring programme, plus a Recovery programme and a Stabilisation programme.

Regional Arts Lottery programmes

The Regional Arts Lottery Programme is administered by the ten Regional Arts Boards (RABs) in England. Importantly, the RABs have taken on funding responsibility for small capital grants of between £2,000 and £100,000. Support is also available for arts projects and organisational development. The programme aims to support five areas of work: access, education, production and distribution, investment in artists, and the development and sustainability of arts organisations. Priorities will vary from region to region, so you are best advised to contact your local RAB.

Applications

To apply for a grant from one of the Arts Councils you should first obtain an application pack which gives full details of the process. Addresses are given at the end of the chapter.

7.5 Sports grants

As with the other Lottery distributors, sport is organised on national lines with each of the national Sports Councils having their own independent budget. The following information reflects Sport England's policies, although there is a broadly similar approach across the UK.

The Lottery funds were originally used to fund capital projects. However, not least because of the poor showing of the British team in the 1996 Olympics, a new strategy was developed of 'more medals, more people, more places', the aim being to increase participation in sport, nurture talent and enhance excellence. New revenue programmes were introduced. In fact, the number of glowing references to Lottery funding by successful British athletes during the 2000 Olympics became a standing joke in the BBC studio!

Sport England now channels its money through two funds: the Community Projects Fund and the World Class Fund, with a broad 75%/25% split in favour of community projects. Also, the emphasis for the Community Projects

Fund is as much on sport as a means of community development as on taking part in sport for its own sake. While non-sports organisations will find it difficult to get sports Lottery funding on their own, by linking in with local sports clubs they can open up new funding options. There are plenty of examples of, for instance, new village halls and community centres being part-funded by the sports Lottery alongside other Lottery distributors, grant-making trusts and such like, with the sports Lottery funding the sports element and the others funding the rest.

The Community Projects Fund has three main elements:

- *Small Projects (up to £5,000).* These are targeted at smaller organisations (gross income £15,000 or under) and are given through the Awards for All programme. The key aims are to promote participation in and lifelong enjoyment of sport. Priority areas include school, after-school and community club links; increased participation among disabled people, minority ethnic communities, women and girls; new or enhanced coaching or other qualifications, and enhanced skills for sports volunteers.
- *Capital (over £5,000).* This programme aims to increase community participation in sport by making money available for pitches, playing surfaces, sports halls, major items of equipment and essential support facilities (such as changing rooms or a creche so that families can access a sports centre). The target groups are similar to those for the Small Projects fund, although there is no upper limit on the organisation's income. However, there is also a strong emphasis on areas of economic deprivation, the promotion of social inclusion, community regeneration and healthy living initiatives, and a partnership approach.
- *Revenue (over £5,000).* Larger-scale projects aimed at tackling social exclusion in sport. Again, the target groups and priority areas are similar to those above.

The World Class Fund is all about elite sportspeople achieving international success. However, local sports and community groups are well placed to work together on initiatives that will help encourage people who don't play sport to play sport. The Lottery funds will want to see clear evidence of sports development plans, particularly for the larger grants programmes. However, they also recognise that while sports clubs may not have good links with disadvantaged communities, national and local voluntary organisations do.

Applications

Applications can be made at any time. For further information, ring your national Sports Council for an application pack.

7.6 Heritage grants

The Heritage Lottery Fund (HLF) is designed to support a wide range of activities connected with museums and galleries, libraries, manuscripts and archives, the national heritage, and transport and maritime heritage. Funding has been given for:

- the buying of property, and the repairing or the restoring of older properties
- acquiring land
- acquiring objects or collections
- improving the public understanding or access to buildings.

Originally only capital grants were made – although the first award, for a National Trust purchase in Scotland, included an endowment element to generate a continuing income for the maintenance of the property. The minimum grant is £10,000, but around half the available funding has in practice been used up each year by a small number of 'big' grants (of more than £2 million). Partnership or matched funding is required and is expected to be in excess of 25%, but there are few restrictions on the type of organisation which is eligible to apply.

As with the Arts Councils, the HLF has come under close scrutiny regarding the extent of the benefit it provides to poorer people and regional inequalities in the distribution of its grants. In addition, there has been debate about the apparent strong emphasis on heritage excellence, which is likely to favour big national institutions, rather than heritage need and the related social and economic benefits. A new strategic plan drawn up in 1999 aimed to address these issues as follows.

- Heritage conservation will continue to be the core of HLF's work and will account for at least 75% of expenditure.
- Up to about £10 million a year will probably be available for acquisitions by or for museums and galleries.
- Half of all expenditure may be distributed to local projects, of less than £1 million, with country budgets set on a value per head basis. Within England there are expected to be regional budgets for this expenditure, intended to bring previously poorly supported regions up to the per capita grant levels of the others.
- 15% or more of overall budgets may go to revenue activities designed to improve heritage education and access, some of it through revenue elements of basically capital projects.
- Up to 25% of the annual budget may continue to be allocated to 'Beacon' projects of £5 million or more (a good term, first appearing in the Select Committee Report), to be selected through a twice-yearly bidding process.

- For three programmes, totalling about £50 million a year or 16% of expenditure, priority will be given to areas of social or economic deprivation (and former coalfield areas, a politically imposed addition). The programmes are: Urban Parks, Places of Worship, and the Townscape Heritage Initiative.
- Separate country committees in England, Scotland, Wales and Northern Ireland are expected to make all grant decisions on grants for less than £1 million, about half the total value of grants. The English committee will probably be strengthened by further non-trustee appointments.

A new strategic plan was being drawn up for implementation from 2002.

Applications

To apply for a grant from the HLF, you should first obtain an application pack, which gives full details of the process.

7.7 The Millennium Commission

The Millennium Commission was set up to help celebrate the passing of the old millennium and the arrival of the new one. By the time the capital programme closed, it had made grants to a small number of very large projects of national importance together with a number of local projects of varying size. Many of these were to do with the environment, including a number of umbrella projects which provided funding across the country for green spaces, community woodlands, floodlit churches, and village halls.

To mark the millennium, the Millennium Commission allocated £100 million towards an Awards Scheme. Awards are for amounts of between £2,000 and £15,000 'to enable individuals to fulfil personal gaols and, in doing so, to make a contribution to their communities'.

The Awards Scheme is run in partnership with around 120 voluntary organisations who applied to the Millennium Commission and were successful with their proposals. Each Award Partner offers awards for a particular purpose and for a particular category of person and in a particular area that relates to their own work. Examples include Groundwork Trust (environmental projects), Age Concern England (projects undertaken by senior citizens) and the British Council (young people travelling overseas).

The awards were offered in the period 1997–2002. To continue the Awards Scheme the Millennium Commission allocated £100 million to endow a new foundation and invited bids to run it. The successful bidder was a consortium of seven organisations that included Comic Relief and the School for Social Entrepreneurs. The foundation they have set up is called 'unLTD'. It will make approximately 1,600 awards per annum in two categories:

- awards of up to £2,500 to cover project expenses and support and training for the award winner
- awards of up to £20,000 for award winners to take a year off to pursue their project idea, including the cost of support and training.

The awards are to enable individuals to create change in their communities and in society generally. They are available to individuals only, but a voluntary organisation can sponsor an individual, helping them prepare and put forward an application and then supporting them whilst they undertake their project.

7.8 The New Opportunities Fund

The New Opportunities Fund was set up in 1998, and has been allocated an increasing proportion of the Lottery 'cake' in order to fund government-determined initiatives in the areas of health, education and the environment. The declared aim of the New Opportunities Fund is to work in partnership with voluntary, public and private sector organisations to support projects that will be sustainable after the funding ends, and which:

- improve the quality of life for individuals and communities
- address the needs of those most disadvantaged in society
- promote social inclusion and encourage community involvement
- complement and enhance relevant national, regional and local strategies and programmes.

The individual programmes are examined in more detail below.

Healthy living centres

There is £300 million available for this programme, which aims to develop a network of healthy living centres across the UK. These are intended to be accessible to the most disadvantaged members of the population and complement government policy in the areas of public health and social exclusion.

Out of school hours activities
Out of school hours childcare

There is £220 million available for this programme, which aims to create new and sustainable childcare places for 865,000 school-age children by 2003. This includes before and after school clubs, holiday playschemes, and childminding facilities.

Out of school hours learning

This programme has £205 million available to fund out of school learning activities in half of all secondary and special schools and a quarter of all primary schools.

ICT (Information and communications technology)

ICT training for teachers and school librarians

This programme aims to raise standards of achievement in schools by increasing the expertise of teachers in using ICT in subject teaching and by improving the competence and confidence of school librarians in this area. It has a budget of £230 million.

ICT training for public library staff

A further £20 million is available for training public library staff.

Digitisation of learning materials

The first stage of the two-stage application process for this programme closed in March 2000, with organisations bidding for £50 million in funding to digitise learning materials which support lifelong learning needs. These will then be made available free of charge to the public.

Living with cancer

£150 million is available under this heading to promote cancer prevention, improve access to screening and treatment, and help individuals and families cope with the impact of cancer in their lives.

Community access to lifelong learning

£200 million of funding is to be devoted to encouraging adults into learning, with a particular focus on ICT.

Green spaces and sustainable communities

NOF is working in partnership with selected Award Partners to deliver this programme, which has a total budget of £125 million available to help communities understand, improve or care for their natural and living environment.

7.9 Awards for All

This is the small grants programme in England and Scotland. The Arts, Charity, Heritage and Sports Distributors, working together, make grants in the range of £500 to £5,000. The programme is open to small charities and community groups with an annual income of less than £15,000. It is administered in England and Scotland by the Community Fund on behalf of the four Boards. Regional committees use a common set of criteria to assess applications locally. In Wales and Northern Ireland separate small grants programmes are administered by the individual Distributors, since they were unable to agree on a common format.

The bulk of the funding is for Community Fund projects (£18 million in year 1), with only £1.2 million allocated to Arts projects, despite the runaway success of the earlier A4E Express small grants programme. Surprisingly, small grants from the Heritage Lottery Fund are not available for conservation, because of a fear that local communities might 'do it wrong'.

Applications

Contact the relevant body for an application pack.

Resources and further information

See also general lists at the end of the book.

Organisations

The National Lottery now has a central website and enquiry line:
www.lotterygoodcauses.org.uk
Tel. 0845 275 0000
Textphone 0845 275 0022

Arts Council of England
www.artscouncil.org.uk/funding
Tel. 020 8973 6517
e-mail enquiries@artscouncil.org.uk

Awards for All
www.awardsforall.org.uk
Tel. 0845 600 2040

Community Fund
St Vincent House
16 Suffolk Street
London SW1Y 4NL
www.community-fund.org.uk
Tel. 020 7747 5299
Application packs: 0845 791 9191

Heritage Lottery Fund
7 Holbein Place
London SW1W 8NR
www.hlf.org.uk
Tel. 020 7591 6000
Fax 020 7591 6001
e-mail enquire@hlf.org.uk

New Opportunities Fund
Heron House
322 High Holborn
London WC1V 7PW
www.nof.org.uk
Tel. 0845 000 0120
e-mail general.enquiries@nof.org.uk

Regional Arts Boards

East Midlands Arts
Tel. 01509 218292
Fax 01509 262214
e-mail info@em-arts.co.uk

Eastern Arts Board
Tel. 01223 215355
e-mail info@eastern-arts.co.uk

London Arts Board
Tel. 020 7240 1313
Fax 020 7670 2400
minicom 020 7670 2450
e-mail chrissie.cochrane@lonab.co.uk

NorthWest Arts Board
Manchester
Tel. 0161 834 6644
Fax 0161 834 6969
minicom 0161 834 9131

Liverpool
Tel. 0151 709 0671
Fax 0151 708 9034
e-mail info@nwarts.co.uk

Northern Arts
Tel. and minicom 0191 281 6334
Fax 0191 281 3276
e-mail info@northernarts.org.uk

South East Arts
Tel. 01892 507200
Fax 01892 549383
e-mail info@seab.co.uk

South West Arts
www.swa.co.uk
Tel. 01392 218188
Fax 01392 433503

Southern Arts
Tel. 01962 855099
Fax 01962 861186
e-mail info@southernarts.co.uk

West Midlands Arts
Tel. 0121 631 3121
Fax 0121 643 7239
e-mail info@west-midlands-arts.co.uk

Yorkshire Arts
Tel. 01942 455555
Fax 01942 466522
minicom 01942 438585
e-mail info@yarts.co.uk

Sport England Lottery Fund
Community Projects Capital Fund
PO Box 649
London WC1H 0QS
www.english.sports.gov.uk/lottery
Lottery line: 0845 7 649 649

unLTD
c/o McKinsey & Co.
1 Jermyn Street
London SW1 (temporary address
whilst the foundation is being set up)

Publications

The following publications are available from the Directory of Social Change.
Prices were correct at the time of writing, but may be subject to change.

A Guide to UK Company Giving, John Smyth, DSC 2002, £25

8 COMPANIES

Companies give more than £400 million a year to charity. About half of this is in the form of cash donations; the rest is gifts in kind, secondments, sponsorships, joint promotions, and goodwill advertising. This chapter covers all aspects of company giving.

Details of organisations and publications referred to in this chapter are on p. 177.

8.1 About company giving

Most companies give out of enlightened self-interest rather than pure altruism or charity, and they see their giving as 'community involvement' or 'community investment'. Their giving is way below what the general public, government or grant-making trusts contribute. However, they are an important target for both national and local fundraising.

The main reasons why companies give are as follows.

- To create goodwill: to be seen as good citizens in the communities where they operate and as a caring company by society at large. They also want to create goodwill amongst their employees, who will get a better impression of the company from the good works that the company is supporting.
- To be associated with causes that relate to their business. Mining and extraction companies often like to support environmental projects; pharmaceutical companies, health projects; banks, economic development projects; retailers and insurance companies, projects working with young people and crime prevention; and so on. This may be to enhance their image, but it can also help build contacts and gain market intelligence.
- Because of pressure from the government to support particular initiatives which contribute to government policy, for example the Education Action Zones.
- Because they are asked and it is expected of them. They also don't want to be seen to be mean. There is also a lot of peer pressure amongst companies in a particular sector of business – banks, oil companies, pharmaceuticals, insurance companies, etc. They are concerned to see that the quantity and quality of their giving is appropriate to their status as a company.

- Because the chairman or other senior directors are interested in that cause (and perhaps support it personally). The chairman's wife (virtually no top companies have a female chief executive) can also play an important part through her interests and influence, although less so as companies employ staff to manage their community involvement programmes.
- Tax. Giving to a charity can be done tax effectively. This will be an added benefit for the company, but seldom the determining factor.

For privately owned or family controlled companies their giving is often little different from personal giving. For public companies, where it is the shareholders' funds that are being given away, the company will want to justify its charitable support. You can help them to do this by telling them not just why you want the money, but why giving you support should be of interest to them. You can also tell them about any benefits they will get in return for their money and about the impact that their donation will make on your work.

Remember too that companies like thanks, recognition and good publicity for their support whether in newsletters, your annual report, or through media coverage.

What companies like to support

There are fashions in what companies like to support. For example, in the 1980s, AIDS/HIV and homelessness were not generally supported, but today companies do support these causes. The following are some of the areas that companies find attractive.

- Important local projects in the areas where the company has a significant presence. Business in the Community organise 'Seeing is Believing' events for business leaders, when they take them to visit local projects to see problems at first hand and explain how they can make a significant contribution.
- Activities that relate to their product. For example, NatWest, now part of the Royal Bank of Scotland, has a schools programme, Face2Face with Finance, promoting financial literacy, and banks in general target their giving at young people (who are potential customers); insurance companies such as Prudential support crime prevention initiatives; BT's £15.5 million community programme supports projects around the theme of communication.
- Economic development projects – because a flourishing economy benefits business. Shell, for example, supports Livewire, an award scheme for new enterprise, and the STEP programme, which provides undergraduates with work experience during the summer vacation.

- Environmental projects – Shell, again, has led the way through their Better Britain awards for local environmental projects; and local Groundwork Trusts are major beneficiaries of company support.
- Educational projects – as education and training are an investment in the future. This assumed added importance under a government whose three stated priorities were 'Education – Education – Education'. Good examples are the Business in the Community millennium programme of encouraging companies to help achieve national literacy targets; and Barclays New Futures, which encourages active citizenship by young people.
- Sporting events and competitions, and other activities that attract keen public interest or mass participation. This would include the London Marathon, the Cadbury 'Strollathon', and Comic Relief's Red Nose Day.
- Initiatives which have the backing of very prominent people. Who knows who is always important in getting support from companies. The Prince's Trust is able to capitalise on this in their fundraising 'finding that doors open for them without having to be pushed'.

FI Group – employee involvement helps homeless people and schools

FI's community programme is focused specifically on employees supporting young unemployed homeless people and education. Priority is given to supporting programmes that will help young people lead successful working lives, particularly through information technology – FI's core business.

All FI offices and several customer-based teams have established programmes of support for local homeless organisations or schools and 70% of FI's Group Board Executive Directors are involved in the programme, either as representatives of FI on national or regional leadership teams or in a personal capacity.

FI's impact on Homelessness and Education has:

- helped raise national and regional awareness of, and support for, voluntary groups supporting young unemployed homeless people;
- provided work placements for eight young unemployed homeless people nominated by FI's community partners. Five progressed into full time employment;
- encouraged and supported its employees to raise over £50,000 for homeless charities and schools.

17% of the workforce nationally has been involved in the programme (1999 survey). In some activities/regions participation is as high as 30%.

There are certain areas that companies will not generally support:

- local appeals outside areas where they have a business presence – there is no business reason for them to do this – although they may well support national appeals;
- purely denominational appeals for religious purposes, although they may well support social projects run by religious bodies;
- mailed appeals, which are printed and sent to hundreds of companies and end up unread in the bin;
- controversial campaigns which might bring them bad publicity, although they may support 'unpopular' causes such as homelessness or mental illness;
- overseas development work, unless the company has a business presence in that country when support will more likely come from a local subsidiary – although some companies do support emergency and aid appeals on the basis that this is the sort of thing that the staff would like to see supported.

Special initiatives by companies in a particular industry

CRASH is the Construction Industry Charity for the Single Homeless. It aims to mobilise support from property companies, construction companies, builders supply companies and builders merchants, architects, surveyors and others with a stake in the construction industry to assist the single homeless.

- Support is mobilised in cash, including asking leading companies to become patrons.
- A CRASH Store is operated for furniture and equipment donated by supporters, including bedding from hotel companies.
- Materials and support in kind is gifted to building projects. As well as acting as a broker for these gifts in kind, a directory of 27 manufacturers and suppliers offering discounts or gifts in kind for CRASH projects is also produced.
- Empty buildings are located for possible use as winter shelters.
- Funds are raised through talks and presentations at conferences and events, such as at the Conference on Women in Property, the British Cement Association Lubetkin Lecture, the annual dinner of the National Housing and Town Planning Council and many others.

WaterAid is a charity set up by the water industry to focus charitable giving and technical expertise for water projects in the developing world. It mobilises support from the water companies, encourages employee volunteering and giving, sends appeals to water customers with their bills. The water industry contributes £1.11 million to WaterAid, and the customer appeal, which is sent to 19 million customers, generates £800,000, together representing 30% of the charity's annual income.

FashionActs is the fashion industry's initiative to raise money for HIV and AIDS. Over eight years it has raised and distributed more than £1 million via a calendar of fashion-related fundraising activities, including a designer jumble sale, an exhibition and sale of signed fashion photographs, a stand at the Clothes Show Live in Birmingham and a sponsored walk.

What companies give

There are a variety of ways in which companies can support charities:

- a cash donation (usually a one-off grant)
- sponsorship of an event or activity
- sponsorship of promotional and educational materials
- sponsorship of an award scheme
- cause related marketing, where the company contributes a donation to the charity in return for each product sold in order to encourage sales
- support in kind, which includes: giving company products or surplus office equipment; making company facilities available, including meeting rooms, printing or design facilities, help with mailings
- 'secondment' of a member of staff to work with the charity, where a member of the company's staff helps on an agreed basis whilst remaining employed (and paid) by the company
- contributing a senior member of staff to the charity's Management Board
- providing expertise and advice
- encouraging employees to volunteer
- organising a fundraising campaign amongst employees, including encouraging employees to give through payroll giving
- advertising in charity brochures and publications.

Companies are increasingly looking for low cost ways of giving support. The 2000 Finance Act has enabled companies to donate listed shares or securities and obtain tax relief in respect of this (see box on page 163). Offering free use of facilities, providing advice, donating product and equipment that is no longer required, encouraging staff to volunteer or collect or donate money will all cost less than making a cash donation.

Companies receive far too many applications. Community involvement budgets have not expanded in line with demands for support. Many now focus their grant-making quite narrowly, whereas a decade ago they were making grants across the whole spectrum of charitable activity. Some of the larger companies now have small grants schemes where they have a major factory or business presence. Some have matching schemes, where they match money collected or donated by employees. Some have developed special grants programmes, like the Shell Better Britain Campaign, which for the past 30 years has supported community environmental initiatives. Some have a 'charity of the year' for a major donation and as a focus for encouraging staff involvement.

British Airways collects money from passengers

'Change for Good', an in-flight initiative run by British Airways for UNICEF, was launched in 1994 at the suggestion of staff and has raised over £13 million to date. An envelope is circulated to passengers, so that their small unwanted foreign currency can be donated, and the message is reinforced with an appeal on the in-flight video. Staff also donate, and run local collections for the fund. Other airlines have now followed the example of BA and run similar schemes.

British Airways also encourages staff fundraising for staff charities such as:

- Dreamflight, where nearly 200 seriously ill children and their helpers are taken on a trip to Walt Disney World;
- Operation Happy Child, which provides holidays for underprivileged children.

Money is raised for these through a range of imaginative fundraising events, including parachute drops, kayak marathons, and celebrity dinners.

There are many ways in which a company can help, unlike other funding sources which only give money. Although you might not get very much in cash donations, there may be better – and equally valuable – ways companies can help you. Try to work out how best they can support you based on their level of giving, what they are interested in and the different forms of support they might give – and then approach them with an interesting proposition which they will find difficult to refuse. You might start by getting some modest item provided free and then try to deepen the relationship and escalate their level of support.

Major company programmes

Some of the largest companies now run large-scale programmes in partnership with a national charity. The following are two examples.

- *Prudential Youth Action Initiative, with Crime Concern.* The aim is to create safer cities by involving young people of middle and secondary school age in crime prevention activities through Youth Action Groups. The scheme publishes a directory of contacts and other publications, organises conferences and training workshops, provides partnership funding to develop local programmes and runs a national award scheme.

- *Barclays New Futures, with Community Service Volunteers*. This scheme offers £1 million a year in cash and professional support to help young people take positive action to benefit their communities. Schemes are assessed on the basis of student learning and personal development, student involvement, social relevance and sustainability. Cash awards of £3,000 (for an individual school) or £7,000 (for a group of schools) are made to 80 projects each year, plus educational resources, professional support and advice.

The different types of companies that give

1 Multinational companies

Most multinational companies have global giving programmes, generally tied to areas where they have or are developing business interests. Some multinational companies, such as IBM and American Express, have an international structure for managing their giving, with budgets set for each country and a common policy for the sorts of activity they are interested in supporting. With others, community involvement policy remains a purely local matter for company management in the country concerned, although some have tried to transfer projects and ideas from one country to another.

Where multinationals give

If you look at the geographical breakdown of a multinational company's giving, you will find the following:

- most money is spent in the headquarters town or region;
- most money is spent in the home country of the company. For example, ARCO, one of the leading oil companies spends most of its budget in the USA, but it has a strategy of trying to spread its giving more evenly in those countries where it does business;
- the North gets more than the South. BP gives most in the UK and Germany, for example. This is despite the fact that money goes much further in the South, where due to currency exchange rates, everything is much cheaper.

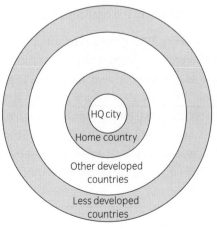

HQ city
Home country
Other developed countries
Less developed countries

The circle of giving
*The further out you are,
the less you can expect to get.*

2 Leading national companies

The giving of leading companies is well documented in *The Guide to UK Company Giving*. This gives information on the scale and scope of the company giving programmes of the top 500 corporate donors, with enough information to be able to identify those companies which might be interested in supporting you.

More than half the top companies are members of the PerCent Club organised by Business in the Community, which has set a target of 1% of pre-tax profit as a recommended level for community support (in cash and kind). Some of the largest companies publish brochures which describe their community involvement programme or specific schemes that they sponsor.

The leading national companies will be supporting large national charities, many of which have whole departments to raise money from companies. They may have their own sponsorship schemes and they will also be making smaller donations to local charities and sponsoring events in the area where they are headquartered or where they have a major business presence. National companies such as BT make grants through regional offices. Retail stores, such as Marks and Spencer or B & Q, often use the store manager to provide advice on a local application and give small budgets to be spent by each store at the manager's discretion.

B&Q – community investment improves customer service

DIY chain, B&Q, has established 300 partnerships nationwide between its stores and local disability groups in order to develop its training on disability awareness and improve its service for disabled people. To motivate and inspire employees it has appointed staff disability 'champions' for each store. This is also designed to empower individual staff to find local solutions to local problems with local partners and to make the relationship sustainable at a local level.

In Salisbury, B&Q gained local group Shopmobility's established expertise and in return provided them with products and assistance. Nationally, the company has also established partnerships with SCOPE and Leonard Cheshire for the same purpose. The function of the partnerships is not charitable. The purpose is to create a better shopping environment for disabled customers. B&Q argues that that if it gets it right for disabled people, then it can get it right for most people. In so doing, it increases sales to disabled people (a traditionally under-served group), increases overall employee satisfaction, retention and productivity rates and enhances its brand.

3 Larger local companies

In any city or region there will be large companies who are important to the local economy. They will often feel a responsibility to support voluntary action and community initiatives in those areas, and value the good publicity this provides. If yours is an important project, make it part of your fundraising strategy to develop a good relationship with the larger companies in your area. Abbey National in Milton Keynes, Boots in Nottingham, Allied Dunbar (part of Zurich Financial Services) in Swindon, Pilkington in St Helens, are examples of this.

There are also companies with a regional remit. The water, electricity and independent television companies all have a specific geographical area within which they operate, even if they are part of a multinational company. Their community support will be confined within these regional boundaries. Brewers are another example; a diminishing number still brew and distribute locally.

4 Smaller national companies

The larger companies, because of their size but also because their giving is well documented, are often overwhelmed with requests for support. But there are also companies that are less well known and with smaller charitable budgets where there are fewer approaches. And there are newly floated companies whose giving will only really develop once they have become public. Such companies can provide opportunities for the enterprising fundraiser.

5 New economy companies

The end of the last century and the early years of this have seen the growth of a new economy based on the IT revolution (the internet, mobile phones etc.) and also on new ways of delivering utilities and other services to consumers. Companies such as Baltimore Technologies and TeleWest have come from nowhere to be included in the FTSE100 in just a matter of years. In 2001, the largest company in the UK was Vodafone. Many of these companies are too busy developing their business to put any real effort into philanthropy. But some – as well as their founders, who now rank amongst Britain's leading rich – are attracted by the concept of 'venture philanthropy', which involves a much more hands on approach to giving. They are prepared to invest substantially in one or more key projects which have the potential to make a real difference and be replicated, providing cash and other support over a longer time frame and becoming personally involved in the development of the project. Others, as their business and profit base are consolidated, may give in a more traditional way.

Examples of new company giving

- New Look Group is a clothing chain with stores throughout the UK. It went public in 1998–99, when it gave only £7,000 in charitable donations. But it then developed the NSPCC as its 'charity of the millennium' and pledged to raise £500,000. By the end of 2000 it had raised more than half of this sum from employee payroll giving, by staging fashion shows, and through the sale of NSPCC campaign T shirts.
- Pace Micro Technology develops and manufactures receivers and decoders for television transmission. It gives small grants to community groups, voluntary organisations and schools within a 15 mile radius of Saltaire, where its head office is located, and Leeds.
- America On Line, which has recently acquired Time Warner, operates three brands, AOL, CompuServe and Netscape Online. In its giving it looks for a synergy with its online services and brand values. AOL supports children and young people; it is interested in online learning and supports Childline, and the Royal Commonwealth Society essay competition. CompuServe (which is targeted at business users) and Netscape Online (which attracts a youth audience) will be developing their giving along similar lines.

Examples of venture philanthropy

- McKinsey & Co, the management consultancy group, has backed the Ashoka Foundation, which supports 'social entrepreneurs', as its world-wide social partner, offering three-year bursaries. It is also backing unLTD, the new foundation set up to continue the Millennium Awards (see chapter 7). In both cases it is providing substantial *pro bono* support and encourages staff to get involved as members.
- The Shine Foundation has been set up by a group of city people as a vehicle for their philanthropy, and is focussing on literacy and numeracy projects with children of primary school age.
- Gary Hands of Nomura, which amongst other activities is the largest owner of pubs in the UK, has commissioned a study of venture philanthropy and the scope for involvement by his company.
- Body Shop International promotes and supports campaigns on the environment and in support of indigenous people, linking together its own giving, its purchasing of the raw ingredients, and the involvement of its staff and customers.

6 Smaller local companies

Smaller, local companies (known in European jargon as Small and Medium-sized Enterprises, or SMEs) are often overlooked. Almost everyone targets the large companies, because good information is available. However, there is a wide range of local companies, from manufacturers on trading estates to accountants and solicitors in the High Street. The majority of SMEs are involved in activities in their local communities. One in six (16%) say they are involved 'a great deal' and 45% say they are involved 'a fair amount' (MORI survey – see box below). Many of these firms are privately owned, and the approach will often be through the managing director or senior partner.

The best sources of information on what companies exist in your area are:

- the local Chamber of Commerce, where most of the more prominent local companies will be members;
- the *Kompass* directory of companies, which is regionally organised;
- the Local Council: the Rating Department might produce a list of major business ratepayers. The Economic Development section may have a list of major employers;
- the local newspaper, which will carry stories from time to time that mention local companies, and may provide information on new companies planning to set up in the area;
- postcode directories, where you can identify large users;
- you – by walking the streets and keeping your eyes open, you can often identify local companies that it could just be worth approaching.

What smaller companies are looking for

A MORI survey of 200 managing directors of SMEs ranging in size from 20 to 1,000 employees in 2000 produced the following results:

1 More than a quarter are motivated by the public relations opportunities which can be generated by their support, so if you want to get and keep a local company on board, make sure you provide press releases and photos to the local press and invite local TV and radio to your events, as well as your local MP and councillors.

2 One in five said that developing the company's relationship with its staff and improving employee satisfaction is important, so team building challenges will be popular.

3 90% said that company directors influence involvement. Around a third are influenced by their employees. So make sure you exploit your local contacts to best advantage.

4 Two of the main barriers to involvement, unsurprisingly, are money and time.

5 81% of those surveyed felt social responsibility will become increasingly important to businesses such as theirs over the next five years.

Most of these companies have no donations policy and give to projects which catch the fancy of the managing director or senior partner. Some may never have given anything before, and may not know about the tax treatment of charitable gifts; so you may need to persuade them to give, and tell them that this can be done tax-effectively.

Some of these companies may prefer to give in kind – for example, a prize for a raffle or advertising in a souvenir brochure for a fundraising event. It might be easier to approach these companies for this sort of support in the first instance; and later on, once they have given something, to persuade them to make a cash donation.

Who decides and who to write to

Larger companies will have a manager who is responsible for dealing with charitable appeals, although a Donations Committee (which includes senior management) may have the final say. The largest companies may also employ specialist staff (rather like a foundation) to assess the applications and make recommendations. Some large companies such as Lloyds TSB operate an independent foundation which sets policy and decides on applications. This is in addition to the company's own community support programme. With medium sized and smaller companies, it is nearly always the top person who decides.

You should write in the first instance to the person who deals with charitable appeals. Make sure that you have the spelling and job title correct. If you have a top-level contact, or if one of your members or volunteers is an employee of the company, then use them. It will always be helpful.

Getting started

You should also try to find out as much as you can about the company, and about its possible interest in supporting your project, but remember that:

- companies generally have less well defined policies than trusts, although you can often determine a pattern to their giving;
- the chance of an application 'out of the blue' getting substantial support is low;
- companies are more conservative in their giving, and are less likely to support innovative projects (at least until they have got established) or anything that is risky or controversial;
- company policies change more frequently than those of trusts, because of mergers, take-overs, or a fall or rise in profits. So ensure your research is bang up-to-date. Consulting a directory, or even having a copy of the company's annual report and accounts is not enough; they may have been taken over since then. Check the financial press on a regular basis.

Nonetheless research is important, not just into policies, but also into contacts. Here are some tips.

1 Find out what, if any, previous contact you have had with companies, any previous fundraising approaches you have made, and with what success.

2 Identify and match possible funders with various aspects of your work. In particular, try to find any local companies that are known for their generosity and might have an interest in supporting your cause.

3 Find out whether any of your Board Members, volunteers or supporters have any personal contact with the companies you plan to approach – and whether they know people who have credibility in the business world, who can help you do the asking.

4 Enlist a senior business leader to assist you with your fundraising. This can be someone to serve as chair of a development or fundraising committee, or just to contact a few colleagues and sign a few letters.

5 Contact Business in the Community to find out about their membership or to help you identify local companies through heir regional network.

6 Contact *bcconnections*, a not-for-profit dedicated to helping charities obtain more support from SMEs.

Ethical issues

Receiving support from companies can be problematic if the business values or practice of the company conflict with what your organisation stands for. There are two approaches. Some organisations will accept money from anyone, on the basis that the money can be used to do good. Others define certain types of company that they will not accept support from. Tobacco, alcohol, gambling, armaments, extraction industries, polluters, companies operating in the developing world that underpay their workforce are all areas of business activity that can cause problems. An ethical stance is of particular importance where the work of the charity is directly connected with the issue or where the relationship is high profile. Health and cancer charities would find it hard to accept money from a tobacco company; peace and international relations organisations have similar problems with arms manufacturers, and so on.

Decide your ethical policy *before* approaching companies. It should be agreed by the Management Committee and minuted. You might want to define and agree a policy in consultation with staff, although sometimes this can be contentious and create divisions. In such cases it may be better to treat each decision on an *ad hoc* basis whilst moving towards some sort of consensus on policy.

Sometimes the issues are clear cut. It is relatively easy, for example, for a health charity to decide whether to accept money from a tobacco company, or a youth charity from a drinks company. The product relationship with the cause is clear, and all the charity has to do is agree a position on the issue.

But what about Nestlé, which sells formula baby milk in developing countries, where the issue and the cause will not be so closely linked?

There are two organisations that chart the ethical behaviour of companies, which can provide you with the information you need to formulate an ethical donations policy:

- New Consumer publishes *Changing Corporate Values*, which explores the ethical performance of 128 leading companies;
- EIRIS, the Ethical Investment Research and Information Service researches companies on the FT All-Share Index. Its main aim is to advise on socially responsible investment. A charge is made for its services.

Nine ideas for getting support from companies

1   Put yourself in the position of the company. Why should they want to give their shareholders' funds to you? Why should they choose your charity, rather than any of the other appeals they receive? Think about the benefits that they will get from supporting you and mention these in your appeal letter. If you are looking for sponsorship, then these benefits will be at the heart of your proposal.

2   Suggest something specific for the company to support, and in your letter tell them why they should be interested. It is often best to think of something quite small if you are approaching them for the first time.

3   Use all the contacts you have in the company to help get your appeal supported. Do you know the chairman, the managing director or any other senior member of staff? Or their spouse, who may be able to put in a good word for you? Or if you telephone, can you get into conversation with the chairman's secretary or personal assistant such that he or she becomes interested and enthusiastic.

4   Think of all the different ways in which the company could help. Cash might not be the best way for them to give their support. Might it be easier for them to offer staff time, perhaps giving you some expertise you lack? Or the use of a vehicle? Or access to company staff to circulate an appeal or to sell your Christmas cards to? It is likely that everyone else will be asking for cash. And the company may find it easier to give in kind, but once they have given in kind and got to know you and your work, cash support may become easier to obtain next time.

5 Consider whether there is a senior executive of the company (the more senior the better) who might become a trustee of your charity – or serve on a fundraising or development committee. They can bring new ideas, good organisation and a wealth of business contacts to your organisation that will be worth many times the value of a donation. Such an invitation, even if refused, may be seen as flattering. If this level of involvement is too much, a request for advice may succeed.

6 Do you have any volunteers who also work for the company? They may be able to help you 'from the inside', and it will do you no harm if you mention their support for your organisation in your appeal letter.

7 Don't assume that every company will give. Make parallel approaches to a number of different companies.

8 Consider who might be the best person to make the approach or sign the letter. It may not be you. Often it is another senior business executive who has already supported your organisation generously. Their endorsement of your work can provide a comfort factor for other companies.

9 Every time you buy anything from a company, ask for a discount. This will save you money, but it is also a way of getting them to support you.

8.2 Cash donations

This is the most obvious way that a company can be asked to support your organisation, but also the most expensive for them, so most cash donations are small (under £200). You are more likely to be successful if you offer a 'shopping list' of specific items, rather than a vague request for general support. Some companies match their employees' fundraising.

Tax and company giving

The 2000 Finance Act made giving tax-effectively straightforward for companies.

1 *Donations*: the company simply pays the full donation to the charity under Gift Aid and then deducts the total amount of their charitable donations from their pre-tax profit calculations at the end of the year. The level of benefit a company can receive in return is restricted on a sliding scale according to the amount of the donation, up to a maximum of £250 in benefits.

2 *Business expenditure*: any expenditure by a company which is wholly and exclusively for business purposes is also deductible against corporation tax liability. This will cover most sponsorship and advertising payments to charity.

3 *Shares*: from April 2000, companies are able to get tax relief for gifts of certain shares and securities to charity. See chapter 4 (page 88) for more on this.

8.3 Gifts in kind

Giving things rather than money is often easier for a company. The value of the gift to the charity will always be much more than the cost to the company. Companies can give:

- products for use by the charity
- products as prizes in raffles and tombolas, or to be auctioned
- old stock and ends of lines for resale in charity shops
- professional and technical advice *pro bono* (without charge)
- facilities such as meeting rooms, conference facilities, training

If a company donates articles that it makes or sells in the course of its trade, or an article that it has used in its trade (this can include computers and furniture), then this can be treated as a tax deductible business expense. Donated items whose 'book value' (value as given in the accounts) is written off before the donation is made (unsaleable or damaged stock, ends of lines etc.) also attract full tax relief. See *The Fundraiser's Guide to the Law* for more detailed treatment of this area.

There are organisations which act as 'clearing houses' for gifts in kind, such as Kind Direct (formerly Gifts in Kind UK).

Some practical tips on how to set about getting support in kind

1 Make a list of everything you need – a 'wish list'. This can include services as well as products (such as the design for a leaflet you plan to produce).

2 Go through the list and try to identify companies that might have what you require. Personal knowledge is fine but you might also want to use business directories.

3 Make contact. Writing a letter does not work well. It is best if you can make personal or telephone contact. State your request, saying that it is for a charity and indicating how well used it will be and how important to your organisation's future.

4 If they refuse to donate it, they might be able to give you a hefty discount. This is worth getting and can be a fall back position in your discussions.

5 Be positive and enthusiastic. It can be very difficult for them to refuse if they know what you want and how important it is for you. It will always cost them far less to donate the item than it would cost you to purchase it.

6 Say thank you. Report back subsequently on the difference the donation has made. Send them your annual report. Try then to recruit them as a cash donor.

8.4 Employee volunteering and secondments

A major resource that companies can offer is their staff time. This can be provided in a number of ways:

- *Employee volunteering*: many of the large companies encourage their staff to volunteer, usually out of office hours, on the basis that this enhances the skills of their employees and promotes good community relations. Some companies make matching donations to the projects their employees are involved with. *Action – Employees in the Community* is an employee volunteering network promoted by Business in the Community.

- *Professional skills*: banks, law firms, accountants, advertising and PR companies can all encourage staff to give their professional skills free of charge or to become trustees. Even where this is not done, you can always ask.

See chapter 16 for more on volunteering.

Another type of support is a secondment, where the company loans you a member of staff full time for an extended period. There needs to be a good reason why the company would do this, as it is an expensive form of support. Schemes might include:

- Challenges for middle and senior managers. These might be in the form of an assignment of say 100 hours to complete a specific task for the charity, which can help the employee develop new skills in a different setting.
- Secondments linked to a major programme which the company is supporting, where the loan of the member of staff is part of the package.
- Pre-retirement secondments as a alternative to early retirement or redundancy. These would normally be on a full-time basis for one or two years. Secondments can also be set up for people 'between jobs' in the company.

Many companies also encourage staff to volunteer after retirement, and REACH (Retired Executives Clearing House) and RSVP (Community Service Volunteers Retired and Senior Volunteering Programme) both act as placement agencies for retired volunteers.

Employee volunteering is not only valuable in itself, but is strategically important since you will be building a relationship with a member of staff who can then act as an intermediary in asking the company for other forms of support, including cash donations.

8.5 Getting companies to advertise

Companies will often take an advertisement in a publication – possibilities include:

- your annual report
- programmes produced for fundraising events
- conference folders and pads
- posters, including educational wall charts.

However, you do need to have thought through whether you actually want an advertisement or company logo to appear prominently in your annual report.

Advertising can be broken down into two categories:

- *Goodwill advertising*, where the primary purpose of the advertiser is to support a charity, and to be seen to be supporting a cause; this creates goodwill for the company rather than selling its products. Companies like it because they get publicity in return for their support and they are asked to give a specific amount that they can afford.
- *Commercial advertising*, where the advertiser wishes to reach the audience that the charity's publication goes to, and the decision is made for purely commercial considerations.

What are you offering to advertisers

Before trying to sell the advertising, you need to recognise what you are offering. If it is goodwill advertising, then the prestige of the event, the nature of the audience, location and any celebrities who will be present will be major incentives. Price is less of an issue than the work of the charity, although the advertiser will want to know the circulation and readership of the publication, any special characteristics of that readership and any particular connection between it and their product. If it is commercial advertising, these details become even more significant.

Pricing the advertising

The first consideration when pricing the advertising is the format of the publication. A lavish souvenir brochure is different from an annual report, and this in turn is very different from a single colour word-processed newsletter. There are two factors to consider when deciding the cost of the advertising:

- How much you want to raise? Divide this target by the number of pages of advertising to get a page rate.
- How much are advertisers prepared to pay? For commercial advertising this is especially important. Try to define the value of your audience to them.

Once you have decided a page rate, then you can then set prices for smaller spaces which are slightly higher than *pro rata*. For example, if the page rate is £250, then a half page might be priced at £150, a quarter page at £85, and eighth page at £50. You can ask for higher sums for special positions, such as the back cover, the inside front cover and facing the contents page. For a regular publication, you could offer a series discount for taking space in several issues.

Getting the advertising

In order to appear professional, produce a rate card which contains all the information that the advertiser needs to know, including:

- deadline for agreeing to take space
- deadline for receipt of artwork and address where it is to be sent
- publication size
- print run
- use of colour on cover and inside pages (four colour, two colour, black and white)
- page rates, including special positions, size of advertising space, and whether VAT is chargeable
- payment details.

The covering letter

On the last Friday of every month, come hail, rain or shine, our team of 150 volunteers pushes a copy of the 'Community News' into each and every one of the 5,000 letterboxes in Newtown. We know our readers eagerly await its arrival, because they write and tell us, telephone us, and stop us in the street to tell us so.

There are many reasons for its continuing popularity – lots of local interest stories, on-the-spot photographs, and our fearless reporting of local issues without political bias of any kind. Our regular features – the crossword, gossip, cookery and gardening columns, the over '60s angle and Young Mum's Forum have all helped us make 'Community News' Newtown's No.1 Good Read, and we aim to keep it that way.

Advertise your company's products and services with us and get your message into 5,000 letterboxes each month. An advertisement rate card is enclosed with full details. If you have any queries, please don't hesitate to call me.

[From *Sell Space to Make Money* (now out of print)]

A simple brochure or covering letter which sets out the reasons for advertising is useful, but posting copies out will generate little response. The way to sell advertising is on the telephone, where you make a call to follow up a letter you have sent. For larger advertisers, you might try to arrange a personal visit. You have to find the right person who can make the decision, grab their attention, persuade them, and not go away until you have a commitment. Of course, the majority of people you approach will say 'no'; but your job is to persuade a significant proportion to say 'yes', and to get them to take a larger space than they might instinctively go for.

A note on VAT

Payment for advertising is not the same for tax purposes as a donation, and you may be liable for VAT if your organisation is VAT registered or close to the VAT registration threshold. Customs and Excise offer two concessions. They treat advertising revenue as VAT exempt if:

- the advertising is in the programme for a one-off fundraising event, where it is treated as part of the income from the event;
- it is paid for by private individuals and at least 50% of the advertisements in the publication are from private individuals.

8.6 Business sponsorship

Sponsorship needs to be carefully defined. It is not a glorified donation, and the fact that you are a charity is largely irrelevant. It is a business arrangement. The charity is looking to raise funds for its work and the company wants to improve its image, promote and sell its products or entertain its customers. The sponsor's contribution is usually money, although it could be a gifts of goods (such as a car), or services (such as free transport), or professional expertise (such as promotion or marketing consultancy), or the use of buildings (such as an exhibition centre), or free promotion (such as media coverage in a newspaper).

Many companies will provide much more in sponsorship than they would as a donation, but only so long as the commercial benefits warrant it. Developing links with the major national and local corporate sponsors could be an investment in your future that is well worth making now. For more detailed coverage of this topic, see *Finding Company Sponsors for Good Causes*.

Who sponsors?

Most sponsors are commercial companies. There are four main options for sponsorship:

- businesses wanting to promote themselves, to create a better image or generate awareness in the local communities where they operate. This includes those companies with an 'image problem' – for example, mining and extraction companies associated with the destruction of the environment who want to project a cleaner image by being associated with a conservationist cause;
- businesses wanting to introduce or promote a product or service. This could include a new brand of toothpaste or beer, or a supermarket opening in the area. Public awareness is important if a product or service is to get accepted, so companies may be open to proposals that give a product or service more exposure;
- companies looking for entertainment opportunities to influence customers, suppliers, regulators, the media and other opinion formers. They may be interested in sponsoring a prestigious concert, a theatrical event, an art exhibition, a horse race or a sporting event, which would provide them with an appropriate entertainment opportunity and the opportunity to meet and mingle with celebrities;
- companies that are committed supporters of your organisation. You may find them something that they would like to sponsor, even if it is partly for philanthropic reasons.

Why companies like sponsorship

- It helps them get their message across.
- It can enhance or change their image.
- It can reach a target audience very precisely.
- It can be very cost-effective advertising or product promotion.
- Further marketing opportunities may develop from the sponsorship.
- It generates good publicity for the sponsor, often of a kind that money can't buy.
- It generates an awareness of the company within the local community in which the company operates and from where it draws its workforce.
- Sponsors can entertain important clients at the events they sponsor.

What can be sponsored?

There is an extremely wide range of things that can be sponsored, including:

- cultural and sporting events
- mass participation fundraising events, such as a marathon or fun run

- the publication of a report or a book, with an attendant launch
- the production of fundraising materials, leaflets and posters, or the sponsorship of a complete fundraising campaign
- conferences and seminars, especially to specialist audiences (such as doctors) where promotional material can be displayed
- vehicles, where the acknowledgement can be painted on the side
- equipment such as cars or computers, produced by the company
- competitions, awards and prizes
- scholarships, bursaries, travel grants.

The bulk of corporate sponsorship money goes to sport, with motor racing, golf, tennis, athletics, football and cricket all receiving huge amounts. These offer extensive media coverage, good opportunities for corporate entertainment and an association with a popular activity. But as a charity you will not be competing for a share of the same budget.

Arts organisations will know that the arts is another big recipient of sponsorship – business support for the arts runs at around £150 million a year. Arts sponsorship is promoted by Arts & Business, which exists 'to promote and encourage partnerships between the private sector and the arts, to their mutual benefit and to that of the community at large'. Social sponsorship is much smaller by comparison, but is a growing area. The 'market' is less crowded and that there are all sorts of imaginative ways in which companies can sponsor events and activities run by charities.

Identifying possible sponsors

First you should decide what benefits your proposed activity can offer a sponsor. Is it access to a target audience? Access to public personalities? A prestigious event with entertainment opportunities? Once you have done this, you can begin to define companies who might be interested. They may be national companies looking for national publicity, or a major company located in your area or a purely local concern looking to develop its local presence. Remember that if you are looking for a substantial sum of money, only the larger companies will be interested.

Then draw up a list of potential sponsors. Do some research to find out what the company has sponsored before, what sort of sums it might possibly provide, and whether it might have any current interests or concerns which could be met through sponsorship. For example, a construction company that has just completed a residential estate will be interested in marketing it, or a new shopping centre may need a promotional event to coincide with its opening. These are opportunities for sponsorship.

You need patience. Sponsorship can take a long time to negotiate, and it is best to plan well in advance. Start discussions at least a year before the proposed activity is to take place.

The sponsorship package

Before you make your approach, you need to prepare a written proposal, which will outline the project, and highlight all the benefits to be gained by the company. It will also have a price for the sponsorship which will reflect as much the benefits to the company as your own need for money. You may be able to get help on this from a friendly marketing/PR firm. In your proposal, you will describe:

- the nature of the project or activity, and how it is likely to work;
- the audiences that will be reached and the publicity that will be obtained. These should be quantified as far as possible (how many column inches of coverage and in which newspapers; how many and what sort of people will attend the event; how many posters will be displayed, how many hits the website will receive etc.). Remember that the company will be primarily interested in reaching those people who are its target audience and you have to demonstrate how you will do this;
- the geographical coverage – is it a national or a purely local activity?
- the image that will be projected through the event, and how this will fit in with what the sponsoring brand or company might be looking for;
- the specific advertising opportunities that will be available on poster hoardings, the sides of vans, in the event programme, on TV and in the press;
- some of the other benefits that the sponsorship might confer on the company – the effect it will have on staff, on business contacts, and on government and other authorities;
- the cost of the sponsorship – and the value of the sponsorship benefits. You can also try to assess how this compares with other ways of achieving the same promotional objective.

All this should be produced in a professional (though not necessarily expensive) way, together with photographs and press coverage from previous sponsored events, and brief background material on your organisation and its work.

Where the money will come from

Which budget head the money comes from is important, as this will determine who will make the decision and what sort of return is needed. The following are the main options.

- *Marketing.* The company may be undertaking all sorts of activity to market its products and brands – all within an annual budget. The marketing manager will be making choices about what promotional options to pursue based on the cost and expected return. If you are asking for sponsorship, then you have to demonstrate the return you can provide – and show that this is a cost-effective option.
- *Corporate image.* Very large companies have a central budget to promote the name, image and logo of the company. Often this is handled alongside their charitable support, and sometimes even out of the same budget. The return to the company may be more intangible than with product or brand sponsorship, but this is all part of the corporate image building process, (which includes corporate advertising and PR as well). A good example of how this can pay off is demonstrated by the following example: Shell was involved in an oil spill on the River Mersey in the 1980s. The judge fining the company said that the fine would have been far larger but for Shell's excellent record in sponsoring the arts and the environment.
- *Employee relations.* The human resources budget is often the biggest single budget that the company has; investing in better staff relations can be a cost effective way of enhancing staff loyalty, retaining and even recruiting staff. The whole community affairs programme of Allied Dunbar (part of Zurich Financial Services) at its headquarters in Swindon (and with its self-employed sales force) can be seen as a way of creating a company to be proud of.

Making the approach

Having identified a potential company and developed your sponsorship proposal, there are a variety of ways in which you can approach the company.

Approach the person who will make the decision directly. For product promotions, this will be the brand manager. For corporate PR, it may be the director of corporate affairs. Try to make an appointment to visit the company to give a presentation of your work and discuss the sponsorship opportunities. Only then will you be in a position to find out about the company's needs and how you can meet them.

- If you cannot arrange a meeting ring the marketing department to find out who to send the proposal to and what sorts of sponsorship they consider. Send a summary proposal to see if it sparks any interest and follow this up with a phone call a few days later to try and arrange a meeting.
- There may be an advertising agency or marketing consultant which will introduce sponsorship opportunities to sponsors. They will sometimes charge you a fee; more usually they will receive a commission from the

sponsor. It depends who retains them, and in whose interests they are acting.

Contractual issues

Sponsorship involves your giving something in return for the money you are receiving, so you need to agree terms through a contract. This can be set out in a legal agreement (for larger sponsorships) or in the form of a letter. You need to be clear about the following:

- How long the arrangement will run. Is it for one year, thus requiring you to find a new sponsor next year? Or can you get a commitment for several years? What happens at the end of this period – does the sponsor have a first refusal on the following year's event? Most successful sponsorship lasts for several years, and the benefit builds up over the sponsorship period, but companies don't like being tied to sponsoring something indefinitely – their sponsorship programme would begin to look stale.
- The fee to be paid, and when the instalments are due.
- What benefits are to be delivered in return for the fee. These should be specified as clearly as possible, so that you know precisely what you are contracted to deliver.
- Whether VAT is chargeable. This will depend on whether your organisation is registered for VAT and the extent of the benefits offered to the sponsor. If VAT is chargeable, this should be discussed at the outset, and the fee agreed should be exclusive of VAT.
- Who will pay for what costs. Who pays for the additional publicity that the sponsor requires is something that is often forgotten. There needs to be a clear agreement as to who is responsible for what, so that you can ensure that everything is covered and there are no misunderstandings later on.
- Who is responsible for doing what. You will need to clarify who will do the public relations, who will handle the bookings, who will invite the guests, whose staff will receive the guests and so on.
- Any termination arrangements in the event of the activity having to be cancelled.
- Who is responsible for managing the sponsorship – a named person on both sides.
- Whether the sponsor is a 'commercial participator' under the terms of the Charities Act, when the requirements of the Charities Act will apply.

If everything is written down and agreed, there will be fewer problems later – and it ensures that everything has been properly thought through at the outset.

8.7 Joint promotions and cause related marketing

Many larger charities are involved in promotional activity to help market a commercial product – this is often known as cause related marketing (CRM). This can bring in large amounts of money and expose the name of the charity to millions of people for little or no cost. The same idea can also be adapted for use by local charities through local promotions.

Commercial promotions can include on-pack and licensing promotional deals, affinity credit cards, competitions and awards, the use of phone lines, and self-liquidating offers. What they have in common is that they present an opportunity to raise money for your cause and to project your charity to new audiences but they require that you work with the company and on their terms to achieve this.

This arrangement benefits both the charity and the commercial partner. It differs from sponsorship in that you are promoting their product or service (for a payment in return) as the primary purpose of the arrangement. But as with sponsorship, you will need to make a business case for it.

Profitable Partnerships

A research report based on a survey of 2000 randomly selected adults conducted by the British Market Research Bureau, found the following:

- Over 65% of the sample had participated in a CRM campaign. Three quarters of them either switched brand, tried out a product or increased their usage because of CRM; four out of five felt more positive about certain purchases, more loyal to a company or brand, and there were clear benefits to the charity, many stating such campaigns provided an easy way for them to give their support.
- Some 90% had heard of at least one CRM campaign and nearly half could spontaneously name a specific company or brand involved in a campaign.
- Two out of three people believe more businesses should become involved. However, a small percentage feel CRM is exploitative or that it is inappropriate for business to become involved in social issues in this way.

Getting started with promotions

Joint promotions are quite difficult to arrange. You must first talk about the possibility of your developing promotional links with companies with a marketing or advertising agency.

You need to decide whether you are the sort of charity which can expect a commercial link of this sort. It has been generally accepted that national household-name charities and those addressing popular causes (such as helping children) are more likely to benefit from this area of fundraising than the less well know charities or those addressing difficult causes such as torture or slavery. However, the success of the CRISIS on-pack promotion with the Covent Garden Soup Company demonstrates that there are no hard and fast rules.

British Gas/ Help the Aged Partnership

In 1998/ 99, winter deaths of 44,000 older people in the UK could be directly attributed to cold related diseases. British Gas embarked on a long-term £5 million cause related marketing partnership with Help the Aged to reduce the number of winter deaths and to make the lives of older people warmer and less isolated. The partnership encouraged consumer donations via a range of customer bill inserts with British Gas matching every pound donated by consumers. It was also integrated throughout the business and supported by employee fundraising, which was topped up by the company, and other community investment initiatives. The promotion is delivering a home insulation programme throughout the UK, funding to heat day centres and lunch clubs, funding for SeniorLine – Help the Aged's free advice line for older people and carers – and funding for a campaign to provide heating vouchers for older people on income support. The partners also lobbied the government over this issue.

More than 200,000 older people have benefited and Help the Aged has received more than £1.5 million, exceeding the contractual commitment. It has generated huge employee support, external media coverage and reinforced British Gas's brand attributes at a time when consumers could choose their energy supplier.

You can wait until companies or their promotional agencies contact you (they may not), or you can try to take the initiative yourself by contacting companies who might be interested. You can also contact promotion agencies (who are not retained by you) to make them aware of the opportunities you are offering which they could include when appropriate in their sales pitch to companies.

If you are approached by a promotional agency pitching for business, this does not mean that anything is certain. They may be working independently, hoping that a good idea that involves your charity can then be sold to a company. In nine out of ten situations, these ideas come to nothing, and you may find you have put in considerable effort without getting any payback.

Issues with sponsorships and joint promotions

Sponsorship involves a close working relationship with a company. This can lead to problems. It is one thing to accept or even solicit money from a company about whose activities you have some reservations; it is quite another when you are actively associated with the work of the company, as you will be in a sponsorship relationship. With commercial promotions the relationship is even closer. The charity is actively promoting the products of the company, so it is important that the product you are associated with is good value and good quality. With both arrangements it is important that you have no ethical problems in associating with that company. You should develop an ethical donations policy before you apply for any sponsorship or suggest a joint promotion – agreeing in advance which types of company you are happy to work with and which you are not. (See *Ethical issues* above.)

There is also the question of who is exploiting whom. How much you should expect to receive from a sponsorship or commercial promotion is also a difficult question. It may be worth a great deal to them to be linked with you. Any negotiation should start from what you think the association is worth to them. Your need for money should not dim the value of your commercial worth.

Finally, there are important legal issues arising from the 1992 Charities Act. The Act defines a 'commercial participator' as 'any person who carries on for gain a business which is not a fundraising business but who in the course of that business engages in any promotional venture in the course of which it is represented that contributions are to be given to or applied for the benefit of a charity'. In other words, high street shops often promote products on the understanding that part of the sale price will go to charity – for example charity Christmas cards published commercially state explicitly that for each pack sold a certain sum will go to charity. The Act also covers advertising and sales campaigns or other joint promotions by companies with charities. If the activity falls within the provisions of the Act, this then requires:

- a written agreement in a prescribed form between the charity and the commercial participator. Model forms of contract can be obtained from the Institute of Fundraising;

- the public to be informed how the charity will benefit from its involvement, which shows what part of the proceeds or profits are to be given to the charity. This is a matter for professional advice.

The Charity Commission also suggests that Trustees should consider the following points before allowing the charity's name to be associated with a particular business or product:

- the relationship is appropriate and will not damage the particular charity or the good name of charity as a whole;
- the proposed fundraising venture is a more effective way of raising money than others that might be considered, and that the terms of the arrangement are generally advantageous to the charity;
- that the arrangement is set out in some detail and kept under review, such that the charity's name is not misused or improperly exploited, and that the charity has the right to prevent future use of its name if the arrangement proves unsatisfactory. It may be worth taking proper legal advice in drawing up the terms of the arrangement.

Resources and further information

See also general lists at the end of the book.

Organisations

Arts & Business
Nutmeg House
60 Gainsford Street
Butler's Wharf
London SE1 2NY
Tel. 020 7378 8143

business community connections
14 Northfields
London SW18 1UU
www.bcconnections.org.uk
Tel. 020 8875 5700
Fax 020 8875 5701
e-mail info@bcconnections.org.uk

Business in the Community
135 Shepherdess Walk
London N1 7RR
Tel. 0870 600 2482

Community Service Volunteers (for RSVP programme)
237 Pentonville Road
London N1 9NJ
Tel. 020 7278 6601

Companies House
Crown Way
Cardiff CF14 3UZ
Tel. 029 2038 0801

CRASH
The Barley Mow Business Centre
10 Barley Mow Passage
London W4 4PH

EIRIS (Ethical Investment Research and Information Service)
80–84 Bondway
London SW8 1SQ
www.eiris.org
Tel. 020 7840 5700

Kind Direct (formerly Gifts in Kind UK)
PO Box 140
4 St Dunstan's Hill
London EC3R 5HB
www.inkinddirect.org
Tel. 020 7204 5003

REACH (Retired Executives Action
Clearing House)
Bear Wharf
27 Bankside
London SE1 9ET
Tel. 020 7928 0452

PerCent Club
c/o Business in the Community

Pro Help
c/o Business in the Community

Publications

The following publications are available from the Directory of Social Change.
Prices were correct the time of writing, but may be subject to change.

CD ROM Company Giving Guide, DSC 2002, £50 + VAT

Corporate Fundraising, ed. Valerie Morton, CAF/ICFM 2002, £19.95

Funding for Change, ed. Susan Forrester, DSC, journal published four times a
year, £40 (voluntary and community organisations) £50 (statutory and
commercial organisations), Issue 1 available April 2003

Finding Company Sponsors for Good Causes, Chris Wells, DSC 2000, £9.95

Guide to UK Company Giving, John Smyth, DSC 2002, £25

A Practical Guide to VAT 2nd edition, Kate Sayer, DSC 2001, £12.95

Other publications

Profitable Partnerships
Business in the Community, £75 (business), £50 (registered charities)
www.crm.org.uk

Kompass (series of directories)
Reed Information Services
Windsor Court
East Grinstead House
East Grinstead
W. Sussex RH19 1XO
www.kompass.com
Tel. 01342 335866

Changing Corporate Values
New Consumer
52 Elswick Road
Newcastle-upon-Tyne NE4 6JH

Yellow Pages
British Telecom
www.yell.co.uk

GOVERNMENT FUNDING

Figures for 2000–2001 show that the money available to voluntary organisations from central government competitive funding programmes in England totalled nearly £300 million, whereas £385.4 million was given as grant-in-aid to individual voluntary organisations. This chapter looks at both types of funding, the new localised partnership initiatives generated by central government, and at ways of accessing support from your local authority.

Details of organisations and publications referred to in this chapter are on p. 197.

9.1 Background to government funding

Grants from government represent a much lower percentage of voluntary sector income than donations from trusts or from the general public – or indeed fees earned from contracts or service level agreements with central or local government. But if you are prepared to research the possibilities thoroughly and tailor your application to meet government objectives, then this can be a worthwhile route to follow.

The relationship between government and the voluntary sector has changed dramatically in recent years. The Chancellor's statement in January 2001 boldly asserted that 'the era of centralising government is at an end', and that 'the way forward is to move power closer to the people'. The new civic patriotism is to be kindled via 'enabling and empowering voluntary action'. He particularly praised the 'greater flexibility to innovate in which voluntary organisations often excel – whether it is coaching teenagers, motivating former truants, or mentoring new businesses' where 'the accent is on the one-to-one approach'. He singled out under-five provision, health, adult learning and the war against unemployment and poverty as areas in which voluntary work can excel. He envisioned a new National Experience Corps for the over 50's to pass on their skills and experience to help others and hoped that within five years most adults would give two hours of voluntary work a week.

A £300 million package was announced over a three-year period to support national and local initiatives:

- £60 million from the Home Office's Active Community budget to increase volunteering in schools, hospitals, and other parts of the statutory sector;
- a matching £60 million from other government department budgets;
- £60 million from the Active Community budget for mentoring, marketing and capacity building;
- £50 million from the Department for Environment, Transport and the Regions for community groups in deprived areas/involvement at the local level;
- £70 million for the Children's Fund to assist local voluntary and community groups to find local solutions to child poverty (announced earlier as part of the 2000 Spending Review).

All this suggests an over-exaggerated view of the part that volunteering can play in the effectiveness of key services. It is also perhaps misguided to think that volunteering can be artificially stimulated by government. However this funding needs to be placed in a wider context.

Behind this fanfare leading up to the 2001 general election, the importance that the Labour government places on the voluntary sector has been reflected in the National Compact drawn up between government and the voluntary sector. This, for the first time, attempted to define their roles and mutual responsibilities (*Compact on Relationships between the Government and the Voluntary Sector*, Home Office and NCVO, 1998). This has been supplemented by a series of Codes of Practice, including one on funding (*Funding: a Code of Good Practice*, Home Office and NCVO, 2000).

However, the most obvious change for the voluntary sector in their relationship with government has taken place at the local level. In the 1990s many services were tendered out to the private and voluntary sector both by local authorities and local health trusts. Many voluntary organisations, particularly in health and social welfare fields, now have contracts or service-level agreements with clear targets and timetables to fulfil. At the same time most local authorities have seriously reduced their dedicated grant programmes for voluntary organisations. Local authorities have been criticised for getting services from voluntary agencies on the cheap, whilst the voluntary sector has been criticised for relinquishing its independence.

In addition, since 1997, an extensive range of area-based programmes have been generated by central government which engage local authorities in partnership arrangements with the voluntary and community sector (see below). The engagement between government and the voluntary sector has become both closer and more complex, with many different relationships and many potential opportunities for funding which bring their different demands and responsibilities.

If you are thinking of applying for government funding, whether from central, local or regional government, or from the many related statutory agencies, known as Non Departmental Public Bodies (NDPBs, formerly known as Quangos), you should remember that it is not enough for you to show that your organisation is doing good and important work. You must be able to demonstrate that the work falls within the government department's own strategies and helps it to meet those aims and objectives. This key point is well stated by John Marshall, head of grants and funding policy at the Active Community Unit of the Home Office:

'Government grants are primarily designed to meet departmental policy objectives and programme outcomes. These should of course be reflected in the published criteria for grant. Applications are, therefore, expected to demonstrate clearly how they will help departments achieve their objectives. Too many applicants seem to assume that the core work of their organisation is reason enough to secure a government grant. I am afraid that no matter how effective or important the work of your organisation, you need to show how it meets the objectives of the funder.'

So firstly find out the strategic objectives of the department or agency, and obtain their strategy documents. Always be absolutely clear about what their mandate enables them to support. This will help you to avoid wasting time on inappropriate applications, and if you do make an application, to stress in it how you will be helping them to meet their objectives.

Also be quite sure you know which department or NDPB you wish to contact. Most central government departments are primarily concerned with national organisations and projects which have a national significance. Devolution has meant that, apart from departments which have a UK-wide remit, such as The Foreign Office, the Ministry of Defence and the Department for International Development, voluntary organisations should approach the relevant departments within their own country – in Scotland and Wales most grantmaking is handled by the departments within the Scottish Executive and the National Assembly for Wales respectively. At the time of writing the Northern Ireland Office was the responsible authority in Northern Ireland. NDPBs have their own geographical areas of responsibility which mostly fall within the four countries, but not inevitably.

Another important and constraining aspect of all government funding at all levels is that it works to an annual timetable ruled by the financial year running from 1 April to 31 March. All grants (excepting contracts) have to be approved within an annual budget. Most departments have firm deadlines for submitting an application, usually in the autumn before the year in which the grant will be made. This means that you have to plan your programmes and budgets well in advance. Since there may be changes to programmes, you must be sure to check these schedules.

Be sure to seek advice from grant officers in a department or agency *before* you send in a completed application form. It is too late to ask questions once you have sent one in. You can't retract and alter it.

9.2 Support from central government

The voluntary sector receives financial support from central government departments and agencies (NDPBs)in a number of ways. The main forms it takes are as follows:

1 funding programmes, directed specifically at voluntary and community organisations (see list below);

2 grant-in-aid to individual voluntary organisations on an annual review basis (see list below);

3 funding programmes, often from NDPBs, covering a wider constituency than the voluntary sector alone. Examples include the Connecting Communities Programme run by the Race Equality Unit of the Home Office, or funding programmes run by NDPBs such as the Arts Councils, the Countryside Agency and English Nature;

4 special departmental initiatives to tackle a problem and to research, test and pilot new approaches/methods, such as the National Disability Development Initiative set up by the Disability Service of the Employment Service;

5 special initiatives, often interdepartmental, and often in selected areas to tackle a problem through local partnerships comprising the public, private and voluntary sectors; these include Sure Start and Health Action Zones;

6 service contracts, which occur most extensively at local authority level and particularly involve voluntary organisations working in aspects of health, disability and social welfare.

These types of support are not listed above according to their relative size. Although central government gives large amounts of money to voluntary organisations each year, most of it goes to organisations already being supported. For instance the available figures for 2000/01 for *1. Competitive funding programmes directed specifically at the voluntary section in England* totalled almost £300 million, which was significantly lower than the total for *2. Grant-in-aid on a annual basis to individual voluntary organisations in England*, which was £385.4 million.

Main competitive funding programmes specifically for voluntary organisations, 2000–2001 – UK-wide and England only

	£millions
Department for International Development	*126.18*
Civil Society Challenge Fund (UK)	20.10
Conflict & Humanitarian Affairs Department (UK)	100.75
Development Awareness Fund (UK)	5.00
Charity Know How (UK)	0.33
Department of Environment, Transport and the Regions	*42.03*
Housing Management and Tenant Participation – Section 16	5.98
Environmental Action Fund	4.21
Special Grants Programme, regeneration/housing	1.44
Housing Corporation Resettlement of Single and Homeless People	9.00
*Rough Sleepers Unit	20.40
Local Heritage Initiative	1.00
(plus an extra £3 million from Nationwide Building Society and Heritage Lottery Fund)	
Department for Education and Employment	*34.08*
Early Education Grants	1.83
Section 64 – Early Years Division	0.78
SEN Small Programmes Fund	1.00
Adult and Community Learning Fund	5.00
National Voluntary Youth Organisations	4.00
Citizenship Education Grants	0.47
Neighbourhood Support Fund	20.00
Community Champions Fund	1.00
Department of Health	*28.10*
Section 64 (health and personal social service)	21.00
Opportunities for Volunteering Scheme	6.60
Black and Minority Ethnic Anti-Drug Grants	0.50
Home Office	*23.33*
Active Community Unit	
Active Community Grants (UK)	18.00
Capital Modernisation Grants (UK)	2.33
Family Support Grant	3.00
TOTAL	**253.38**

*One-off funding, not available in subsequent years
[*A Guide to Funding from Government Departments and Agencies*, 2nd edition, 2001]

Annual grants-in-aid to voluntary organisations outside competitive programmes

The distinction between grants and grants-in-aid is not always clear even within the Civil Service. Grants-in-aid tend to be on a continuing basis to bodies towards their operational costs. These organisations are closely linked to particular government policies and interests and many have owed their genesis as voluntary organisations to joint initiatives arising between government departments and/or their agencies and voluntary sector interests.

Much of this funding is given to the work of organisations which are themselves funding bodies, providing financial and other support to people and young children with physical problems, such as the Independent Living Fund, Motability and the Family Fund Trust.

Grant-in-aid, 2000–2001 – UK-wide and England only

Department	£millions
MAFF	**0.30**
DCMS	**7.17**
Governing Bodies of Sport	7.17
Defence	**55.45**
(*including* Army Cadet Corps – £40,079)	
DfEE	**2.37**
including	
National Mentoring Network	0.60
Basic Skills and Adult Further Education	0.60
(7 organisations including National Institute	
for Adult Continuing Education – £0.445)	
Learning Alliance	0.85
Voluntary Sector National Training Organisation	0.20
DETR	**17.79**
including	
Encams (Tidy Britain Group / Going for Green)	3.76
Groundwork	7.50
RoSPA	0.41
DfID	**48.00**
Partnership Programme Agreements	48.00
Foreign	**6.55**

Health	**29.60**
including	
Family Fund Trust	25.36
Sexual Health Promotion	2.10
Home	**55.82**
including	
Refugee Integration	2.10
(*including* Refugee Council – £1.3)	
Refugee Reception and One Stop Services	14.00
Refugee Legal Centre & Immigration Advisory Service	18.00
Victim Support	18.30
National Family and Parenting Institute	0.67
HM Prison Service	**0.65**
Commission for Racial Equality	**4.30**
(for Racial Equality Councils)	
Lord Chancellor's	**3.64**
Funding for Marriage Relationship Support	3.64
Social Security	**139.21**
including Independent Living Funds	131.30
Trade and Industry	**14.60**
including NACABx	14.42
Total	**385.44**

[*A Guide to Funding from Government Departments and Agencies*, 2nd edition, 2001]

Joined up thinking

The Social Exclusion Unit within the Cabinet Office has been a key player in the government's drive to achieve more co-operative working between departments on cross-sectoral issues and has taken a major part in the thinking behind the development of the two new funding streams, the Children's Fund and the Neighbourhood Renewal Fund, mentioned below.

Specific interdepartmental units have been established to administer programmes such as Rough Sleepers, New Deal for Disabled People, New Deal for Lone Parents, and Connexions. The Neighbourhood Renewal Unit set up to co-ordinate the work of the various departments and agencies concerned with the National Strategy for Neighbourhood Renewal became operational from April 2001.

Partnerships and special initiatives

There has, over recent years, been a proliferation of initiatives generated by central government to tackle specific problems in areas of particular disadvantage. Through these central government has sought to stimulate new initiatives and cooperative work at the *local* level through the development of a variety of partnerships across all sectors, public, private and voluntary/community. These often involve huge amounts of money. They include:

- New Deal for Communities
- Health Action Zones
- Education Action Zones
- Sure Start

More recently the Legal Services Commission (successor to the Legal Aid Board) has been developing Local Legal Services Partnerships throughout the country.

For many of these programmes certain localities, or zones, have been selected in areas of particular need to receive additional funding for innovative approaches. You can find out if your area has been selected from your local authority (full lists can also be obtained from the department and via its website).

These initiatives do not operate like competitive funding programmes. In general they run to the following pattern.

- Each selected area is allocated a certain tranche of money by the lead central government department to reach particular objectives with clearly targeted outcomes.
- A partnership is formed of the public, private and voluntary sector organisations with a clear interest in the programme.
- A separate managing body is set up responsible for drawing up a strategy and budgeted programme of activities over the lifetime of the scheme.
- Within this programme voluntary organisations may be funded for an agreed activity or service which forms part of a wider strategic plan.

Although the opportunity to join such a partnership may seem attractive, the many additional administrative tasks and incessant meetings can create a very heavy workload, so you need to be sure that your organisation has the capacity to cope.

Local voluntary and community groups within the location of a special initiative should be alert to the possibility that the partnership body may decide to provide a community fund in their area. See chapter 6 (section 6.2) for more on community foundations. Some HAZs and Sure Start partnership programmes have done so.

The plethora of partnerships has led to a new community planning duty by which service providers across the country are being encouraged to establish *Local Strategic Partnerships* i.e. a 'single co-ordinating partnership for an area ... linking the neighbourhood to the regions, co-ordinating across and between partnership activity'.

In addition to the partnership arrangements noted above, the voluntary sector has also been playing a major part in helping to implement particular central government programmes such as the New Deal for Unemployed People and the Strategy for Rough Sleepers.

Regionalisation

The introduction of Regional Development Agencies (RDAs) has added an important new tier to government, but one which is not democratically accountable except in Greater London. RDAs have been given specific statutory responsibilities for economic development and regeneration, competitiveness, business support and investment, skills, employment, sustainable development. Whilst their thinking seems to be business led, their decisions will increasingly affect the work of voluntary organisations which have formed into regional networks to be able to make an input into their thinking and their work.

Already RDA demands have had an impact on funding sources accessed by voluntary groups. RDA responsibilities included overseeing the Single Regeneration Budget. They called for freedom from restricted budgets and power to decide their own spending priorities, according to regional needs as expressed in their strategic plans. As a result the Single Regeneration Budget, the massive fund jointly supported by many departments particularly DETR, DTI and DfEE, will not continue after the transition year, 2001–2002. From 2002–2003, this funding will go directly to each RDA into their 'single spending pot'. Voluntary groups have spent many arduous years working to get their projects supported via this fund only to find the ground rules are being rewritten.

A cross-departmental unit, the Regional Co-ordination Unit, has been set up to give more coherence to the work of the Government Offices for the Regions. A particular aim will be to introduce better co-ordination of area-based initiatives many of which, at the time of writing, overlap and make competing demands on local partners.

Funding to local groups

Whilst, as a general rule, central government departments support national work or initiatives with a national significance, and leave the funding of local and community activities to local government, in recent years a number of time-limited programmes have been initiated by central government departments, administered on their behalf by agencies 'closer to the ground'. These included at the time of writing:

- Community Resource Fund administered by community foundations for the Active Community Unit of the Home Office;
- Neighbourhood Support Fund, administered for the DfEE by Community Development Foundation, National Youth Agency and Youth Alliance;
- Community Champions Fund, delegated from the DfEE to the Government Offices for the Regions and then to local administrators;
- Adult and Community Learning Fund, administered for the DfEE by two national agencies.

These programmes have varied greatly in size. The largest, the Neighbourhood Support Fund, has made no less than £60 million available over three years.

These precede major interdepartmental initiatives of importance for the voluntary and community sector which will come on stream during 2001.

- The Children's Fund will release £70 million of its allocation to be administered by and for local voluntary and community groups over a period of three years. In the third year, £40 million will be distributed, and there is clearly an intention that funding will continue.
- The Neighbourhood Renewal Fund, as part of the National Strategy for Neighbourhood Renewal, is expected to help fund capacity building and fund additional training of key individuals as well as community chests to assist local communities. Funding may also be available to enable community inputs to Local Strategic Partnerships (LSPs). At the time of writing the details about this had not been announced. Certainly LSPs in the most deprived areas will receive start-up funding through the New Deal for Communities to help empower local people and communities to play their part in setting local priorities and determining local action for their neighbourhoods. Funds should help cover the cost of residents' and groups' participation, and allow LSPs to use 'innovative approaches to involving local people', alongside funding for small 'Community Chests'.

Non Departmental Public Bodies (NDPBs)

The official definition of an NDPB is 'a body which has a role in the process of national government, but is not a government department or part of one, and which accordingly operates to a greater or lesser extent at arm's length from ministers'. Their boards, which are charged with the responsibility for their work, are comprised of appointees. Increasingly board members are being selected through open competition. Much of the work of government is carried out by these semi-autonomous bodies.

It would be foolish to attempt too many generalisations about NDPBs, they are so many and so varied. Regional Development Agencies are NDPBs. The main point for the fundraiser to remember is that they also operate according to the annual financial round (1 April to 31 March). They receive their funding from the government department to which they are related and they are accountable to its minister, who may exert pressure on them as considered necessary.

Like central departments they disburse funds according to their strategies. It is important to understand these and to obtain full details of their funding programmes along with their annual report. Be sure to check on their deadlines for grant applications, their grant conditions, the range within which grants are made and any requirements for match funding. You will face strong competition. NDPBs usually fund local authority initiatives and well as those from the private sector, so it is important to appreciate and be able to demonstrate the particular strengths of your voluntary organisation in meeting the agency's objectives and grant criteria.

Many national NDPBs such as the Countryside Agency and English Nature have regional offices which decide on grantmaking through close contact and understanding of their local constituency. It is important to build up a good working relationship with these officers. With all agencies it is best to discuss your proposals first with relevant grant officers.

The largest group, by far, are the Health Authorities and the Hospital Trusts. Others are listed overleaf.

Non Departmental Public Bodies and the departments which fund them

Department of Culture, Media and Sport – related agencies
The Arts Council of England
Regional Arts Boards
Resource: The Council for Museums, Archives and Libraries
Area Museum Councils
Arts and Business
National Heritage Memorial Fund
English Heritage
Sport England
Institute of Sports Sponsorship

Department for Education and Employment – related agencies
Learning and Skills Council
National Youth Agency
Connect Youth International, formerly Youth Exchange Centre
Commonwealth Youth Exchange Council
Employment Service

Department of Environment, Transport and the Regions – related agencies
Housing Corporation
Home Improvement Agencies
Housing Action Trusts
English Nature
Forestry Commission
National Forest Company
Countryside Agency
Landfill Tax Credit Scheme and ENTRUST

Home Office – related agencies
Prison Service
Youth Justice Board Development Fund
Alcohol Education and Research Fund
Commission for Racial Equality

Foreign and Commonwealth Office – related agencies
Charity Know How (UK-wide)
British Council Arts Group (UK-wide)
Visiting Arts (UK-wide)
Connect Youth International (UK-wide)
Commonwealth Youth Exchange Council (UK-wide)

Lord Chancellor's Department – related agency
Legal Services Commission (covers England and Wales)

The list includes UK-wide departments and central government departments in England. There are equivalents in most cases in the other three countries of the UK, for example the Scottish Arts Council, Historic Scotland, Scottish Homes, Scottish Law Commission, Scottish Natural Heritage, Scottish Museums Council; the Arts Council of Wales, Countryside Council for Wales, Council for Museums in Wales, Welsh Historic Monuments, Housing for Wales; the Arts Council of Northern Ireland, Northern Ireland Museums Council, Northern Ireland Community Relations Council; Northern Ireland Environment and Heritage Service, Northern Ireland Housing Executive. In addition there are agencies specific to that country, for example the Welsh Language Board.

Getting information and using websites

If you don't know the relevant internet address the following are good starting points and have links to other sites:

- *www.open.gov.uk* The government information service site provides an index of sites including departments, councils, NHS Trusts and non-departmental public bodies.
- *www.coi.gov.uk* The Central Office of Information site for English departmental and non-departmental public bodies' press releases updated daily.

The departmental websites often contain detailed criteria and often downloadable application forms. Although the quality of information and regularity of updates varies, they contain information on government policy, recent press releases, transcripts of speeches and consultation papers.

For central government and NDPB funding in England, you can consult the latest edition of *A Guide to Funding from Government Departments and Agencies*. It is particularly useful in displaying the full range of sources, giving details about the programmes and examples of beneficiaries. It may also help stimulate some lateral thinking about fundraising. In addition, there are specialist sources which concentrate on particular areas of funding, such as the National Youth Agency.

9.3 Local government

Local government reorganisation has led to a confusing variation in the types of local authority. Unitary authorities (which carry out the full range of local government responsibilities) have been introduced. Whilst these have been uniformly introduced in Scotland and Wales, unitary authorities now co-exist in England alongside county and district councils. No changes have been made in Northern Ireland or the metropolitan areas of England (and the London boroughs already carry out the full range of local authority duties).

The situation in England seems complex, arbitrary and piecemeal. The population size of unitary authorities varies considerably as does their geographical area. There are 47 shire unitary authorities (in addition to Metropolitan Authorities and London Boroughs) – they include cities and towns and areas such as York, Derby, Plymouth, Luton, West Berkshire, Bath and NE Somerset, the Isle of Wight, and Telford & Wrekin. Some counties and districts have been abolished and replaced entirely by unitary authorities (Berkshire) whilst other counties remain (Surrey).

In many counties new unitary authorities co-exist alongside the counties of which they had formerly been a part. For instance two new unitary authorities were created from within Leicestershire – Leicester City and Rutland – leaving a smaller Leicestershire County Council with seven district councils. However, to put the situation in perspective, there are still 34 county councils and 238 district councils (as at winter 2000–2001).

An understanding of the different responsibilities of the different types of authority is obviously useful (see box).

In addition many local authorities are reorganising their styles of operation and are developing cabinets of executive councils and an increased role for other councillors as 'backbenchers' scrutinising and influencing policy. It is important for local organisations to understand the system operating in their authority.

Also local compacts are being developed as part of the National Compact initiative. It could be useful for organisations to know their local authority's progress on this.

The creation of a range of local area strategies by central government (see 'Partnerships and Special Initiatives' above) has inevitably bought many voluntary and community organisations into a closer working relationship with their local authority since these initiatives are governed by boards with voluntary sector representation.

	Met/London[1] Authorities			Shire/Unitary Authorities		
	Joint Authorities	Met Councils	London Boroughs	District Councils	Unitary Authorities	County Councils
Education		●	●		●	●
Housing		●	●		●	●
Social Services		●	●		●	●
Libraries		●	●		●	●
Leisure & Recreation		●	●		●	●
Planning Applications		●	●	●	●	
Strategic Planning		●	●	●		●
Transport Planning		●			●	●
Passenger Transport	●				●	●
Highways		●	●		●	●
Fire	●				●[2]	●
Waste Collection		●	●	●	●	
Waste Disposal	●	●	●		●	●
Environmental Health		●	●	●	●	
Revenue Collection		●	●	●	●	

[1] Greater London Authority (GLA) functions need to be born in mind. It has duties particularly concerning Transport, Economic Development, Environment, Planning, Fire and Culture.

[2] Joint Fire Authorities operate in counties with unitary authorities in them.

[Source: Local Government Association]

Local contacts

For grants and other forms of advice and help, get in touch with the range of local authority officers who are responsible for information and support services relevant to your organisation. You may also need to develop working relationships with officers dealing with regeneration, employment and training and with links to European Structural Funds. The Government Offices for the Regions and the Regional Development Agencies have key roles in these areas, and any contacts you can develop will be helpful. However officers in your local authority may also be able to provide you with advice and act a good starting point to direct you as necessary to relevant officers in the regional bodies.

Whilst it is vital to contact the specialist grants officer (if there is one) or to find the officers responsible who service the committees relevant to your work, it is also vital to find out the names of the councillors serving on committees, particularly the chairperson. You should also try to enlist the support of your local councillors, whether they are from the party in overall control of the council or in opposition.

Find out their interests

Before approaching councillors and council officers, it is sensible to find out how much your local council gives for your area of interest and the particular projects it supports. This information is readily available in the minutes of local meetings.

It is also interesting to find out what comparable councils give. If yours is one of the councils which is spending very little on voluntary organisations, it may be useful long-term ammunition to be able to underline this point to your council by making suitable comparisons – though this will probably not help you much in the short term where changes in council budgets are unlikely.

Vital research

You should get to know the working procedures of your local council. Find out:

- What principal responsibilities each tier of local government in your area has, particularly with regard to your area of activity.
- What each relevant council's stated policies are. If, for example, a council lays strong emphasis on providing educational facilities and services, you may be able to take advantage of this when applying for a grant for an educational component of your work.

- How and when decisions on grants are taken. You need to know both the procedure and the timetable.
- What organisations they have funded in the past, and the amounts they have given in individual grants. This more than anything else will give you a picture of their general approach and preferences.
- Which councillors and council officers will be involved in the decision to fund you, and which are likely to be sympathetic to your organisation.

Making your case

Once you have identified the councillors and council officers whose support you need, it is advisable to spend time interesting them in your organisation. Invite them to events, which will also be a good opportunity for them to meet your colleagues. If there are people with local influence on your board or who support you in some way, persuade them to talk to some of the key councillors and officials about the value of your work. (Check these local VIPs' political persuasions first, and 'match' them with councillors with similar political views.)

It is a good idea to prepare the ground in this way before a formal application is made for a grant, so that you have a fair idea of what will be acceptable and what will not. Make sure that all those responsible for contacting and lobbying councillors are properly briefed: first, on the local importance of the organisation (backed up by figures, analysis etc.); second, on how this work relates to the policies and priorities of the council; and third on what the council can do to help. If councillors receive conflicting or muddled statements from a variety of sources, this can do considerable damage to your case.

Particular considerations

Apart from information particular to your council, there are criteria which all councils are likely to use when considering your proposal. You should take these into account at an early stage.

- How well does the work and objectives of your organisation fit in with your council's stated policies and priorities?
- Are there any organisations in the area doing similar work? If there are, do these organisations receive local authority funding? Are there sound reasons why the authority should fund your organisation as well as, or instead of, those it is already funding?
- How successful are you? Is your work of a high calibre? And what outside evidence can you provide to support this? How many people do you serve? And how many of them come from the local authority area? Are there

other ways in which you can demonstrate local community support, such as membership or local fund-raising?

- How well organised are you in terms of financial and administrative control? Are you reliable? Is your work endorsed by way of grants from other official bodies?
- How strongly do the local people feel about you? Would local opposition be strong if you were forced to disband from lack of funds?

Media coverage

While you are talking privately to council officers and councillors you should also be directing your efforts at your local media to reinforce your message. Items on local radio and in the local paper about the importance and quality of your work, reviews and interviews in which you outline future plans of benefit to the community should also have an effect on councillors' opinions.

Support in kind

Local councils may be able to offer you gifts in kind as well as cash grants: second-hand office equipment and furniture; premises for your use either free or at a low rent; help with transport maintenance; staff secondments (though these are rarely made in the arts field); access to the council bulk purchasing scheme which may offer lower prices than elsewhere. But you will only be able to find out if such support is available if your contacts with councillors and council officials are good.

Regular contact

Whatever support you are looking for, you should be talking regularly to councillors and council officials, especially those who are of particular importance to you. Keep them informed of your activities throughout the year, not just when grant application time looms again.

Acknowledgements and personal thanks

And, as always, you must say thank you for any assistance you receive from them. Remember too, to credit the council in publicity material, in media interviews and in formal speeches. The council (as well as councillors, who will always have one eye on the next election) needs a good press as much as you do.

Rate relief

In addition to giving you a grant, the local authority can also give you relief on your Business Rates. If you are a registered charity you are entitled to 80% rate relief on any premises you occupy for charitable purposes. This relief is reimbursed to the local authority by central government. Your local authority can also at its own discretion give you relief on all or part of the remaining 20%. Rate relief is given only if you apply for it and only for the current and following rate years (1 April to 31 March). It cannot be granted retrospectively. You can still apply for rate relief, however, even if your charitable status has not yet been officially approved by the Charity Commission (the Inland Revenue in Scotland and Northern Ireland).

Once you have been granted rate relief, you should continue to obtain it automatically, but check your annual rates bill to make sure this is happening. Because of pressure on financial resources, many councils are now less willing to give discretionary relief. But it is certainly worth applying for it. And continue to apply for it each year, if you are unsuccessful at the first attempt.

Getting information

The Local Government Association puts out some very useful factsheets about the structures and responsibilities of local authorities which are also available on the web. More importantly, the funding advice officer in your local Council for Voluntary Service, Rural Community Council or their equivalents, should be able to inform you about the committee structures of the council in your area, provide you with contacts, funding programmes, etc.

Resources and further information

See also general lists at the end of the book.

Organisations

Local Government Association
26 Chapter Street
London SW1P 4ND
www.lga.gov.uk
Info line 020 7664 3131

National Youth Agency
17–23 Albion Street
Leicester LE1 6GD
www.nya.org.uk
Tel. 0116 285 3700
Helpline 0116 285 3792

www.open.gov.uk
The government information service site provides an index of sites including departments, councils, NHS Trusts and non-departmental public bodies.

www.coi.gov.uk
The Central Office of Information site for English departmental and non-departmental public bodies' press releases updated daily.

Publications

The following publications are available from the Directory of Social Change. Prices were correct at the time of writing, but may be subject to change.

Guide to Funding from Central Government Departments and Agencies 2nd edition, Susan Forrester and Anthony Stenson, DSC 2001, £18.95

10 THE EUROPEAN UNION

The European Union (EU) provides a huge amount of money for social and economic development in member states, a small part of which is available to voluntary organisations. The amount received by the UK through the European Social Fund alone is estimated at £1.6 billion a year, which goes to regional and local government, regional regeneration initiatives, Learning and Skills Councils, as well as to voluntary organisations. The top 500 charities receive around £50 million annually from Europe (1997–98 figures). This chapter gives you an overview of what is available and how to access it.

Details of organisations and publications referred to in this chapter are on p. 212.

10.1 About EU funding

There are three main types of funding available from the EU.

- *Structural Funds*. The most important of these are the European Social Fund (ESF) and the European Regional Development Fund (ERDF). They are controlled by member governments and need to be matched by funding from within the UK. The European Social Fund is of particular interest to voluntary organisations – see 10.2 below.

- *Budget line funding*. There are some 150 further budget lines which offer opportunities for voluntary organisations to apply for funding, although eligibility is not necessarily limited to the voluntary sector. These budgets are controlled by officials in Brussels operating within one of the Directorates General (DGs) of the European Commission. A full list of budget lines for 2001 is given below – see 10.3. To an extent decisions on funding can be influenced by MEPs in Strasbourg, who can lobby on your behalf. Almost all applications have to have a significant trans-national dimension and UK-only projects are not normally funded.

- *Contract and research funding*. This is for specific work which the European Commission wishes to commission, on behalf either of itself or another government. It is usually put out to tender and can support research across a range of issues in the areas of health, environment, socio-economic affairs, energy, transport and medicine. There are also opportunities to host European Commission conferences and events.

Getting money from Europe can be a long, slow and painstaking process. There is increasing competition for the available funds, and the programmes, priorities and guidelines are constantly changing. Each year, the EU agrees its budget. The budget year runs from 1 January to 31 December and you need to keep up to date and to make contact as early as possible, ideally a full year in advance. Although the budget is adopted in December, it has been under discussion for the whole of the preceding year and so it is never too early to begin your research, although you will be unable to apply until an official invitation to tender has gone out. More information is available from the publications and organisations listed at the end of the chapter. Where matching funds are required, then you need to make sure that these are committed before you apply.

10.2 The Structural Funds, including the European Social Fund

The Structural Funds account for over 40% of the EU budget and, unlike the other EU budgets, the programme for the UK is wholly administered within the UK.

The European Regional Development Fund (ERDF) aims to reduce the gaps in development between different regions in the EU and so it is only available in certain regions of the UK. It is administered by the Department of Trade and Industry, from whom more information is available.

What ERDF can pay for

- To create and maintain permanent jobs
- To develop infrastructure
- Community development / capacity building
- Education
- Research and Development (R & D), technology transfer
- Environment
- Tourism
- Support for Small and Medium Enterprises (SMEs)
- Environmental image improvement

The European Social Fund (ESF), the other main structural fund, aims to promote training and job opportunities. The emphasis of the programme is on economic regeneration rather than social welfare, despite the name

European *Social* Fund. You will therefore be asked to show key economic outputs (such as the number of people emerging from your training with work-related qualifications) rather than the social or human benefits of counselling and confidence-building activities, for example.

ESF supports projects which help people back into work either through direct provision or by giving guidance, and projects aimed at preventing redundancy – for example retraining and upskilling of employees. It is of far more interest to voluntary organisations than ERDF.

European Social Fund 2000–2006

The central aims of the fund will be:

- developing and promoting active labour market policies to combat unemployment;
- promoting equal opportunities and social inclusion for all in gaining access to the labour market;
- promoting and improving education, training and counselling, as part of lifelong learning policy;
- promoting a skilled, trained and adaptable work force;
- improving women's access to and position in the labour market.

[*A Guide to European Union Funding*]

ESF is split into three Objectives:

- **Objective 1** support is directed at the most deprived areas. In the UK, these are Cornwall and the Isles of Scilly, South Yorkshire, West Wales, and Merseyside.
- **Objective 2** supports areas facing structural difficulties. It is targeted at specific geographical areas. Objective 2 regions include:
  - rural areas in decline
  - urban areas in difficulty
  - depressed areas which depend on fisheries
  - areas going through changes to their society and economy in the industrial and service sectors

  Objective 2 will support projects which develop human resources.
- **Objective 3** aims to support adapting and modernising policies and systems of education, training and employment. It will support projects working with both employed and unemployed people.

  Objective 3 funding is available in all areas except Objective 1 areas.

What ESF can pay for

Getting unemployed people back to work

- Careers advice, counselling and other measures to prepare the unemployed for work or study
- Vocational training
- Work placement
- Start-up aid for the unemployed
- Wage subsidies for employing the unemployed
- Capacity building for local and interest communities

Training in firms threatened by change

Any type of training which contributes to local economic development

---

The management of ESF now rests with the Government Regional Offices in England, the Welsh European Funding Office in Wales, and the Scottish Objective 3 Partnership and the Strathclyde European Partnership (Objective 2 only) in Scotland. Applications for funding have to be made to these bodies. The application form, guidance notes and other relevant documentation are all available online at: www.esfnews.org.uk

Each English region, Scotland and Wales all operate their own application processes, and you are advised to check with your relevant body for application deadlines and to obtain copies of any relevant regional guidance and information.

10.3 Budget line funds

The following is a provisional list of the budget lines in 2001, which gives an indication of the many and varied fields of activity where the EU has an interest in providing funding. The list will vary from year to year and up-to-date information is normally available from ECAS or IDs in Brussels.

At the time of writing €1 = 61p.

p.m. stands for *pro memoria*, meaning that no budget has as yet been established for the relevant programme.

Budget line	€
A-30 Community subsidies	
A-3015 European Bureau for lesser used languages and Mercator	1,000,000
A-3021 Grants to organisations advancing the idea of Europe	1,800,000
A-3022 Study and research centre	1,500,000
A-3024 Associations and federations of European interest	1,260,000
A-3029 Support for international non-governmental youth organisations	1,400,000
A-3035 Preservation of Nazi concentration camp sites as historical memorials	350,000
A-3038 Other general grants	148,000
A-3042 Subsidy to cultural organisations advancing the idea of Europe	3,754,000
A-321 Town-twinning schemes in the European Union.	10,000,000
B2-1 Structural funds	**30,005,000,000**
B2-10 Objective 1	20,832,000,000
B2-11 Objective 2	3,613,000,000
B2-12 Objective 3	3,575,000,000
B2-13 Other structural measures	164,000,000
B2-14 Community initiatives	1,683,000,000
B2-140 Leader	329,600,000
B2-141 Interreg	777,000,000
B2-142 EQUAL	464,600,000
B2-143 URBAN	111,800,000
B2-16 Innovative measures and technical assistance	138,000,000
B2-300 Cohesion fund	2,715,000,000
B3-10 Education, vocational training and youth	
General and higher education	
B3-1000 Cooperation in the fields of education and youth policy	5,910,000
B3-1001 Socrates	239,306,000
B3-1003 Promotion of the linguistic diversity of the Community in the information society	7,550,000
Youth Policy	
B3-1010 Youth	66,753,000
Vocational training and guidance	
B3-1020 Promotion of European pathways in work-linked training	1,030,000
B3-1021 Leonardo da Vinci	142,397,000
B3-20 Culture and audiovisual media	
Culture	
B3-2008 Programme in support of culture	31,580,000
Audiovisual media	
B3-2010 Media Plus (measures to promote the development of the audiovisual industry)	55,370,000
B3-2011 Media Training	19,000,000
B3-2017 Other measures in the audiovisual sector	2,010,000
Campaigns to combat drug taking in sport in Europe	
B3-2020 Campaign to combat drug taking in sport in Europe	4,955,000
B3-30 Information and communication	
B3-300 General information work concerning the EU	12,900,000
B3-301 Information outlets	12,640,000
B3-302 Information programmes for non-member countries	4,955,000
B3-303 Communication work	14,330,000
B3-304 European integration in universities	3,559,000
B3-306 Information programme for European citizens (Prince) – Information activities in connection with specific policies	36,160,000
B3-309 Special annual events	1,250,000

B3-40 Social dimension and employment
Social dialogue and the Community social dimension

B3-4000 Industrial relations and social dialogue	11,190,000
B3-4002 Information and training measures for workers' organisations	11,000,000
B3-4003 Information, consultation and participation of representatives of undertakings	3,910,000

Labour market

B3-4011 EURES (European Employment Services)	12,460,000
B3-4012 Measures to achieve equality between men and women	9,710,000

Social protection and cooperation with charitable associations

B3-4102 Analysis of and studies on the social situation, demographics and the family	2,035,000
B3-4105 Preparatory measures combating and preventing exclusion	15,640,000

Freedom of movement

B3-4110 Free movement of workers, coordination of social security systems and measures for migrants, including migrants from third countries	2,550,000

Measures in the field of public health protection

B3-4308 Public Health (2001–2006)	44,574,000

Health and safety at work

B3-4310 Health protection, hygiene and safety at work, incl. a subsidy for the European Trade Union Technical Bureau for Health and Safety	3,500,000
B3-4314 Health and safety at work for SMEs	5,000,000

Energy
Measures to improve the Community's energy balance

B4-1030 Altener – Promotion of renewable energy sources	17,378,500
B4-1031 SAVE – Promotion of energy efficiency	10,838,000

Cooperation and observation of markets in the energy sector

B4-1040 ETAP – Studies, analysis and forecasts in the energy sector	423,500
B4-1041 Synergy – promotion of international cooperation in the energy sector	3,410,000

Environment

B4-304 Legislation and other general action based on the Fifth Action Programme on the environment	14,400,000
B4-306 Awareness and subsidies	7,000,000

LIFE (financial instrument for the environment) – Projects on the Community territory

B4-3200 LIFE III – Part 1: Nature protection	25,590,000
B4-3201 LIFE III – Part 2: Environmental protection	25,590,000
B4-3300 Community cooperation on civil protection, marine pollution and environmental emergencies	1,419,000
B4-3400 Decommissioning of nuclear installations and waste management	7,100,000

Consumer protection, internal market, industry and trans-European networks

B5-100 Community activities in favour of consumers	21,726,000

Internal market: Strategic implementing measures

B5-3001 Implementation and development of the internal market	12,288,000
B5-303 Customs 2002	23,645,000
B5-313 Standardisation and approximation of legislation	17,015,000

Promotion of growth and employment: measures to assist firms

B5-326 Industrial competitiveness policy for the EU	7,000,000

Promotion of an information society: measures to assist citizens

B5-331 Information Society	5,000,000

Labour market and technological innovation

B5-502 Labour market	13,020,000

B5-510 Programme for enterprises and entrepreneurship, particularly for SMEs	22,500,000
B5-511 Programme for enterprises – improvement of the financial environment for SMEs	71,500,000
Trans-European networks	
B5-700 Projects of common interest in the trans-European transport networks	572,165,000
B5-720 Trans-European telecommunications networks	34,460,000
Area of freedom, security and justice	
B5-802 Measures for combating violence against children, adolescents and women	4,676,000
B5-803 Measures combating and preventing discrimination	12,800,000
B5-810 European Refugee Fund	34,190,000

Research and technological development

B6-6111 Quality of life and management of living resources	603,326,000
B6-6121 User-friendly information society	867,672,000
B6-6131 Competitive and sustainable growth	665,763,000
B6-6141 Energy, environment and sustainable development	273,459,000
B6-6211 Confirming the international role of Community research	123,139,000
B6-6311 Promotion of innovation and encouragement of participation of SMEs	103,800,000
B6-6411 Improving the human research potential and the socio-economic knowledge base	305,746,000

Relations with the rest of the world – external actions

B7-0 Pre-accession strategy

B7-01 The Sapard Pre-accession instrument: Agriculture	540,000,000
B7-020 ISPA: Instrument for structural policies for pre-accession	1,080,000,000
B7-030 PHARE: Economic aid to the associated countries of Central and Eastern Europe	1,365,910,000
B7-310 Cross-border cooperation	153,000,000
B7-0311 Cooperation in the Baltic Sea region	10,000,000
B7-040 Pre-accession strategy for Malta	7,500,000
B7-041 Pre-accession strategy for Cyprus	11,500,000
B7-050 Pre-accession strategy for Turkey	p.m.

B7-2 Humanitarian and food aid

B7-20 Food aid	455,000,000
B7-21 Humanitarian aid (ECHO)	
B7-210 Aid, including emergency food aid to help populations of developing countries after disasters and other third countries hit by disasters or serious crises	456,000,000
B7-219 Operational support and disaster preparedness	8,000,000

B7-3 Cooperation with developing countries in Asia, Latin America and Southern Africa, incl. South Africa

Asia

B7-300 Financial and technical cooperation with Asian developing countries	262,150,000
B7-301 Political, economic and cultural cooperation with Asian developing countries	88,000,000
B7-302 Aid to uprooted people in Asian countries	36,000,000
B7-303 Rehabilitation and reconstruction operations in developing countries in Asia	15,000,000
B7-304 Aid for the rehabilitation of East Timor	28,380,000

Latin America
B7-310 Financial and technical cooperation with Latin American
developing countries 167,775,000
B7-311 Economic cooperation with Latin American developing countries 83,060,000
B7-312 Aid to uprooted people in Latin American countries .... p.m.
B7-313 Rehabilitation and reconstruction operations in developing
countries in Latin America 71,800,000
South Africa
B7-320 European programme for reconstruction and
development (EPRD) 121,100,000

B7-4 Cooperation with Mediterranean countries and the Middle East

B7-410 MEDA (Measures to accompany the reforms to the economic and
social structures in the Mediterranean non-member countries) 712,770,000
B7-420 Community operations connected with the Israel/PLO
peace agreement 47,950,000
B7-431 Rehabilitation and reconstruction operations in the Mediterranean
and Middle Eastern Countries 5,000,000

B7-5 Cooperation with countries of Central and Eastern Europe, the Balkans, the New Independent States and Mongolia

B7-51 European Bank for Reconstruction and Development Community
subscription to the Capital
B7-52 Assistance to partner countries in Eastern Europe and Central Asia
B7-520 Assistance to partner countries in Eastern Europe and Central Asia .. 382,280,000
B7-521 Cross-border cooperation 23,000,000
B7-5211 Cooperation in the Baltic Sea region 6,000,000
B7-522 Rehabilitation and reconstruction operations in the partner
countries of Eastern Europe and central Asia .... p.m.
B7-54 Cooperation with Countries of the Western Balkans
B7-541 Assistance for the countries of the Western Balkans 304,000,000
B7-542 Assistance for the reconstruction and democracy in the Republic
of Serbia 240,000,000
B7-546 Aid for the reconstruction of Kosovo 175,000,000

B7-6 Other cooperation measures

B7-60 *Community measures to support NGOs*
B7-6000 Community contribution towards schemes concerning developing
countries, carried out by non-governmental organisations 199,400,000
B7-6002 Decentralised cooperation in the developing countries 3,230,000

B7-61 Training and promotion of awareness on development issues
B7-610 Training and promotion of awareness on development issues
including periods of training at the Commission for nationals of third counties .. 3,730,000

B7-62 Multisector issues
B7-6201 Environment in the developing countries and tropical forests 40,830,000
B7-6211 Aid for poverty related diseases (malaria, tuberculosis) in
developing countries .... p.m.
B7-622 Integrating gender issues in development cooperation 2,020,000
B7-624 Grants to ngos which combat child discrimination in
developing countries .... p.m.
B7-626 Campaign against sex tourism in non-member countries 1,000,000
B7-63 Social infrastructure and services .... p.m.
B7-6310 North-south cooperation schemes in the context of the campaign
against drug abuse 5,176,000

B7-6312 Aid for population and reproductive health care, including HIV/AIDS — 20,704,000
B7-6313 Aid for basic education in developing countries — p.m.
B7-64 Specific aid schemes in the field of development
B7-641 Rehabilitation and reconstruction measures for the developing
countries, particularly ACP states — p.m.
B7-66 Specific measures involving third countries
B7-6600 External cooperation measures — 17,500,000
B7-661 Community participation in action concerning anti-personnel mines — 11,460,000
B7-671 Rapid reaction facility — 20,000,000

B7-7 European initiative for democracy and human rights
B7-701 Promotion and defence of human rights and fundamental freedoms — 35,010,000
B7-702 Support for the democratisation process and strengthening
the rule of law — 35,010,000
B7-703 Promotion of respect for human rights and democratisation by
preventing conflict and restoring civil peace — 19,100,000
B7-704 Support for the activities of international criminal tribunals and
for the setting-up of the International Criminal Court — 3,000,000
B7-709 Support for democratic transition and the supervision of electoral
processes — 5,000,000

B7-8 External aspects of certain community policies
B7-81 External Aspects of Environment Policy
B7-810 LIFE – Operations outside Community territory — 3,285,000
B7-811 Contribution to international environmental activities,
including the Global Environment Fund — 4,840,000
Cooperation with third countries on education and vocational training
B7-830 Cooperation with third countries on education and vocational training — 2,350,000

B8-0 Common foreign and security policy
Conflict prevention and crisis management
B8-0100 Conflict prevention and crisis management – Existing measures — p.m.
B8-0101 Conflict prevention and crisis management – New measures — 10,600,000
Non-proliferation and disarmament
B8-0110 Non-proliferation and disarmament – Existing measures — 6,000,000
B8-0111 Non-proliferation and disarmament – New measures — 3,000,000
B8-0120 Conflict resolution, verification, support for the peace process
and stabilisation – Existing measures — 5,000,000
B8-0121 Conflict resolution, verification, support for the peace process
and stabilisation – New measures — 5,000,000
European Union special envoys
B8-0130 European Union special envoys – Existing measures — 900,000
B8-0131 European Union special envoys – New measures — p.m.
B8-0140 Emergency measures – Existing measures — p.m.
B8-0141 Emergency measures – New measures — 5,000,000
B8-0150 Preparatory measures – Existing measures — p.m.
B8-0151 Preparatory measures – New measures — 500,000

[Source: IDs]

Accessing the budget lines

Budget lines are handled in Brussels by the various Directorates General (DGs) of the European Commission (see box on page 210), or through their Technical Assistance Offices. In order to get access to these funds, there are a number of fairly straightforward but lengthy processes.

1   Read the Vade-mecum (see web address at the end of the chapter). Since 1999, all DGs are required to meet the minimum standard set by the Vade-mecum on Grant Management, which was produced to deal with earlier problems of fragmentation and lack of transparency.

2   Find out as much information as you can about the many programmes and budget lines that connect with your work. Be prepared to look behind the official label at examples of work that has actually been funded under a particular heading. There are considerable opportunities other than ESF, and it is often those organisations that find out about these first and make their approaches before others do that are successful. Useful starting points are suggested at the end of the chapter. The internet is perhaps the single most useful research tool when you are dealing with Europe. There is an enormous amount of information published on the main Europa website, and your biggest difficulty will be in navigating through it all. You can find your way to the websites of the relevant DGs, where background information and lists of current and previous grants are often available. But you can also ask people in other organisations where they have made approaches, and try to learn from their experience.

3   Once you have identified a suitable budget line or lines, make an initial contact with the relevant DG or Technical Assistance Office. The system appears to work in a rather more open manner than British government departments. Telephone systems are good and everyone speaks English. Fax and e-mail can also be useful at the preparatory stage. Establish whether what you have in mind fits in with the conditions of that particular programme. This can be done by asking for any written conditions or criteria. In addition, ask for the application deadlines and for information on how soon after the deadline a decision might be made. The 'call for proposals' will be published in the Official Journal of the EU, but by that time there may only be a couple of months left in which to submit an application. It is therefore useful to find out what calls for proposals are in the pipeline so that you can have a draft ready in advance.

4   At this stage, you may decide either to send in a firm application or to submit a brief outline of what you are proposing. Firm proposals are most suitable where you are approaching a large funding programme

with tight requirements. Where this is not the case, it may be better to submit an outline in order to be able to discuss what you are planning with the relevant officials. It may be useful to meet officials in Brussels or the UK. This can be arranged simply and at relatively low cost. It will give you a chance to explain your ideas, and find out their priorities and any special requirements. Officials are accustomed to being seen in their offices and happy to discuss ideas – indeed many welcome it.

5   You will inevitably then be required to send in a formal application – and this is where the system can break down. The time it takes for a decision may well exceed one year (by which time your need may have altered). This is something that officials are only too well aware of and they will generally let you know the latest lead times.

6   Lobby. There may be value in lobbying MEPs – if you can find one interested in your project. They do not have any control over the budget, but officials are often influenced by their interest. It is however a risky undertaking, since it may be viewed by officials as interference.

Tips on making applications to Europe

- Don't expect clarity. Procedures vary from one office to another and even published guidelines change from time to time. Careful research is well worth the time and effort involved.
- Talk about ideas not money. Officials are there to develop their programme areas, not yours. You should be prepared to understand the wider picture, discuss your ideas and adapt them to meet their interests as well as yours for those budget lines and programmes where there are no clearly set out guidelines.
- Don't be in a hurry. Expect to be talking to officials early in one year to be getting money in the next year. Sometimes it can take far longer than this. Response times in some departments are very protracted. In other words, plan ahead.
- Think partnership. This is becoming increasingly important for projects. It takes more time, but adds strength to your application.
- Consider using an expert to help you make your initial approach: there are now a good number of people based in Brussels and elsewhere who specialise in this sort of work. There are also a number of liaison groups who can advise you, such as the Euro Citizen Action Service (ECAS).
- Observe the deadline.
- Be clear where your co-funding will come from.
- Don't underestimate the red tape. Ensure that you begin nothing before you have a signed contract, and make sure everything is fully documented.

Directorates General and services of the European Commission

SG	Secretariat General
SJ	Legal Service
PRESS	Press and Communication Service
ECFIN	Economic and Financial Affairs
ENTR	Enterprise
COMP	Competition
EMPL	Employment and Social Affairs
AGRI	Agriculture
TRANS	Transport
ENV	Environment
RTD	Research
JRC	Joint Research Centre
INFSO	Information Society
FISH	Fisheries
MARKT	Internal Market
REGIO	Regional Policy
ENER	Energy
EURATOM	Euratom Supply Agency
TAXUD	Taxation and Customs Union
EAC	Education and Culture
SANCO	Health and Consumer Protection
JAI	Justice and Home Affairs
RELEX	External Relation
TRADE	Trade
DEV	Development
ELARG	Enlargement
EACO	EuropeAid Co-operation Office
ECHO	Humanitarian Aid Office
ESTAT	Eurostat
ADMIN	Personnel and Administration
IGS	Inspectorate General
BUDG	Budget
AUDIT	Financial Control
OLAF	European Anti-Fraud Office
SCIC	Joint Interpreting and Conference
SDT	Translation Service
OPOCE	Publication Office

After your application is approved

Once you have agreement from the appropriate DG to support your project, you will be asked to sign a contract with the Commission with a number of conditions. Possibly the most onerous of these are the reporting requirements, which are especially complicated as they need to be done in sterling and also in euros. You should always get professional advice about the problems of fluctuating exchange rates, which can leave you with either less or more money to spend than you had planned for. Make sure also that you only charge for expenses that were included in your original project budget. If changes to this become necessary, get agreement from the Commission first; you do not want to be put in the position of having to refund money. Finally, it may appear obvious, but do submit your report and evaluation on time and in the required format, particularly if you expect to be applying for EU funding again.

If your application is not approved

As with other sources of funding, the DGs receive more applications than they can accept, so failure need not mean that your project was completely unsuitable. You can ask for feedback, for information about successful applications, and for the percentage of successful applicants. You may be able to revise your proposal and try again under a different heading or indeed the same heading next year.

10.4 Issues around European funding

1   **Contract funding:** European funding is contract funding, not grant funding. If your project application is approved, you *must* do what you said in the application. If you use the money for activity not detailed in the application form you may be deemed to be in breach of contract and thus have to pay back any European monies claimed.

2   **Matched funding:** European funds rarely pay 100% of the costs of running a given project. The money given to top up the European money is known as *match funding* or *co-financing*. It is the applicant's responsibility to find this money, and this should be done as part of the project planning process *before* an application is made. There are strict guidelines on what can and cannot be used as match funding. You are strongly advised to read the latest guidance notes relevant to the European funding stream that you are applying for.

3   **A European dimension:** Many of the budget line funds are conditional on you working in partnership with like-minded organisations in other

Member states. In most cases you will be expected to name these *transnational* partners in your application.

The implication of this is that you should build relationships with like-minded organisations across Europe even before you consider submitting a proposal. Go to conferences, use e-mail, and develop contacts by joining any relevant European networks and liaison groups. If you do not have a transnational partner, you can also ask officials of the relevant DG to help you find one.

4 **Delays in decision making and payments:** Applications can take a long time to process. For budget line funds this can be as long as a year. For ESF funds a delay of three months is not unusual. You are strongly advised not to start your project until formal approval has been received.

Different European funding streams have different payment systems. The relevant guidance notes should give you details. However, be aware that the reality does not always follow the theory. Payments may be delayed for a number of reasons, the most common being that the claimant organisation has not provided all the required information.

Resources and further information

See also general lists at the end of the book.

Organisations

Department for Education and Employment (DfEE) – for ESF
European Social Fund Unit
Caxton House
6–12 Tothill Street
London SW1H 9NF
www.esfnews.org.uk
Tel. 020 7273 5032/5926
Fax 020 7273 5540

Department of Trade and Industry (DTI) – for ERDF
1 Victoria Street
London SW1H 0ET
Tel. 020 7215 5000
Fax 020 7215 6749

European Briefing Unit
University of Bradford
Bradford BD7 1DP
Tel. 01274 235821
Fax 01274 236820
e-mail ebu@bradford.ac.uk
Provides training courses on applying for European funding.

European Citizen Action Service (ECAS)
53 Rue de la Concorde
B-1050 Brussels
Belgium
www.ecas.org
Tel. + 32 2 548 04 90
Fax + 32 2 548 04 99
e-mail admin@ecas.org

European Commission
Tel. (main switchboard)
+32 2 299 1111
Websites
main site: http://europa.eu.int
for Vade-mecum:
http://europa.eu.int/comm/secretariat_
general/sgc/info_subv/vm_gm.htm
Official Journal:
http://europa.eu.int/eur-
lex/en/index.html

**Industrial Common Ownership
  Movement (ICOM)**
74 Kirkgate
Leeds LS2 7DJ
Tel. 0113 246 1737/1738
Fax 0113 244 0002
e-mail icom@icom.org.uk
Has published guides to ESF finance
and project monitoring.

**Information Diffusion Europe
  Associations a.s.b.l. (IDs)**
Avenue Voltaire 135
B-1030 Brussels
Belgium
Tel. +32 2 735 13 01
Fax +32 2 735 53 09
e-mail id.s@skynet.be

Publications

The following publications are available from the Directory of Social Change.
Prices were correct at the time of writing, but may be subject to change.

A Guide to European Union Funding, Peter Sluiter and Laurence Wattier, DSC
1999, £12.50

Your Way through the Labyrinth, A Guide to European Funding for NGOs, 8th
edition, ECAS 2002, £20, 9th edition in preparation for summer 2003 (check DSC
website for information)

11 INCOME GENERATION AND CONTRACTS

More and more voluntary organisations now earn income as well as raise it. This doesn't simply mean charity shops in the high street. There are all sorts of ways in which modern charities charge for services. The top 500 charities earn some £1 billion in fees from local and central government, while charity shops bring in £270 million and other forms of trading nearly £243 million on top of that (1997–98 figures). Although this book is aimed primarily at fundraisers, developing earned income streams can be a key element of your fundraising strategy.

Details of organisations and publications referred to in this chapter are on p. 224.

11.1 Why income generation?

For a long time charities have drawn the bulk of their income from grants and public fundraising. Earning income through charging for services, for example, has traditionally been viewed as a private sector activity and this kind of entrepreneurial approach has been regarded as inappropriate for charities. Over the past decade, however, there has been a major shift in attitudes. The contracting out of services by government (see chapter 9) has meant that many charities have become adept at tendering for business and drawing up service level agreements; alongside this development, more and more charities have developed income streams from trading activities whether these be charity shops or charging for services. This kind of income generation strategy can bring various key advantages.

- You are helping to create a more robust organisation with a wider range of income options and funds for expansion and development. Within reason, the more income streams you have, the greater your ability to withstand losses or downturns in individual areas. You also have more development potential.

- You can make a better case to funders by showing the breadth of your income and your ability to turn work funded by short-term grants into longer term trading activities.
- The more you earn the less you will have to raise and the more viable and sustainable your organisation will become. Income generation can take a lot of pressure off your fundraising, especially as competition for grants is so fierce.
- You can only sell services if they are needed, are of sufficiently high quality, and if someone is prepared to pay. This can add an important dimension to your quality standards, strengthen the link between the service you provide and the user on the receiving end, and help build a constituency of support in your local community. This in turn can add greatly to the user's contribution to your work.
- Income generation reduces dependency on outside support and major grant sources, gives you much greater independence from funders and freedom to speak out on behalf of your organisation – and, more importantly, its users.

11.2 The options

Income generation means developing or participating in a commercial enterprise to make a profit. This could include:

- charging the users of a service for providing that service
- providing a service under contract for a body like a local authority
- selling items made by the beneficiaries of the organisation
- selling items to members, visitors and supporters
- earning money through selling publications, running conferences, providing training, undertaking research or selling consultancy within the organisation's area of expertise
- entering into a commercial activity completely unrelated to the work of the organisation simply to make money. The profit from your commercial activity is then used to support the main work of the organisation.

Put like that it sounds a simple and logical thing to do – and, in the right hands and under the right management, it can be – but many find that successful income generation is more difficult than it seems. Some even make heavy losses on their trading. It certainly requires lots of planning and discussion before you get going.

Furthermore, and fundamentally, the enterprise is only a means of earning money to support the mission or work of the organisation. If the enterprise becomes too demanding in time and resources, if the income it generates is relatively small or non-existent, or if it diverts you from your real work, then stop.

In this section we will look at the different ways of generating income, and the risks and opportunities involved in each.

Advantages of income generation

- It can provide an additional independent source of income for the charity's work.
- It forces a more commercial approach to the management of the organisation, such that the cost and value of each product is known.
- It creates a more lively entrepreneurial approach.
- There is positive feedback – the more successful you are, the greater the income return.
- It fits within current culture and attitudes.

Arguments against income generation

- Asking donors for money is easier.
- With income generation, it's only the surplus (after all costs) that is available to support the charitable work.
- It makes the organisation too commercial, distorts priorities and distracts from the real agenda.
- Too often it *loses* rather than makes money.
- Many organisations do not have the skills, the management capacity or the organisational structure to undertake income generation activity successfully.

Charging for services

You can ask beneficiaries to contribute towards the cost of the services that they are receiving (possibly where these were previously provided free of charge). There is no problem under charity law with a charity charging for its mainstream services (this is called 'primary purpose trading'). Much depends on the nature of your clientele. Many theatres and opera houses, for example, are constituted as charities, and people expect to pay for attending a performance (as well as for a programme, a drink at the bar and other income generating activity). All this also helps make a better case to sponsors – income generation can reinforce other fundraising.

The main argument against charging is that it can exclude those unable to pay (creating a charity for the rich). Your trustees should consider carefully the implications of charging a fee for your charity's services. However, it can bring a number of benefits.

- It forces the organisation to calculate the real cost of providing the service. Oscar Wilde once said that: 'a cynic is somebody who knows the price of everything and the value of nothing'. Conversely, many charities know the value of everything but the cost of nothing.

- Once you know the cost you can decide a subsidy policy. You don't have to provide the service free or at full cost. You might want a differential pricing policy (special rates for local residents, concessions for the unwaged and over 65s) – this can be an extremely effective marketing tool.
- You can set a marketing budget. You will need to invest in promoting the service to potential 'customers'.
- It creates a different and possibly more equal relationship between the service provider and the service user.
- There is a demonstrable commitment from the service user, and an indication that what is being provided is what is needed and wanted.

Contracts for services

The contract culture has brought massive changes into the voluntary sector. Voluntary organisations are now key providers of mainstream services in the health and social care fields. The government body becomes the 'purchaser', providing the funds and setting the guidelines for how the service is to be run and who is to benefit. The charity is the 'provider', running the service and hoping to make a surplus.

Take, for example, residential care for the elderly which used to be provided by the local authority but which is now contracted out to a range of commercial and not-for-profit providers. The purchaser selects a provider (either by negotiation or through a tendering process). The contract is not awarded on price alone, but also on quality and the provider's ability to run the service. The contract (sometimes called a service agreement) is then issued which defines the service to be provided and the payments to be received.

The contract culture opens up a range of income streams, but requires certain skills and you need to be aware of potential pitfalls.

- The arrangement is quite different from a funding relationship. The payment is not a grant; it is for a service and may have penalties for non-performance, which increases the level of risk. The price is fixed at the outset and the terms are set by the provider (which is the other way round from a funding application where the applicant sets out what they want to do and seeks funding for it).
- The fact that you are a charity is often irrelevant. The purchaser is buying the best available service at the best price. You won't get anywhere by saying 'give it to us because the charity benefits'.
- Costing the bid is vital. A charity could submit a bid at cost or to make a surplus. Some have submitted bids at below cost, hoping to raise the balance

through fundraising – don't! It is not a proper use of charity funds to sub-sidise public sector services, and underfunding can soon lead to financial crisis.

- The contract work may be a diversion from the real mission of the charity, and be undertaken solely because the money is there.

There are examples of charities being bullied by purchasers. One charity was asked to provide a complete statement of costs incurred in running a highly successful contract. A renewed contract was then offered at cost price. Desperate to get the work, the charity agreed to it. This should not be allowed. Organisations cannot survive on this basis. Commercial providers would not tolerate this sort of behaviour.

Exploiting skills and expertise

Many voluntary organisations have developed specialist skills and expertise which they can sell. This could be part of the dissemination process, encour-aging better working practice and enabling similar projects to be developed. Or it could be done simply to generate income. Home Start Consultancy, for example, is a resource centre for local Home Start projects, providing them with training and support – for a fee. Child Poverty Action Group provides training on welfare matters and publishes the *National Welfare Benefits Handbook*. Both these organisations are exploiting their expertise whilst directly pursuing their mission.

Think about whether you could:

- organise training courses
- organise conferences
- sell publications or information sheets
- offer consultancy.

You also need to think about these questions:

- Is there a market for what is being offered? If so, will it pay an economic price? As with other forms of income generation, it is vital to know the costs involved.
- Does the organisation have the marketing skills and the administrative capacity to make it a success? Could you link up with another organisa-tion, maybe a specialist training organisation or publisher?
- Have you got a marketing budget and strategy? Too many organisations produce a publication, for example, and only then think about what to do with it. It often proves to be an expensive mistake.
- Is what you are planning one off or can it be repeated? If so, you will be able to spread your start-up costs over a longer period.

Example

A women's training charity, which was already funded to run courses for unemployed women who wanted to return to paid work, negotiated a contract with a big local employer to run a version of their 'Moving into management' course for selected employees. The employer paid the charity the market rate for the training, rather than a subsidised charity rate, because it recognised that it was buying a high-quality service, the employees acquired new and very relevant skills, and the charity had found a new source of income (and surplus) from selling its existing skills to a new market.

Selling products made by beneficiaries

Do you have or could you develop any of the following?

- products made in sheltered workshops by people with disabilities or impairments
- products made in the developing world
- training programmes for the long-term unemployed or people with special needs
- produce from a city farm or community garden

This may be the main purpose of your organisation, or simply a spin-off benefit. You must ensure that what is being sold is of marketable quality, and that there is a market which can be reached – whether through a retail outlet, by mail order to supporters or by wholesaling the merchandise to a retailer.

Selling gift items to supporters

Some of the larger charities raise money through catalogue trading, where new goods are offered to supporters and to the general public by mail order or through local agents. Even successful, well-resourced national charities with a strong track record in this kind of trading may still earn as little as a 10% profit from trading in this way, since merchandise, marketing and management costs have to be taken into account. The following are some key points.

- The merchandise must be of a high standards and live up to its catalogue promises. The goods should also reflect your values – either in the materials (recycled paper, for example) or through the design. The catalogue should form a range of products rather than a collection of unrelated items, and the range must appeal to the target market. The goods must be available in sufficient quantity to meet likely demand, or there will be a serious loss of confidence. And you must give yourself a profit margin.

- Promotion. You can sell successfully through charity shops, but there are tax implications unless the shop is selling mainly donated goods or items produced by the beneficiaries of the charity. Generally you will sell through a catalogue. Unlike a charity shop where customers can walk in off the street, a catalogue needs vigorous promotion, usually by direct mail, to build up a list of regular purchasers which will create an assured market. Some sales will be made through word of mouth and personal contact; most will come from sending the catalogue to previous purchasers, to your supporters and to other likely mailing lists.
- Control and administration. Catalogue trading involves a major buying, warehousing and order processing operation, with all the associated control and cash flow worries. You will need good pricing and cost control, and to be able to finance a fluctuating business, where you will be buying in stock well in advance of getting sales income.

On a more modest level, many smaller charities produce and sell some of the following in an attempt to raise money:

- Christmas cards and gifts to their supporters;
- souvenir items to visitors (at heritage sites, museums, arts centres, etc.);
- publicity material, such as tee-shirts and lapel badges.

Done well, these can generate useful income and carry a logo, a slogan or a message, thereby publicising the cause. You need to be clear at the outset whether you are producing and selling the items to raise money or generate publicity. Sometimes a charity gets into this sort of trading because they believe their supporters want them to, or they see other charities doing it and feel that they ought to. They can end up selling quite small quantities of Christmas cards, for example, and be making a loss and involving themselves in a lot of worry and management time. This becomes a waste of effort, which could better be used more effectively to ask people for money.

Promotional items that can be sold to raise money with the charity's name, logo and message

- Greetings cards
- Calendars
- Diaries
- Address books
- Pens and pencils
- Tee-shirts
- Wallets
- Mugs
- Posters

This form of trading does not directly further the work of the charity and its success should be judged by the amount of money generated in return for the effort, capital, risk and management time put in. It is also an activity which cannot always be carried out directly by the charity itself, and a separately managed and funded trading company may need to be set up (see below).

Charity shops turning donated gifts into cash

Charity shops selling donated items such as second hand clothes are routine high street presences. Most charity shops are simply retail outlets, selling merchandise to generate a profit for the charity. Some aim to be information points, promoting the cause and the work of the charity, and perhaps recruiting new supporters. Whatever the purpose, running a shop requires a considerable management effort, and it is increasingly difficult to attract customers and make money now that charities are in competition with so many commercial discount outlets for clothing and other goods. Some major charities are even starting to close down at least some of their shops. The following are some of the key factors for success.

- *Location*. Finding the right location is essential. The shop must be sited in a place that can attract passing trade. It must be near enough for the voluntary helpers who will staff it. And you have to balance these needs with the rent.
- *Staffing*. Most charity shops depend extensively on volunteers for their staffing. The usual pattern is to employ one professional manager for a shop of any size, who will co-ordinate a team of 20–40 volunteers. Some shops have a separate volunteer committee which runs the shop. Training, recruitment, supervision and management are vital to success.
- *The merchandise*. Charity shops tend to sell three types of merchandise: goods donated to the charity by well-wishers in order to raise money (such as second hand clothing, household items and jewellery); goods produced by the beneficiaries of the charity (for example in sheltered workshops and rural development projects); and goods produced by the charity (such as greetings cards). Quality is important, particularly when the shop is selling donated goods which should be cleaned, repaired or checked, sorted and priced before they are sold.

For further information, read *The Charity Shops Handbook*. Also, contact the Association of Charity Shops, a forum for those charities (large and small) which are running charity shops.

Letting space in a building

Some charities have premises which they can use to generate an income, whether by hiring out office space, conference or seminar rooms, or by running a commercial service on the premises (such as a print shop or community cafe). Again, there are major questions around your management capacity to do this, whether it is financially worthwhile and the risks involved. For further information, Community Matters produce a book on *Managing your Community Building*.

Sources of capital

You may need money to invest in your income generation activities. There are various options:

1 *Borrowing*: You can only borrow money if your constitution allows you to. There are a number of socially responsible banking services that specialise in borrowing and lending out money to good cause organisations at below commercial levels of interest and without the onerous guarantees or security that commercial lenders may require. The pioneer in this field was Mercury Provident, now operating as Triodos. The Charities Aid Foundation is also developing a charity banking service, and Business in the Community has helped develop Local Investment Funds. A wealthy trustee or an outside benefactor may also be prepared to advance you the money.

2 *Savings*: You may be able to use some of your free reserves to invest in income generation, or allocate some of your annual surplus to an income generation fund. You must use your charitable money for charitable purposes. Investing in income generation is acceptable if this is a primary purpose activity. If it is a commercial rather than a charitable activity, then the money will need to be supplied as an investment, and this requires an assessment of risk and returns and independent professional advice on whether this is a reasonable way to invest the charity's funds.

3 *Grants*: Most funders are very cautious about financing commercial activities, even though the money will be used to help the charity. However, you might be able to submit an application for development funding to help you get your trading off the ground. You will need to convince the funder not only of your ability to trade successfully, but also that it represents a really good and secure investment in your future sustainability and development.

11.3 Problems and issues

1 The need for an entrepreneurial approach

Reliance on grants has discouraged an entrepreneurial approach amongst many voluntary organisations. Voluntary organisations have usually been run by budgeting their expenditure against available funding – the idea of a revenue budget with income generation targets is often an alien concept. The idea of using marketing and selling techniques to generate income, and of strategic investment (spending money now to produce a return later on) will need new skills and new approaches. It also requires a change in attitude.

2 Kinds of people and skills needed

You will also need to recruit people with the relevant skills and approach. This may mean moving outside your traditional networks and recruiting from the private or social business sectors.

3 Losing the vision

Voluntary organisations are driven by a shared vision of a better society. The work that they do, for the most part, reinforces that vision. When the main purpose becomes making money, a new set of attitudes starts creeping in and many organisations become concerned that they will lose their internal cohesion.

Some organisations prefer to separate out their income generation work, even where there is no legal requirement to do this. They recognise that they will need a different kind of staff, possibly with different reward systems and salary structure, incentives and benefits.

4 Charity law

When your income generation activity involves the pursuit of your charitable objectives (often called primary purpose trading), the sale of products made by beneficiaries, or the sale of donated goods, there are no problems. But if it involves activities outside these three categories, there may be charity law problems and tax problems. But this will only be significant where:

- the trading activity is substantial and involves the use of the charity's assets (it is not a proper function of a charity to get substantially involved in a non-charitable activity – trading – or to apply its assets for this purpose);
- a profit is being made, which would be taxable if generated directly by the charity. Very often after allocating all relevant overheads, a charity will find that it is not making any real profit from the activity. If a substantial profit is being earned, you might need to set up an associated but separate trading company to avoid paying tax;

- the charity's resources are being put at risk. Substantial trading activity involves risk. There are cases, including some large well-known national charities, where large losses on trading have had to be made good out of charitable funds.

In such circumstances, you may need to trade through a separate trading company. This is tax effective, as the profits can be Gift Aided to the parent charity. This is an extremely technical area and you will need good professional advice on the best structure. See *The Voluntary Sector Legal Handbook* for more information.

Resources and further information

See also general lists at the end of the book.

Organisations

Association of Charity Shops
224 Shoreditch High Street
London E1 6PJ
Tel. 020 7422 8620

Business in the Community
135 Shepherdess Walk
London N1 7RR
Tel. 0870 600 2482

Charities Advisory Trust
Radius Works
Back Lane
London NW3 1HL
Tel. 020 7794 9835

Community Matters
8–9 Upper Street
London N1 0PQ
Tel. 020 7226 0189

Triodos
Brunel House
11 The Promenade
Bristol BS8 3NN
Tel. 0117 973 9339

Publications

The following publications are available from the Directory of Social Change. Prices were correct at the time of writing, but may be subject to change.

A Practical Guide to VAT 2nd edition, Kate Sayer, DSC 2001, £12.95

Voluntary Sector Legal Handbook 2nd edition, Sandy Adirondack and James Sinclair Taylor, DSC 2001, £42 (voluntary organisations) /£60 (others)

Other publications

The Charity Shops Handbook, Hilary Blume, Charities Advisory Trust 1995, £10.95

Managing your Community Building, Community Matters 1996, £15.95

PART
three

TECHNIQUES

12 FUNDRAISING FROM THE GENERAL PUBLIC

Some of the most traditional forms of fundraising remain the most effective, both in terms of amounts generated and the ability to give again and again. This chapter looks at a range of methods of fundraising – public collections, events, raffles and lotteries – which can involve the general public in your work and, potentially, turn them into long-term givers to your organisation.

Details of organisations and publications referred to in this chapter are on p. 251.

12.1 Collections

Collections are still a very popular and effective way of raising money locally. They require a good deal of planning, a well briefed and enthusiastic team of volunteers and some equipment, for example collection boxes. The main benefits of a collection, aside from the money raised, are that it reminds your local volunteers about your cause, and gives your organisation a noticeable presence for the period of the collection. This type of fundraising can be done in various ways:

- house-to-house collections, where you knock on doors and ask for support, or leave an envelope and information about your work, and call back next day;
- street collections and collections in public places. Typically here a collector will have a collecting box, and may give some token in return for the donation (such as a sticker);
- collecting boxes placed on shop counters, in pubs and in restaurants for people to leave their small change;
- static collecting devices placed outside shops;
- collecting boxes in supporters' homes, where they can leave their small change or ask their friends to contribute.

Organising a house-to-house collection

my Grandma is happy

Jimmy Sheals
Aged 3

Some are not so lucky

Please moisten and seal

Help the Aged

Home Truths

Millennium Campaign

We aim to raise an extra £10 million by the end of this century towards:

Security of the home

Safety in the home

Contact from the home

Mobility beyond the home

Just 5p more in each envelope would enable us to help lots more elderly people in need. Please give as much you can. Thank you

Help the Aged

An example of a house-to-house collection envelope produced by Help the Aged.

A successful house-to house collection requires:

- carefully recruited volunteers
- well chosen streets in which to collect
- good advance planning
- delivery of collecting materials in good time
- reliable collection of envelopes
- careful recording of donations.

House-to-house collections are very popular with both national and local charities, and are a good way of asking everyone in a specified area to give their support. The collectors need to be well briefed. They are the link between your organisation and the public, and may be asked all sorts of questions about the work of the organisation and how it spends its money, which they will need to answer accurately and enthusiastically.

The first step is to obtain a permit from your local council. You will need to specify the date or time scale of the collection, the localities in which you intend to collect and the manner in which the collection will be carried out. A licence may be refused on several grounds including that:

- it will cause inconvenience to the public;
- it is on the same day or the day immediately before or after another collection;

- the expense is too high or too little will be generated for the cause;
- the promoter has not acted properly in past collections.

The detailed requirements for conducting a collection are set out in the regulations attached to the 1992 Charities Act. These cover such things as who can collect money and how the collection has to be run. You only need a licence for a collection in a public place (a place to which members of the public have access) or when you are collecting in more than one location. A collection restricted to a private house, school, office, public house or hospital does not require a licence. However, even if you are not collecting cash (if you are going from house to house asking for jumble or paper, for example), you still need a licence to collect in a public place.

If you are organising a national collection (throughout the whole or a substantial part of England and Wales) then you can obtain an order from the Charity Commission authorising the collection. For details of the rules on collections in Scotland and Northern Ireland, consult the Scottish Council for Voluntary Organisations and the Northern Ireland Council for Voluntary Action.

Before applying for a permit, you should plan how you will run the collection. Local knowledge should help you decide which sorts of houses are likely to be responsive. For larger collections you may want to collect throughout the area.

An important factor is the group of volunteers that you have. Typically you may want one volunteer to take responsibility for one street, probably the street they live in or one nearby. Volunteers can be recruited on a networking basis or by telephoning. Ideally you will want to approach people for this activity who have identified themselves as having an interest in your organisation – they might have made a donation or got involved in some other activity. There may be too many to approach face to face or, if you are carrying out a national campaign, may be spread over too large an area, so the most practical way to ask them to get involved is over the phone – see chapter 14, section 14.3, for more information on using the telephone.

Once you have recruited your volunteers it is important to provide training and induction. For example, a general briefing about the charity and its work; the purpose of the appeal; when they should collect; how they introduce themselves; what to say; what difficult questions to expect, and so on. You can arrange a training session, brief people individually, or prepare a pack containing all necessary information.

The collectors' main function is to deliver an envelope on which there is a message, possibly with an accompanying brochure or letter from the charity. A couple of days later, the collector should return to collect the envelopes. At this point they will encounter responses ranging from hostility through apathy to enthusiasm. There will be those who refuse to help you and those who choose to be abusive. Most will be polite. Some will try to justify their decision not to give (generally it is not worth trying to change their minds). Some will be genuinely interested in what you are doing, which is a good opportunity to give more information and even recruit a new member or volunteer.

The returned envelopes should be handed in to a central point, and opened under the supervision of two people, with the amounts from each address logged in a register. Try to keep track of how much money comes from each area, for future reference. If you can, have your collectors make a note of those giving money who show a particular interest in the organisation, as you might want to approach them to do something else for you. However you may find that this is difficult with larger collections in more than one area.

There is always the possibility of fraud by someone carrying out an unauthorised collection in your name. If you receive any reports of unauthorised collecting, investigate it as fast as you can, as any bad publicity will damage your organisation and the voluntary sector as a whole. Under the 1992 Charities Act you now have the power to prevent unauthorised collections by seeking an injunction from the courts.

Checklist for organising a small scale, local collection

1 Make sure your chosen date does not clash with holiday periods or other collections.
2 Seek any authorisation you need: from the police or local authority.
3 Identify your target areas and locations for collecting and what time to carry out the collection.
4 Recruit your volunteers.
5 Prepare any materials you need, such as collecting boxes or envelopes, leaflets about your work, details of any membership scheme, and stickers.
6 Brief your volunteers about the work of the charity, and provide some basic training in effective asking.
7 Organise how the money will be received and accounted for. Bank all proceeds immediately upon receipt.
8 Thank volunteers, telling them how much they raised and how important this will be to your work.
9 Follow up on those donors who have been noted as being particularly interested in your organisation.
10 Debrief your volunteers. Find out what went well, and what not so well. Suggest ways of doing better next time. Keep a record of which locations or neighbourhoods did best.

Organising a street collection

Running a street collection is in some ways more difficult than a house-to-house collection as volunteers tend to be less enthusiastic. The collecting has to be concentrated into one day and you, the organiser, have to provide enough collectors to cover the whole of the collecting area.

As with a house-to-house collection, you will need a permit and should apply to your local council for this. Do this well in advance, as others may have already laid claim to particular collection dates and sites. If you have an annual flag day or collection week, you will need to apply each year.

There are two main requirements for a successful collection.

1 You need plenty of volunteers to carry out the collection. Draw up a rota for each collection point, using people for not more than an hour or two.
2 Choose locations to give collectors access to the maximum numbers of people. The high street or shopping centres are usually best, though collecting at well populated events, such as outside a football stadium, can also work well. The ideal site is one where you are visible to passers by as they walk up a street. This gives the potential donor time to think about giving. If you are stationed immediately outside a busy entrance to a shop, people have to make a split second decision to give. If you make it difficult, this gives them a reason not to give.

You also need to cultivate a positive attitude in your collectors. Although they are not allowed to solicit on the streets, they should not shrink back from passers-by. A collector who is prepared to look people in the eye and station themselves in the middle of the thoroughfare – being careful not to cause an obstruction – will do much better.

You will need a sealed collection device that is easy to carry, convenient for the public to put money into, and easy to get the money out of again after the collection. The main choice is whether to go for a more expensive plastic collecting box that can be reused, or whether to use a cheaper disposable box. This will depend on your future plans. A number of commercial suppliers now provide a range of collecting receptacles which can be personalised with your charity's name and logo.

It is a good idea to have your collectors wear a sash or some other highly visible item with your charity's name on it. Then people can see at a distance what cause is being collected for. It is not good enough to hope that passers by can see the label on your tin. You may wish to offer sticky lapel badges indicating that someone has given. This can help spread the idea in a busy town centre as well as alerting other collectors that these people have donated already. It is also useful to carry some general leaflets about your organisation for donors who are interested in knowing more about what you do.

Checklist for a street collection

- A good date and location for the collection
- Lots of enthusiastic volunteers
- The right equipment: stickers or flags to offer people, and collecting boxes suitably labelled to advertise your organisation
- Printed information about your appeal to brief the volunteers, and to hand out to interested passers by
- Local publicity
- A proper system for receiving and banking all the cash that has been collected

---

Static collection devices

Static collection devices are large, often brightly coloured, free-standing collecting boxes placed near the exit or just outside shops in high streets, pubs, cinema foyers, superstores, service stations and other similar locations. They can provide a regular, though usually quite small, source of income for a charity. Suitable locations are anywhere where people are paying for things and the device is visible. It must be on private property, although the street outside a shop may be within the boundary of the premises.

If the collection devices are not looked after regularly, they can be vandalised or stolen. Larger devices should be chained so that they cannot be removed. It is always worth checking up regularly to see how they are being displayed, and taking the opportunity to chat to the shopkeeper and enthuse them about your cause.

Many shops are happy to have one or more smaller collecting boxes on their counter for customers to put their change in. As with the larger collecting devices, these need to be properly maintained and managed. The box needs to be durable. If it is falling apart, it gives out a message that the charity does not look after its money properly. The box needs emptying regularly, as it can fill up quickly with smaller coins.

Considerable care needs to be taken to ensure that the money reaches the charity. One approach is to make the box the responsibility of the proprietors of the establishment. For example in a pub, it would be the responsibility of the landlord or landlady to send in a cheque when the box is full. This would be inappropriate in shops, where the turnover of staff is high. In such places, volunteers should arrange to make regular collections and keep in touch by telephone.

It is also helpful to write a thank you letter showing how much has been raised and what has been done with it. This can encourage the shopkeeper to take pride in the collecting box. The letter can be displayed to encourage further giving.

12.2 Organising a fundraising event

A successful and repeatable fundraising event can be extremely valuable for you. It brings all kinds of direct and indirect benefits. However, for every successful event that attracts new supporters, another collapses, is rained off or has the sponsor pull out at the last moment. You must always evaluate the fundraising potential against the risk of losing money. A well-run event can make money, take your message out to a wider public and bring in new supporters. But many absorb a great deal of energy for very small returns. This section is concerned mainly with ticketed events, while mass participation sponsored events are dealt with in 12.3. For more detailed information, see the 'How to' guide *Organising Special Events*.

Objectives of an event

If you decide to hold a fundraising event you must be very clear what you want to achieve with it. Is it mainly to raise money or to interest new people in your organisation? Set a clear primary objective for the event. This will help define it and create measurable targets for what you want to get out of it.

Events can be of any size and complexity. The main idea is to offer an enjoyable experience in return for the participants' money. Both elements are important. It is not just about generating as much money as possible; if everyone has a good time, they will be happy to participate on another occasion.

In 2000 the Medical Foundation for the Care of Victims of Torture organised an auction where people paid to have well known authors, such as Nick Hornby and Kathy Lette, use the successful bidder's name in their next novel. This is a particular type of event that will attract a particular type of person and is likely to both raise money and generate publicity.

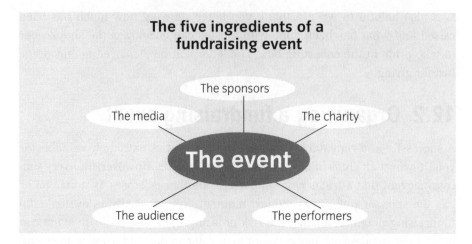

The five ingredients of a fundraising event

The sponsors

The media

The charity

The event

The audience

The performers

Whatever your event, there are five principal groups of people likely to be involved: sponsors, the media, the performers, the audience and the charity. Get them working in harmony and you are well on your way to success.

1 Sponsors

Your sponsors will support the event in order to meet their own business objectives (for example it gives access to their target audience – such as car buyers for auto dealerships – or key opinion formers, celebrities, etc.). In order to attract sponsors, you will need to show them how your event can help them achieve their objectives. If you make the most of the next ingredient (the media), then your sponsors will regard the event even more enthusiastically.

2 The media

The media are in business to report events such as yours, especially if there is a star performer or if the event is genuinely newsworthy. Star names and celebrities attract the media more than anything. You may be able to get some coverage by talking about the good work you do or the fun of the event. If the event is considered significant enough, a newspaper, radio or television station may become a 'media sponsor', offering you free advertising and press coverage to promote the event in advance, thereby extending your audience reach, in addition to providing a good picture feature of the event itself.

3 The performers

The performers are central to the event itself: the band booked to play at a ball; the auctioneer undertaking the sale; or the football teams and celebrity players playing in a charity match. They also have something to gain from participating. It could be a fee (although try to get a reduced fee or a free performance), or good publicity and an association with a good cause – which is good for their image.

4 The audience

About 10% of the public attend charity events. Some go simply because they want to participate in the event; many consider it a way of supporting a charity. People do not go to a charity auction feeling the same way as if they were going to a commercial auction. They are much more likely to bid generously. People going to a charity concert expect to hear something about the organisation involved or be asked to give to a collection. Their enjoyment of the occasion will in part be determined by the quality of the performance (get that wrong and you risk your reputation), and in part by the degree to which the charity benefits.

5 The charity

The final ingredient is you and your organisation. Your involvement gives the event a focus – the main reason for its happening is to raise money to support your work. The audience may come because they are your supporters, or because they are interested in your cause. The performers will not come to just any event, because they may have many other commitments. An event for your organisation should be something that strikes a sympathetic chord with them. The sponsors will decide to back the event because of your reputation and the audience that you can deliver for them. Your contacts with royalty, celebrities and other important people can be a further incentive.

Deciding what to organise

One starting point for deciding the sort of event you want to have is to examine your market. What will have the most appeal for your supporters or the group you want to target? Who is likely to attend the event? What are their interests? Will they bring their friends? Are they old or young? Active and energetic? How much do they know or care about your cause? How much disposable income do they have? What are you and your helpers interested in – and what contacts do you have (access to performers, for example)?

Alternatively, think about the major types of event and see whether any seem appropriate. A short list might include:

- sporting events
- musical and cultural events
- balls, dinners, auctions and other entertainment events
- exhibitions, festivals and fairs.

Most events are run on a one-off basis – although you may want to repeat one if it is successful, thereby creating a regular source of income for your charity. The first time you hold an event, it will take longer to organise – so try to develop events that can be repeated. Some events take place over a period of time – for example, a knockout football competition or a film festival. More complicated (and more risky) events should be left for when you have more experience.

Depending upon your plans, you may need some sort of licence (to run the event, to collect money in a public place, or to run a bar). Check the legal requirements with the local authority before you start any detailed planning. There may also be tax implications.

Event management

It is important to allow enough time to organise your event, as it often involves more effort than you think. There are three main ways to do this, each with their own drawbacks and advantages.

1 Doing it yourself (or getting another member of staff to do it) will help you learn how it should be done and provide you with the experience to do it better next time. However, if you haven't run an event before you may jeopardise the chances of success by your inexperience. You would certainly need to take advice from more experienced people.

   The single biggest problem of doing it yourself is the time investment. How much money could you be raising if you were not organising this event? All events require attention to detail, checking and double checking at every stage. If you are in the middle of a busy fundraising programme, then being responsible for something that requires so much of your time may not be sensible.

2 Engage a professional. Sometimes an event will be run through a sporting or theatrical body which does this on a regular basis. You could engage them to do the whole thing (and try to persuade them to do it free as a charitable contribution). If not, there are professional event organisers in the musical, sporting and entertainment fields who will do all the day-to-day organisation for you – for a fee. If you hire a commercial event organiser on the basis that a proportion of the ticket price or the proceeds goes to them, they will be a 'professional fundraiser' under the terms of the Charities Act, and certain requirements will need to be met to comply with the Act. See chapter 14, box on page 279, and also *The Fundraiser's Guide to the Law* for more information.

3 Establish a committee of volunteers. The key appointment will be the chair, which could be you. This need not be someone who has run an event before, but they do need to have strong leadership qualities and the good management sense to link the commercial needs of the event to the requirements of the charity. You will probably then need to select a multi-disciplinary team that embodies all the skills necessary to make

the thing work: from people with the sporting or musical background to deal with the programme, to the accountant who will tell you whether VAT is chargeable on the ticket sales and what the legal requirements are. Give yourself plenty of time to find the right people.

Fundraising events and tax

When income to a charity is given freely there is no tax payable on it. However, many events involve the sale of tickets to the public. This is considered trading rather than fundraising and may be liable to tax. This is a complicated area involving both VAT and income tax. There is a tax concession (ESCC4) for those organising occasional events which allows the income from such events to be treated as a donation and be free of tax. For further information, see the Inland Revenue publication *Trading by Charities*.

For VAT, there is also a concession. Normally the sale of a ticket to an event would be treated as a taxable supply and be subject to VAT if the seller is registered for VAT (or obliged to register because the ticket sales take total taxable income above the VAT registration threshold). However, if the ticket price is split into two components, a reasonable price for attending the event and a donation, and if the wording is such that the donation element is optional, then only the attendance price would be treated as taxable income for VAT purposes. It is worth taking professional advice or consulting your local VAT office if you are in any doubt.

There are several important aspects of successfully managing the event.

- *An accurate budget.* You have to control costs if you are to run the event profitably. Your budget will show how many people you will need to attract and what price to charge for tickets. You will need to make an early assessment of all the likely costs and the potential sources of income and include something for contingencies. On the income side it is worth making a high and low estimate to illustrate what may happen in different circumstances. This will highlight the risk involved.
- *Time.* You can organise an event in a short space of time, but the longer you leave yourself the better. The best is an annual cycle, with the planning of the following year's event starting just after the completion of the current one. Booking a venue or obtaining the services of star performers may take a lot longer and may dictate how far ahead you need to plan.
- *Legally binding contracts.* You will need to set up arrangements with performers, the venue and any sub-contractors, expressed through some formal written agreement. This sets out precisely what has been agreed and is signed by both parties to confirm the agreement and to avoid disagreement later on. It is especially important to agree how any money is to

be split (both expenditure and income); who has the rights to any record-ing of the event; who is responsible for what costs, and what the obligations are in the event of cancellation. Where considerable sums are involved, the agreement should be drawn up by a lawyer.

- *Good administration and record keeping.* For your first event, you will have to start from scratch; but the next time will be much easier, since you will be building on experience. Keep records of everything – for example, whether insurance is needed, where to go for it and how much to pay. Immediately after the event, have a de-briefing – find out what went really well, what went wrong or could be improved, what suggestions there are for doing better or raising more money next time.

Reducing the risk

Apart from accurate budgeting and cost control the best way of reducing risk is good planning, organisation and marketing. However, things have a habit of not going to plan, so you need to think about your exposure to risk and how to reduce it. There are several ways of doing this.

- *Financial sponsorship.* Get all the costs of the event covered by a sponsor, so that any money raised goes to your cause, a message that is likely to encourage ticket sales.
- *Commitments and guarantees.* One way of running a charity ball is to have a committee of say 20 people, each of whom agrees to get 12 people to come to the ball. They take responsibility for selling the 12 tickets, or for paying for them themselves if they are unable to find others to contribute. This means that you have a guaranteed attendance of 240 people – enough to fill the venue or make sure that the event is a success.
- *Cost cutting.* You can try to get as much as possible lent, donated or spon-sored for the occasion, so that you do not have to pay for it. Venue costs, performer costs, and the cost of prizes can all be substantial, and if they are too high can jeopardise the success of the event. Not having to pay or paying much less is a simple way both to get more out of the event and to reduce risk at the same time.
- *Insurance.* It may be possible to insure against public liability, theft or damage (in case something goes wrong), and even against the possibility of bad weather for an outdoor event.

Strip 4 Shelter

In 1999 Shelter, the UK's largest national charity working with homeless and badly housed people, launched its annual football fundraising event Strip 4 Shelter.

Strip 4 Shelter taps into people's love of football and aims to raise money by asking people from all walks of life to pay £2 to wear their favourite football team's shirt or colours to work, school, the game or the pub. Many also get involved in fun footie events organised in their school (as in the photograph) or workplace.

Sponsored by Nationwide, the building society and sponsor of the football league, and supported by partners such as UCI Cinemas and the Scottish and Newcastle pub chain, the campaign has raised £500,000 to date. Celebrities have also been attracted to support the event; not just footballers like Kevin Keegan and Les Ferdinand, but many MPs, and television personalities including Chris Evans and Ant and Dec.

There is also a dedicated website for the event, www.strip4shelter.org.uk

Promotion

Effective promotion can turn an event from a modest success into a really profitable one. Decide who will want to come to the event – your target market – and how best to reach them.

Local radio can be a powerful promotional tool for local events. Many radio stations send mobile recording studios; others may send a reporter to cover the event live. This sort of link creates a promotional momentum. The station will want to give frequent plugs during the run up to the event, mentioning the date and how to get tickets. Another possibility is to offer free tickets as prizes to be given away by the radio station.

You can also advertise. Think about posters and handbills displayed or distributed locally, advertising in the press and being included in listings magazines.

One way of encouraging publicity is to feature celebrities who may be attending the event or performing at it. For sporting and musical events, the performers will be one of the main attractions. Alternatively, you can invite a celebrity to act as compere, to open the event, to present the awards or to announce raffle winners at the event. Having famous names adds credibility to the event, and encourages people to come along and stay until the end.

You also need a strategy for getting people to come if ticket sales are slow, but not so disappointing as to have to cancel the event. Once you are sure the event is going to run, it is important that the event is well attended. At that stage it is more important to see that people are there than that all the tickets are sold. This means that you should be prepared to give tickets away free to groups who might be interested in coming – through schools and student unions for young people's events, through hospitals and other institutions for other events, or via a media promotion.

Sponsorship

Events offer a sponsor a range of facilities and benefits. Sponsors need to know a good deal about the event and its expected audience before they will make a commitment – how many people are expected, who they might be and how they will be exposed to any advertising messages.

You should have a clear idea of how much money you need from a sponsor and what you can give in return. You might be offering special hospitality facilities, opportunities to meet famous people, to place the sponsor's message in a prominent place, or the chance to publicise the sponsorship through the advertising or public relations undertaken for the event. See chapter 8 for more on company sponsorship.

One of the key items that can carry a main sponsor's message, and those of other advertisers too, is the brochure (this is known as 'goodwill' advertising, as the advertisers are seen to be supporting a good cause). Almost every event needs a brochure or programme containing details about it, which can also generate income. Each copy can either be given away free (to create maximum circulation) or be sold on the day to generate further income.

Also, if the event requires prizes these can be asked for and provided as a form of sponsorship from either a local or national company depending on the size and potential of your event.

Developing extra income

For many events, such as a dinner dance or a ball, the ticket price will cover the cost of putting on the event and not much more. If you want to generate money for your work, you will need to devise ways of getting those attending to give or spend while at the event, such as:

- holding an auction, raffle or prize draw;
- giving out donation forms for each person to fill in, making an appeal during the evening, or collecting money from those present. To make sure that people respond generously, you should say what the money is for and perhaps suggest a level of donation. You could also offer a prize for the table that contributes the most.

Spin-off for future fundraising

A great advantage of a successful event is that you can build up an audience for future occasions. By keeping the names and addresses of those who have attended, you can invite them to participate next time.

Try to capture the interest of the people who attend so that they learn about your cause and understand the importance of your work. You can also add the participants' names to your database, although if you are planning to send them other fundraising appeals not directly connected to the event, you may need to make sure that they are happy for you to do this. See Appendix 2 for information on the requirements of the Data Protection Act.

Organising a particular type of event can help you reach out to a new audience. For example, if you are interested in people involved in education you might think about an exhibition of children's paintings; or if you want to appeal to people who have an interest in the arts you might organise a benefit screening of a film or performance of a play.

However, you need to be careful. People attend or take part in charity events for many different reasons. It may well be that a substantial number of those attending do not and will not care about your charity but were attracted by the event itself. Therefore, sending them expensive appeal literature over a long period of time may simply be a waste of money. It is much better to ask them what they want to receive from you – if anything – and give them that. The response rates to this kind of strategy are usually as high (if not higher) than the blanket approach, but at a lower cost to you.

12.3 Walks, runs and challenge events

Another traditional but highly successful fundraising method is an event where participants are sponsored by their family and friends depending on what they achieve. Almost anything can be sponsored, for example:

- giving up smoking (number of days without a cigarette up to a specified limit)
- slimming (amount of weight lost during a set time)
- marathon runs (kilometres raced plus a bonus for completing the course)
- penalty shoot outs (goals scored if you are the penalty taker, or goals saved if the goalkeeper)
- even cycling in the Himalayas!

In deciding on what sort of event to organise, find something that will be sufficiently popular to attract lots of participants as well as something that is straightforward to run. You also want something that you can repeat, building on your experience and success to achieve greater returns the next time you run it.

A sponsored event can be used to get across an important message about your cause. For example, an environmental charity might organise a sponsored clean up of litter from an area of countryside; or a health charity might organise a fun run. However, remember that people often feel they are supporting their friends' participation in an event rather than making a donation to your charity.

If the event does not attract enough participants, or they cannot generate the sponsorship money, you may not hit your target. So think carefully about what will attract your target audience, and whether you can reach them. If it is young families, think of something that will involve the whole family during the weekend. Family strolls, fun runs and sponsored swims are all popular – you are only limited by your imagination.

You will have four main audiences for your event:

- those who have participated and enjoyed the experience before – so it is important to keep a record of who has participated in previous years;
- your supporters. Mail your members and donors – they may be interested in doing something to help raise money;
- those who are interested in the particular activity you have chosen (cycling, walking, marathon running, etc.), but who may not know about your work – although their participation gives you the opportunity to interest them in it;

- those involved in your organisation: your management committee; your staff (their involvement in a sponsored event can improve morale and teamwork); and your beneficiaries.

The National Deaf Childrens Society (NDCS) and Charity Challenge Events

NDCS started doing charity challenge events in 1996 with an Arabian Nights Bike Ride to Jordan. The event was a huge success with 150 people getting involved, raising £300,000. They made the event deaf friendly, tying it in with their cause, by taking a sign language interpreter and got the television programme *See Hear* involved, who publicised and filmed the event. Their next event, in 1997, was Cycle Cuba and national press advertising was used to broaden the audience getting involved. Their target was three trips with 200 riders; instead 650 people were recruited and there were seven Cycle Cuba trips! These raised £1.7 million.

NDCS have carried on organising these hugely successful events (on a recent Cycle India, 60% of the participants raised more than their minimum £2,000 donation) and at the same time have involved a very different, younger audience in their work with deaf children.

Organising a mass participation event

Break up your plan for the organisation of your event into three parts.

1 Before the event

At this stage, you will need to:

- decide the event and agree the route or venue;
- get necessary permissions and insurance;
- plan the promotion and recruitment of the participants. Since the ultimate success of the event depends on the amount raised, it is important to have your target number of participants. You can then encourage them to raise more money by: setting a minimum sponsorship requirement which they guarantee to pay; giving them a target, both in terms of the number of sponsors they should aim to get and how much to ask for; having an entrance fee for participating in the event;
- carefully prepare the sponsorship forms and explanatory materials about the work of your organisation. The form must describe exactly what is being done, but should also say why the money is needed. It should list the names and addresses of sponsors; a phone number to contact the sponsor if they fail to produce the money they have promised; and the amount pledged. You want to encourage sponsors to be generous. They need to know how many miles (or whatever) they are likely to be paying for. Most

sponsors do not know what level of sponsorship is expected, and are guided by what others have written before so encourage participants to approach their more generous supporters first. Alternatively you might indicate some preferred amounts. Some people may prefer to give a fixed sum. The form should allow for this too;

- provide advice and support to participants to help them collect pledges;
- organise volunteers and stewards to help on the day;
- confirm the route;
- prepare a certificate of completion for participants to take away after the event.

You will be surprised by the range of sums people raise. This depends as much on the effort put in by the participant (which you can of course encourage) as on their financial circumstances.

2 On the day

You need to make sure that everything runs smoothly, that there are sufficient helpers, and that they are properly briefed. You also need to ensure that participants are welcomed (especially any celebrities who are participating), that newspaper and radio reporters are met on their arrival and briefed about anything unusual (including anyone participating in fancy dress, any stunts, anything unusual about what the money will be used for), that there is information at the start of the event to advise performers and the public what the route is, where the refreshment and toilet facilities are, and for events that involve physical exertion, where medical help can be obtained. You will need to have sufficient helpers to staff the various check-in procedures, to mark the route and to certify completion.

3 After the event

Key activities at this stage are:

- collecting the money. This is primarily the responsibility of the participants. Keep a register of all those who took part and stress the importance of collecting the money by a deadline date. Follow up by phone or by letter. You can also provide an incentive by offering a prize for the largest amount actually raised by an individual or a team;
- thanking those who helped;
- recording the names and addresses of those who took part.

Finally you should review the whole event from planning through execution and follow up. This is important as it will enable you to identify your successes, but also your weak points and problems, so that you can improve on everything the next time you do it.

Sponsored event checklist

1 Make sure you plan well ahead.

2 Choose the right activity for your target audience and cause.

3 Set a date and find a suitable venue.

4 Get any permissions you need, for example to use a public place.

5 Produce sponsorship forms.

6 Involve other organisations, as they can be a good source of participants.

7 Organise local publicity and get media sponsorship.

8 Get local business sponsorship to cover costs and pay for any prizes being offered.

9 Prepare for the day: ensure you have all the stewards, equipment and information that you need for the event.

10 Thank all the participants.

11 Chase up all uncollected pledges.

12.4 Raffles and lotteries

Raffles and lotteries are a commonplace method of fundraising and can be used successfully by both large and small organisations. All lotteries are regulated, but the regulatory authority depends on the status of the activity (see below).

Who regulates lotteries?

Activity	Definition	Authority	Act
Raffle	No skill with entry fee	Gaming Board	Lotteries Act
Scratch cards	No skill with entry fee	Gaming Board	Lotteries Act
Slot Machines	n/a	Gaming Board	Gaming Act
Prize Draws	Skill with entry fee	Advertising Standards Authority (ASA)	Code of Advertising Practice (CAP)
Free Draws	No skill, no entry fee	ASA	CAP

Some definitions

Lotteries come in many forms, and have different names.

- *Lottery*: formal name for a game of chance by sale of tickets. This could be a private lottery, a small lottery, a society lottery, a local authority lottery or the National Lottery.
- *Raffle*: colloquial name for a lottery, usually with non-cash prizes.
- *100 Club*: a group of 100 people participating in a lottery on a monthly basis. Tickets are purchased by monthly subscription and the draw is each month.
- *Tombola*: a small scale game of chance at an entertainment event, usually involving the purchase of tickets to win bottles and other donated goods. Each ticket usually wins a prize.
- *Sweepstake*: a lottery where the winner is decided by drawing lots; for a sweepstake on a horse race, for example, the winner is the participant who has drawn the name of the horse that wins the race.
- *Skill Game*: where the outcome is decided by some measure of skill (including a tie break to choose the winner from all those submitting correct answers). Sometimes the element of skill required is very small, and the format is used to get around lottery regulations.
- *Competition*: the same as a skill game. Skill games and competitions can also be free entry, where they are used extensively in sales promotions. A recent variant requires entrants to ring a premium telephone number, where the cost of doing so generates a return for the promoter. Because a measure of skill is involved, these are not technically lotteries, which are games of chance.
- *Free entry draw*: this is a skill game or prize draw used in sales promotion, where there is no charge for entering.

An example of a raffle ticket produced by Crusaid, a charity working with people with HIV and AIDS.

For the purpose of regulation, lotteries are divided into four categories (apart from the National Lottery which is separately regulated by the National Lottery Commission): small lotteries, private lotteries, society lotteries, and local authority lotteries.

Each type of lottery has a different set of regulations which are covered in full in the Gaming Board's publication *Lotteries and the Law*. See box *Basic lottery rules* for general descriptions of each type of lottery.

Basic lottery rules

- **Small lottery**
  Incidental to entertainment; £1 maximum per ticket; no registration required; sale of tickets on premises only; no money prizes, and £250 maximum on purchase of prizes.

- **Private lottery**
  Limited to one group of people or one location; £1 maximum per ticket; no registration required; sale of tickets only to members.

- **Society lottery**
  Promoted by one society; £1 maximum per ticket; sales up to £20,000 requires registration with Local Authority; sales over £20,000 requires registration with Gaming Board; returns and audited accounts must be submitted.

- **Local Authority lottery**
  Promoted by a Local Authority; £1 maximum per ticket; sales up to £20,000 registration and reporting requirements as for Society Lottery.

Prizes

Some people buy tickets to support your charity; others may be attracted by the prizes. As a lottery gets bigger, the lure of prizes becomes more important. You can either offer cash (though not for Small Lotteries) or non-cash prizes.

Getting goods or services donated as lottery prizes can be a good way of getting support from companies. For a small or a private lottery, prizes can be collected from local companies and shops, and need not be more than £5–£20 in value. Having a wide range of prizes that you can display at the event will help sell the tickets. It is not usually necessary to offer cash prizes.

For larger raffles you need to focus on a smaller number of better prizes. The main prizes are what will encourage people to buy tickets. An unusual and imaginative prize is more attractive than a money prize, and sometimes will not cost a lot to organise. For example, a museum supporters group might arrange a personal tour with the director followed by a dinner. Allow plenty of time to find good prizes which are consistent with your organisation's aims. Prepare an outline of your plans, or for major raffles, a special brochure highlighting the advantages to being associated with the raffle. You should contact potential prize donors well before the event and companies will want crediting for their support, possibly on the tickets themselves, at the prize giving, and in any press coverage.

Promotion

Everything hinges on selling tickets. If the prizes are right and the price not too high (£1 per ticket is the current maximum that you can charge), tickets are best sold on a personal basis. For small raffles where the tickets are sold at an event, this is not difficult but needs careful planning. Identify a group of key volunteers for the evening and ask them to go round and visit everybody at the venue. You can also contact supporters prior to the event, and ask them to ask their friends at their place of work.

For a society lottery where you aim to sell tickets to a wider public, more will need to be done. You can send tickets to your supporter base. Although some may be irritated by this, enough usually accept the tickets and sell them on or buy them themselves. In one raffle 20,000 members were sent two raffle books each. This resulted in 100 people returning their books and a total sale of 96,000 tickets. The end result was an income of £60,000 with costs of £12,000.

Local groups or volunteer fundraisers are often excellent at selling raffle tickets, especially when they actively sell in their workplace or neighbourhood. Ring them up to see if they will do it, and to offer encouragement.

Some organisations offer incentives to those selling lottery tickets. In one example, a computer was offered to the person who sold the most tickets – although the organisation could not tell whether this incentive made any difference to the number of tickets sold.

The draw

In a small raffle, the draw for the prizes is the moment of drama. Build the timing of the draw into your plans for the event. It should be announced at regular intervals leading up to the draw as an aid to selling tickets. Ideally, the draw should be the finale, thus encouraging people to stay to the end of the event. Getting a celebrity to present the prizes can add to the excitement. This is a good opportunity for a photograph. Invite a photographer, or arrange for a member of staff to take pictures of prizes, prizewinners and celebrities.

For a larger raffle the situation is different. Few members of the public will want to attend the draw, although the date and place should be clearly publicised on the tickets. There is an opportunity to use the draw to invite donors and sponsors to meet senior staff and trustees, and to try to enlist their support for the next year.

To gamble or not to gamble

Organisations with a strong religious tradition (and some others) may find this area of fundraising problematic. Even with the prevalence of the National Lottery, they may not wish to be involved in any form of gambling. It is not important what you personally think about selling lottery tickets, or whether there is any evidence that links buying lottery tickets with addictive gambling. What is important is that you are clear about your organisation's attitude. If there are good reasons to believe that gambling might be a contentious issue, you should make sure your organisation has an agreed policy on it.

12.5 Working with patrons and celebrities

Association with a well-known personality can lift your organisation from obscurity into the limelight. Celebrities can help in many ways. For example, their presence at an event will be a potential draw. They can inspire members and donors, and can turn your fundraising event into a roaring success.

Probably most important though, is their potential for attracting media coverage. If a well-known broadcaster is prepared to lead a press conference announcing a new campaign, the press is going to be much more interested than when an unknown charity executive says the same thing. Similarly photo editors are more likely to publish a photo of a well-known and attractive actor opening some new facility, than when a local councillor is doing the same thing. So use all your networking skills to make connections with people who will attract positive media attention.

A local charity can of course get good local coverage by using people who are well-known in their own area. You may not be lucky enough to have a world-famous musician or footballer living in your village, but it is still worth cultivating contacts such as councillors, business people or local TV and radio presenters, who may be pleased to get involved.

Celebrities give their time for the same reasons that anyone else wants to support the charity – they think it is worthwhile and that their contribution can make a difference. However, it is not just having celebrities associated with your organisation, but the way you use your celebrities that will have an impact.

Using celebrities effectively

Try to find a relevant celebrity. People who have had direct experience of an issue or problem will be a much more powerful advocate for the organisation and the cause. For example, the actress Susan Hampshire is dyslexic and has supported the British Dyslexia Association for many years. Celebrities should also be matched to your target donor audience.

Well-known people can be used in a wide variety of ways – from becoming a patron or joining your board of trustees to appearing in photo calls, launching publications, giving out prizes or participating in fundraising events.

When asking a celebrity to help, you need to think carefully and discuss with them the best way for them to get involved. They want their association with you to be a success, but not to take too much time.

You also have responsibilities to them. Celebrities have their reputations to consider, so they do not want to be associated with bad publicity or with controversy. They may be used to a level of personal support and attention that is difficult for small organisations to sustain – everything from being given detailed instructions for what they are expected to do, to having speeches written for them, being collected by taxi or car and driven back after the event, and being accompanied and looked after whilst they are there.

Managing celebrities

It is often said that celebrities are the most difficult of people to work with. Some well-known people demand to be treated as celebrities in all aspects of their lives; others can be deeply appreciative of the opportunity to be involved at all. It is important to build your relationship with such people carefully, as indeed you should do with anyone who contributes to your organisation in any significant way.

Because celebrities can bring you great benefits, you should treat them professionally and politely, and try to make sure that their contribution is meaningful for you and satisfying for them. Control access to your celebrities tightly. You must prevent them being asked to do too many things too frequently, or even being asked to do things that they have specifically declined to do.

Appearance fees are always an issue. Most performers do not expect or want to take fees from charity events, and certainly should not be encouraged to do so. You should be prepared to pay reasonable expenses – and only consider paying the most nominal amounts as a fee, and then only in exceptional circumstances and possibly as a donation to a charity of their choice (hopefully that will be you!).

If you are recruiting a celebrity for an event, they will need to have a very clear idea of what is going to happen and precisely what is expected of them. Will they be making a speech? Who will write it for them? Will a car be provided? When must they arrive? When can they discreetly slip away? Who will greet them and look after them whilst they are with you? Will there be a presentation of flowers or a public thank you? Do they have to shake hands, speak to and be photographed with your main sponsor? Who will brief them on what to say? Who will be responsible for formally thanking them afterwards on behalf of the organisation? And so on. They will also want to be told how much their presence has helped; how many extra people have come this year; how much extra money was raised, and how many reporters covered the story.

Sometimes you have to deal with them via an agent or personal assistant. Working with an agent can be both a help and a hindrance. They will be more concerned with fees and payments, and may not want their client to do something for nothing. On the other hand, being associated with you can bring the celebrity a lot of good publicity and help create an image of a caring person. So there is some benefit to their client. Try to get a direct line to your celebrity as soon as you can. But the agent can be helpful in identifying long-range opportunities and availability; they can also help you get an idea of what the celebrity is looking for from the arrangement, as well as their likes and dislikes.

Resources and further information

See also general lists at the end of the book.

Organisations

Angal Service to Fundraisers
(produce and supply collecting boxes)
Building A
91 Ewell Road
Surbiton
Surrey KT6 6AH

Customs & Excise
(for VAT matters)
www.hmce.gov.uk
Find your local office in the telephone
directory under Customs and Excise
Vat Business Advice Centres.

Inland Revenue
(for tax matters)
Inland Revenue (Charities)
St John's House
Merton Road
Bootle
Merseyside L69 9BB
Tel. 0845 3020203

**Northern Ireland Council for
 Voluntary Action**
127 Ormeau Road
Belfast BT7 1SH
Tel. 01232 321224

Scottish Council for Voluntary
  Organisations
18–19 Claremont Crescent
Edinburgh EH12 5EZ
Tel. 0131 313 2488

Publications

The following publications are available from the Directory of Social Change. Prices were correct at the time of writing, but may be subject to change.

The Fundraiser's Guide to the Law, Bates, Wells & Braithwaite and Centre for Voluntary Sector Development, DSC 2000, £16.95

Good Ideas for Raising Serious Money, Sarah Passingham, DSC 1995, £9.95

Organising Local Events, Sarah Passingham, DSC 1995, £5

Organising Special Events, Stephen Elsden and John Gray, DSC/CAF 2000, £10.95

A Practical Guide to VAT 2nd edition, Kate Sayer, DSC 2001, £12.95

Tried and Tested Ideas for Raising Money Locally 3rd edition, Sarah Passingham, DSC available autumn 2003 (check our website for information), c. £14.95

Voluntary Sector Legal Handbook 2nd edition, Sandy Adirondack and James Sinclair Taylor, DSC 2001, £42 (voluntary organisations) /£60 (others)

Other publications

Institute of Fundraising Code of Practice on House to House Collections

Institute of Fundraising Code of Practice on the Telephone Recruitment of Collectors

Institute of Fundraising Guidance Note on the Management of Static Collection Boxes

Institute of Fundraising Code of Practice on UK Charity Challenge Events

Institute of Fundraising Code of Practice on Charity Challenge Events

Institute of Fundraising Code of Practice on Raffles and Lotteries

13 CAPITAL AND BIG GIFT CAMPAIGNS

In addition to your regular fundraising activity, your organisation may need to raise money to launch a major new service or embark on a large-scale building programme. This chapter gives a brief introduction to when and why you might undertake a capital campaign, and how capital and big gift campaigns tend to be structured.

Details of organisations and publications referred to in this chapter are on p. 260.

13.1 The case for a capital or big gift campaign

With responsibility for care and welfare shifting away from the state, either because of increasing expectations and rising costs or as a consequence of the contract culture, charities are going to find themselves needing more and more capital funding. Schools and hospitals need money to develop their facilities and for equipment; organisations caring for the elderly need to meet the needs of a growing older population. The National Lottery continues to fund (or part fund) national, regional and local arts, heritage and sports projects where there is a requirement for matched funding (see chapter 7). All this suggests that capital fundraising will continue to grow. This increase in the demand for funds could result in a decline in response rates and a resistance to giving. It also means that those seeking funds in a highly competitive climate will have to look for ways of improving their effectiveness.

Charities have always been able to attract big gifts, and in recent years attention has turned to using big gift fundraising as one of the principal components of a capital campaign. The techniques tend to be used in the context of a large single one-off appeal for a particular project, such as Shelter's nationwide telephone helpline Shelterline, the NSPCC Full Stop Campaign to end child abuse, the £300 million raised for Oxford University through the Campaign for Oxford, and the £134 million raised for the conversion of Bankside Powerstation into Tate Modern.

Campaign phases

A campaign to raise a significant sum must be properly planned and is likely to go through a number of clearly defined phases:

- the planning stage
- the case document, which sets out and justifies the purpose of the fundraising
- the business plan or feasibility study, which sets out the plan and time scale for the fundraising
- the research
- the recruitment of an appeal committee
- the private giving phase, in which major gifts are sought
- the launch
- the public giving phase
- the consolidation.

Going through all these stages not only ensures that the appeal is properly planned and organised. It also allows a reasonable timescale for the appeal, links it with your expenditure plans and alerts you to any cash flow shortfalls. It may take over two years from start to finish; a very large target may well take longer. You need to consider the question of investment and risk. When plans have been approved and the staff have been taken on, trustees can get nervous about the chances of the original outlay being recouped. This demands an understanding of the appeal process and faith in the people charged with its success.

Issues to consider

One issue is the degree to which a capital campaign will interfere with your ongoing fundraising and affect future fundraising prospects. This will vary with each organisation, and depends on the campaign strategy and the relative sizes of your capital and revenue fundraising budgets. For a £50 million a year charity raising £5 million of capital, there is likely to be some overlap. And if your existing supporters have made a substantial donation, they may want to be left alone for a while. However, for a small charity raising a relatively large sum, the momentum, excitement and interest that is generated by the campaign will probably add to the regular income received rather than detract from it.

Difficult cash flow decisions may need to be taken. There will be considerable costs involved in the early months, especially if a professional fundraising consultant is retained. No campaign is cost-free; there will need to be budget for administration and publicity material. A properly planned and resourced campaign will stand a much better chance of success.

However, there may come a point at which you question whether the campaign will succeed. If you take the view that it will not, then you should pull out. This is not an easy decision to take but it is better to withdraw at an early stage than to be seen to fail publicly.

13.2 Planning a campaign

Planning a capital campaign involves the following stages.

1 *Planning the project for which the funds are being raised.* You need to be able to justify the need for the project as vital both to the work and future of the organisation; otherwise, people won't give. You will need to prepare a business plan for the project, to assure yourself that you can raise the money and that you will have enough to keep going once it has been completed. Major campaigns are by definition very public, so potential failure is also public. It would be highly embarrassing if the project folded after completion for lack of the funds to run it. You will need detailed costings and drawings.

2 *Doing a feasibility study.* Many organisations take on a consultant to get advice on how to conduct the campaign. One of their first steps will be to conduct a feasibility study to identify whether the campaign is likely to be successful. This is important, as it will also highlight any inconsistencies or ill-conceived ideas.

3 *Planning the structure of the campaign.* At this stage it is advisable to recruit a campaign committee to lead and oversee the fundraising. The key appointment is the chair. The committee's function is to raise big gifts, so people should be appointed for their asking capacity and their networks, as well as their interest in your organisation. You may also want to establish sub-committees to oversee the running of other elements of the campaign such as events, publicity and media coverage, and to harness volunteer help. These committees will need to be supported by an office staffed by paid or volunteer workers who are well-briefed, efficient and available.

4 *Reviewing likely funding sources.* A vital planning tool is a table setting out the number and size of donations needed. This lists the gifts that you plan to acquire, helps you identify possible donors and sources, and gives guidance on the level of support to ask for. Always start from your existing donor base and contacts. Who do you already know with the ability to make a big gift? Then move on to other strategic sources of funding. Is there a well-known trust whose support would act as a lever in approaching other funders?

5 *Documentation and research to back up the above.* For major gifts, you should undertake some preliminary work on likely sources. You should certainly explore possible government and trust grants.

6 *Preparation of the case statement.* This is a vital document, which will be the strategic plan for the appeal. It will include sections covering the following.
- a background to the charity and its history
- a description and justification of the project
- the costs of the project
- a costed breakdown of the individual components of the project
- the gifts needed to achieve this target
- the plan for raising the money (including any fundraising events)
- the sources of money expected.

This report needs to be professionally presented.

7 *Identifying the people who will provide the lead gifts for the campaign, and approaching them to see if they will help.* This is usually done by drawing up lists of leading business people and other influential people gleaned from a wide range of sources, including personal knowledge and contacts. They will meet infrequently, but are there to help solicit the largest gifts through their contacts and credibility. Once again, the appointment of the chair is critical as they will be the public figure leading the campaign. These first large gifts will set the tone for the appeal and boost your confidence.

8 *Ensuring the support of your trustees.* One key issue is the degree to which your trustees are committed to the campaign. It will be extremely difficult to approach people for support if the trustees are known to be unenthusiastic.

Leadership

The leadership of the campaign is extremely important. There are two key principles to bear in mind.

- People respond better when asked by their peers, that is those who are at or above their own level in business or society.
- Response will be better if the person asking has already given and given generously. One question they are very likely to be asked by those they are approaching for donations is if they have given themselves.

The qualifications to look for in the chair and in campaign committee members are that they have the resources to give major gifts on the scale you need (either personally or through the company or foundation they are associated with); that they have good networks which will provide important potential givers; and that they are able and willing to ask others to support the appeal both in person and by letter.

The first stage is to identify people to help you plan the campaign. Since initially you are asking for advice rather than money, it will be easier for them to agree – but they will probably expect to be asked for a donation later on. A group of two or three senior people with an interest in your work can form the planning group. Their role is either to act as the formal leadership of the appeal or to select that leadership. They should be well-respected in the community and, if possible, not have been associated with a similar appeal in the recent past – if they have, their asking capacity may have been diminished. As already mentioned for other groups, they also need to have a good network of contacts to draw on.

You need to understand why such important people might want to work for your cause. There are many reasons. Some people will do it because they genuinely believe in and support the cause; others find an approach from a senior person in the community difficult to resist; others find the link with other business people attractive for their own purposes; some are motivated by the notion that they might get recognition; and some just like the challenge of achieving something worthwhile. They will appreciate efficient administration and being provided with the back up they need. This will ensure that their time is effectively used (and not spent in lots of committee meetings).

Many people will not know how to ask effectively, so you may need to provide some training in the principles of effective asking and an induction to the work of your organisation.

13.3 Managing the campaign

The private phase

With all the building blocks in place, you should be ready to begin the task of asking for money. At this stage, everything is still done privately, without fanfares of publicity. You need to make sure of a core of funding before you go public.

The first step is to get the financial commitment of your campaign committee. It is important that your early gifts are of a sufficient size to give a lead to those that follow. Through the process of developing and refining the appeal document, most committee members should already be aware of the scale of donations that are needed. They will have been engaged in discussions about what is expected of other prospective donors, and will be familiar with what might be expected of them.

Once they have made their own commitment, they should move on to the task of approaching others. You will already have drawn up lists of prospective donors. They can add new names from their own contacts and decide how best to approach them.

The task of asking for big gifts is best done by the committee members themselves, with you, the fundraiser, providing smooth administration. Once you have identified who should approach a potential donor, a wide variety of methods can be used from an informal sounding out at a dinner party to a personal letter to an invitation to see the project – whatever the person asking feels most comfortable with.

People usually take time to decide on big donations, and this is especially true for large public sector grants. Do not expect a decision within the course of a single meeting. You might need a series of meetings – starting perhaps with a reception, followed by informal chats – that culminate in the prospective donor being asked to help and offered a range of possible ways of doing so. In addition to money, they can be asked to give support in kind and the names of others who might be approached.

The objective of the private stage of the appeal will be to collect pledges of between 25% and 50% of the appeal target. This will give a real boost to the appeal when it is launched. It is wise to launch your appeal to the public only when you are confident of its success.

Table of gifts needed for appeal

It is always sensible to break down the total appeal target into the numbers of gifts of different sizes that you will need to raise. This table is an example showing how this might be done.

No. of gifts	Amount p.a. £	4 year value £	Total over 4 years £
2	25,000	100,000	200,000
8	10,000	40,000	320,000
20	5,000	20,000	400,000
40	2,000	8,000	320,000
70			**1,240,000 TOTAL**

The public phase

The public phase should start with an official launch. This can be done in a number of ways depending on how the campaign is structured. It should certainly include a press conference and might also involve an event to which you can invite prospective donors.

In the public phase of the appeal, much of the money will be raised from larger numbers of people making smaller donations. This phase will have several objectives: to take the appeal to a wider audience; to assist the task of the big gift fundraising; and to give those who were unable to give at a high level the opportunity to give at a more modest one.

A press and public relations campaign is important to raise the profile of your appeal. Some big appeals recruit PR committees or involve PR professionals on a voluntary basis. You should certainly have someone working hard on public and media relations, as this will underpin your other fundraising activities.

Events are an important component of your campaign, as they attract media coverage, and reach out to a wider audience. You may want to set up a volunteer committee to take responsibility for events, as they take a good deal of time to organise. (See chapter 12 for more on event management.)

Direct mail can also be used, targeted at people your personal approaches have not yet reached. It is important, though, that this be left towards the end, so that nobody gives a small donation in response to a letter where they might otherwise have given a bigger donation if asked personally. A mailing is also more likely to produce results if people can see that the target has nearly been reached.

For very large national campaigns, you may need to have a regional committee structure to harness opportunities at a regional level. The regional chairpeople should be appointed as part of the campaign structure, and they then recruit people in their area. In this public phase their role will mainly be helping to stimulate and co-ordinate events to raise support and get publicity for the campaign in their area.

The consolidation phase

Consolidating what has been achieved in the first stages of the campaign will ensure that you make the most of the efforts and the contacts you have made for your continuing fundraising. This phase includes a number of key steps:

- bringing in all the money that has been pledged. During the campaign you will have received promises of support which may not yet have materialised. This is the point to chase these up;
- closing the campaign. When the target has been realised there should be an announcement (to get publicity for the success of the venture) and a celebration involving some sort of reception or event. Key volunteers, prominent supporters and sponsors, staff and others who were centrally involved in the appeal can all be invited;

- thanking those involved;
- setting up a development committee for the future. You may have generated your income on a somewhat *ad hoc* basis up to this point; the creation of the right structure for the charity and its future fundraising can help ensure that the momentum is not lost. This may involve setting up a permanent development committee to carry on the fundraising, or a high level advisory committee. During the course of the campaign, you will have gained the confidence and enthusiasm of a number of key contacts. Those who have been particularly effective should now be encouraged to take more permanent places within the structures that you have created so that they can continue to help you;
- further fundraising. With these people and structures in place, you are in a position to approach people who did not give to the campaign, and to begin to go back to those who did give for further support.

Resources and further information

See also general lists at the end of the book.

Organisations

The following organisations advise on capital and big gift campaigns:

The Factary
The Coach House
Upper York Street
Bristol BS2 8QN
Tel. 0117 924 0663

Oxford Philanthropic
36 Windmill Road
Headington
Oxford OX3 7BX
Tel. 01865 744300

FR & C Ltd
Tebbit House
Winchcombe Street
Cheltenham GL52 2NE
Tel. 01242 522323

Publications

The following publications are available from the Directory of Social Change. Prices were correct at the time of writing, but may be subject to change.

Find the Funds, Christopher Carnie, DSC/CAF 2000, £12.95

14 DIRECT MARKETING

Marketing is not just for commercial companies, nor is it only about selling. Fundraising demands a range of marketing skills. In a sense, this whole book is about marketing – marketing a cause to someone who can contribute money and time to supporting it. This chapter looks at the link between marketing theory and fundraising and covers some basic fundraising methods and media.

Details of organisations and publications referred to in this chapter are on p. 299.

14.1 Marketing – a brief introduction

Marketing is often described in terms of the four P's – product, price, place and promotion. For this chapter, one more has been added, planning.

Planning and market analysis

Marketing planning starts with a clear understanding of an organisation and its work, the market in which it is operating, the competitor organisations (in the non-profit, the public and the private sectors), and the attitudes of potential supporters.

Useful tools for this include:

- doing a SWOT analysis for your organisation, in which you concentrate on what the internal strengths and weaknesses are, and the external opportunities and threats (see chapter 3 for more on this);
- market share analysis, which measures what proportion of a given sector of donated income you are currently receiving – for example, how much support is given by local companies, and how much of this your organisation is receiving;
- market research, which identifies the attitudes of your potential or actual supporters to giving to the cause in general, and to your particular charity.

All this will give you a better idea about those people and groups you should be targeting.

Product

The service your organisation provides is, in marketing terms, the product. It consists of the following ingredients:

- the actual 'tangible' product or need which your charity exists to meet;
- what the donor gets from association with you;
- any extra benefits: for example, an invitation to meet a child that has been helped or attendance at a special function each year.

You are competing for a share of your supporters' disposable income. You have to tempt them to buy your product rather than someone else's, so you need to make your product as attractive as you can.

Each product you create will have a life cycle. According to marketing theory, you will need to re-promote your product from time to time to keep it up to date, attractive and in people's minds.

Charities also have a range of fundraising products which they market to their donors. These might include a major donor programme; membership subscriptions for broader support; a regular giving scheme to increase committed support, and a schools fundraising scheme for younger people. These can all happily co-exist, so long as they are not in competition with one another.

Price

Donors do not automatically know how much to give. You need to steer them towards what is likely to be achievable and affordable to them, while also meeting your own requirements.

The most obvious way of doing this is to ask for a precise amount, for example, 'We are asking each person to give £10'. However this can beg the question, 'Why £10?'. The response to that is to give an idea of what the money can achieve – '£10 can buy a new walking frame for a disabled child'. The donation may not actually be spent on that, so be careful that the wording does not create a binding obligation to spend the money in a certain way. You may commit a breach of trust if you say you are definitely going to buy walking frames and then use the money for play equipment instead.

There are three useful approaches in this type of situation.

- A shopping list of tangible items, illustrating a range of things at different prices that the donor's money might be spent on.
- A range of levels of support from which the donor can choose.
- A range of possible frequencies (annual, quarterly, monthly). You will find that smaller amounts given more frequently are likely to yield larger

annual donations. This is because people respond to the headlined figure more than to the actual cost.

The price you ask determines both the type of supporter you get and the amount of benefit you generate for your organisation. This will be the donation minus the cost of fundraising and administration. A monthly £5 donation will cost as much to service as a £25 donation, and might be immediately swallowed up by administration costs. There can be a tendency to ask for too little. People are more generous than you think, so you need to make sure you ask at the right level. For example, with potential major donors you will do yourself a disservice asking for only £50 – not because it is expensive to administer, but because they might have given a great deal more.

Place

Place in marketing terms refers to the means by which people give. It will usually be closely linked to promotion. For example, a personal request to help provides an opportunity to write a cheque and hand it over. A request made in a speech or over the radio should also include a way of giving support (for example, a return address or a telephone number). Think carefully about how people are expected to get their money to you, whether it is through a donation form, a bucket at the door at an event, a credit card hotline, a well-placed advertisement or a secure website.

The place will determine not just what you can ask for, but how people view your organisation. For example, if you decide to raise money from a series of balls or dinner dances, you will only interact with a certain range of people in a particular atmosphere. You could also appeal to a wider audience by running a series of special coffee mornings (like Macmillan Cancer Relief's 'World's Biggest Coffee Morning'). The two approaches might ultimately achieve the same result in terms of money raised. However, they would have done this by using completely different techniques, from quite different sources, using different resources and helpers, and in the process creating a completely different perception of your organisation by the participants.

Promotion

How do you project yourself to the public? It is not only the medium, but the message too. The message is conveyed by a whole range of things within your control. Your name – or at least the title of your appeal – sends an important message, particularly if you have made this name well-known. People recognise World Wide Fund for Nature (WWF) or Save the Children, and these names evoke images of what the charity is doing.

How you present yourself creates an impression of credibility, urgency, dynamism, and so on. Most important is how you express your needs in your written and visual material. Is it a rational or emotional appeal? Is it supported by human content? Good designers and copywriters can create the image you require for your organisation, if they are well briefed. See chapter 15, section 15.3 for more on this.

The medium of your promotion is another important ingredient. Are you going to rely on personal recommendation to get your message across? Or are you going to use TV, radio, newspaper advertising, direct mail, posters, house to house visits, exhibitions, company promotions, booklets, events, one-to-one approaches (by telephone or face to face)?

These five P's are interdependent, if one factor is changed then it will affect all the others. The rest of this chapter looks in more detail at the key marketing techniques used in fundraising.

14.2 Direct mail

The post provides one of the most flexible and powerful tools in fundraising. A postal appeal or direct mail programme can provide both regular and immediate income. The key is to build up and maintain an active and enthusiastic base of supporters. This takes time, effort and money to get started. Postal appeals will not provide immediate income for organisations which do not yet have an active supporter base. This will need to be developed, in order to provide an audience for your appeals.

The three main elements of a mailing programme

- *The audience*. There can be an enormous variation in the response rates you achieve, particularly between cold audiences (who you are trying to recruit as new supporters) and your existing donors (who are more likely to respond).
- *The message*. What you tell them and what you ask for are extremely important. You need to devise a powerful message that will move people to give. The creative approach, that is the way you angle the story you are telling them, and the 'offer', what you are asking them to do, are the two most important components of the message.
- *The timing*. Some times of the year may be better than others. For example the period leading up to Christmas is a good time for charity appeals, as it is a time when people feel predisposed to give. If there is a good reason for the appeal, for example as a response to a natural disaster, then the immediacy of the need and demonstrating that you are responding efficiently and effectively means that you should get your appeal out as quickly as you can.

Good direct mail entails sending a clear personalised message of the length you want, to whom you want, when you want. It will need:

- a selection of people to send the appeal to;
- a mailing pack – often a leaflet with a covering letter, some mechanism for replying (also known as a response device) and an envelope for the donation to be returned in;
- a system for dealing with the response.

There are three broad categories of direct mail which fall into two types of promotion:

Acquisition (or recruitment) of supporters
- 'cold' mailings to people with whom you have had no previous contact;
- 'reciprocal' mailings, where you mail sections of your supporter base with another organisation's appeal and they do the same.

Supporter development
- 'warm' mailings to your existing members and supporters.

Response rates on warm mailings are the highest, and can vary dramatically depending on what you are asking for – legacies, committed gifts, one-off donations – and the creative treatment you decide to use – for example, is it an emotive, hard hitting story? Reciprocal mailings to other people's supporters also work relatively well – these people are known charity supporters and already respond to direct mail. Response rates on cold lists also vary enormously, from virtually nothing to as much as 3%, depending on the cause and the list you are mailing to. The average seems to be around 0.5% to 1.5%. However, once people have given, they become part of your warm list and your next challenge will be to motivate them to give again.

The power of the medium comes not only from the ability to target your message precisely, but also because you can get the same message out to large numbers of people, which provides an economy of scale. The idea is to make the medium as personal as possible, as if you are writing to a friend or colleague. However, as your supporter base gets bigger, the opportunities for making your mailings personal diminish. This depersonalisation will inevitably have an impact on your returns, but one way of addressing this is to break down your base into smaller groups and send them slightly different messages.

This is called segmentation. You will certainly want to say something different to your existing donors from what you say to those who have not yet given. You may then want to subdivide further – for example, separating higher value donors and those who support you with a monthly direct debit, from people who make lower value one-off donations.

Ways to personalise mailings

A personalised communication works far better than a general 'Dear Supporter' letter. If you are writing to thousands of people, you may have to make it more general in appeal but there are still ways to make it appear more personal.

1   Mailmerge your letter or have it laser printed so the donor is addressed by name, for example 'Dear Mr Radcliffe'. Alternatively if you are writing to a small select group you could handwrite the donor's name in the salutation at the start of the letter and your sign off ('Yours sincerely') as well as your signature.

2   Personalisation is not just a matter of name and address. It also includes any detail about them or their giving which you can incorporate into the body of the letter – such as the amount of the last gift and the purpose for which it was given.

3   Use an ordinary stamp rather than having the letter franked. If it is an urgent appeal test using a first class stamp, which can further increase the returns.

4   Have a handwritten postscript at the end of the letter which reinforces the message. This can be printed.

5   Ensure that the response device has the donor's name on it.

6   Use a reply envelope with your name or that of the appeal letter's signatory on it (as well as the organisation and reply address), so that the reply letter is addressed to someone and not to an anonymous organisation.

Components of a mailing

The components of a mailing vary widely. A well used model consists of five parts:

- an outer envelope, with a window to show a name and address on the reply device or at the top of the letter. The envelope can be overprinted with a message to encourage recipients at least to open the letter;
- the letter as the main communication, which should be written to interest and involve the prospective donor as much as possible;
- a coupon or reply device to summarise what the appeal is about, give examples of expected donation levels, and carry any codes and donor identity so that you can keep track of the response;
- a reply envelope to return the reply device and donation. Use Freepost if you can. Making it easy for the donor to reply will increase the response considerably;
- a leaflet: this can help to provide more detail and illustrations of the need that are highlighted in the letter. A leaflet is not always necessary but can be helpful in building a clearer picture for the donor.

This type of pack allows you to include as much information as you feel you need. However, be careful of over-wordy appeals, as they may well go unread. Use pictures to tell the story, case studies and quotes to illustrate that you can make a difference, and graphic devices to break up the text. Think carefully about the envelope and external appearance. This is essential to increase the chances of people opening it rather than putting it straight in the bin. The best-planned and most attractive appeal letter will be completely wasted if no one gets as far as reading it.

Getting the message right

Like any other printed communication, getting the message right is at least half the battle (the other half is getting it to the right people at the right time). For a mailing however there are a number of other things to be aware of.

- *The proposition*. Each mailing should have a central proposition. It might, for example, be '£21.60 can help a child in distress' or 'urgent action is needed to save the rainforests of Brazil'. This central idea should be the visual and verbal theme throughout the mailing pack.
- *The request*. You must be absolutely clear what you want. A good letter will repeat the request for help several times. Then there can be no mis-taking what you really want the reader to do.
- *The length of the message*. There is no rule about this. The important thing is to say what you want to say, and say it effectively. Focus on qual-ity rather than length.

Warm mailings

Sending appeals to your own donors is one of the most profitable ways of raising money. Not everyone can expect to raise £1 million by mailing 80,000 people, although it has been done. The principle is to get the audience, the message and the timing right.

The relatively high response that you can get from warm mailings (to previ-ous donors) is the main reason for building a supporter database. When you include the longer-term support from regular givers and membership sub-scriptions, you might be able to raise as much as £10 for each £1 of fundraising costs. However, you are communicating with one of your most committed audiences. Get the approach and message right and you will raise money; get it wrong, and you can lose support from those you rely on.

There are varying views about how often you should write to your donors. Some people feel that twice a year is an invasion of privacy, while other organisations keep in touch at least once a month (when all the different com-munications from them are included). Trustees often take a very conservative view of this, which can effectively block the sensible development of your direct mail income. Testing is sometimes the only way for you to prove the point that more frequent mailings will be productive. If you find it cost-effective to mail more frequently, then do so; if not, then don't. Alternatively, ask your donors how often they would like to receive information from you. If your supporter base is large enough, divide it into different segments depending on how often each group wants to hear from you. However frequently you plan to contact people, you need to develop a mailing strategy and have a good idea of your programme for the year.

A sample annual mailing plan

A – appeal, R – Annual Report, I – Information Mailing/Survey, U – Upgrade mailing

	April	June	Aug	Oct	Dec
Committed Givers	U	A	I	A	A
Major Donors	U	R	I	A	A
Active Donors	U	A	I	A	A
Lapsed Donors	A		I		A
Enquirers/Prospects	A		I		A

An example of a possible mailing plan, taking into account the need to appeal regularly to good but uncommitted supporters, report back to major donors with an annual report, give core donors an opportunity to upgrade the value or type of their support and to approach lapsed or prospective donors less frequently. Each of the different segments in the plan will require a different package, even if appeals are going out at the same time.

You could develop a newsletter or magazine to keep your regular donors or members informed about and involved in your work. This will be useful in creating a context within which you continue to solicit their support. However, most organisations will be using direct mail to seek money directly. It is beneficial to vary what you are sending them in order to make a high frequency mailing programme less repetitive. For example:

- invite them to become regular givers. This can be extremely effective and very appealing to donors if you start by asking for a small sum each month. But the response rates will be smaller than for a single donation;
- ask them to organise an event or participate in a local collection. This can help get new initiatives going locally. The majority of Oxfam shops started with an appeal for volunteers in the locality;
- suggest that they leave you a legacy. This will not produce cash now, although you can offer an extra option of making a donation as well or instead.

Cold mailings

It is all very well to dream about the returns you could get if only you had a active supporter base of 10,000 people – you have to acquire them first. One of the main ways of doing this is through cold mailings ('cold' because the person receiving your letter has not demonstrated any warmth to your cause before).

You will need to compile names and addresses from available sources or rent lists from a list broker. The main differences between warm and cold mailings lie in the cost and the message. Because the people you are contacting are not your existing supporters, you can expect a poorer response from them. Thus to get the same amount of money you may need to mail to ten times as many cold names at ten times the cost. Then there is also the cost of renting the list. This often forces fundraisers to look for a cheap way of reaching the large numbers necessary to get a response of any size.

Most of the recipients of a cold mailing will not know much about you, so you will need to give a basic description of your work and some reassurance about its value and importance. This may be through endorsements from well known people, or giving answers to frequently asked questions (like the amount spent on administration), or by highlighting your achievements and successes.

Not all of the people on any purchased list will necessarily be unknown to you. Some may be existing supporters and you should check for these before mailing. You could find yourself in an awkward situation if what is perceived as an inappropriate message is sent to one of your major donors.

Other ways to identify good lists in advance are to find out whether the list is already mail responsive, whether there are a high percentage of people on your own list of donors who are also on this list and whether they seem to be the same sort of people as your typical donor.

Before you purchase or rent a new list, you should check whether the list has been used recently, how old it is, whether it has been updated recently (you do not want to be sending letters to out of date addresses or people who have died). Also check whether the list has been regularly checked against the Mailing Preference Service list, in order to remove all those people who have asked not to receive unsolicited mail.

Evaluating mailing lists

Eleven questions to ask before you buy a mailing list:

1   Are the people your supporters or someone else's? If so, could you get them to endorse your appeal?

2   Are they mail order responsive? If this is a list of mail order buyers or postal donors they will be more used to responding in the post.

3   Is this a compiled list or a list of someone's customers/ supporters? Compiled lists do not respond well.

4   Are the people on the list similar to your own donors: by age, gender and attitude?

5   How up-to-date is the list and when was it last updated? Don't buy names of people who are no longer there.

6   Is there a name and home address for each person?

7   Are these people buyers/donors or just enquirers?

8   Have these people bought or given recently? Can you take only the recent ones?

9   Is there any information on frequency of activity? The more frequent the better.

10   When was this list last mailed? The more recently the better.

11   What was the amount of money on average that was given/paid? Are these people likely to be able to give what you need?

Getting the right mailing lists is essential when you are trying to find new supporters. The difference between getting a good mailing list and a poor one may be as much as five times.

[*Commonsense Direct Marketing*, Drayton Bird]

Cold mailings rarely pay for themselves, but if you are not continually adding to your supporter base it will gradually decline as existing supporters die, move or lose interest. You have to balance the cost of acquisition against the likely support you will receive from those who respond. If half the donors continue to support you your original acquisition cost is easier to justify. Some may even go on to leave you a legacy.

When starting from scratch, a direct mail programme will need a certain amount of initial investment. Depending on the sort of response rates you get, you may find that the programme does not begin to generate any surplus for three to four years. However, at that point the income should gradually build up, given good management of the programme.

Local charities may have a significant edge here. It may be easier to find suitable local lists, the local connection can generate additional interest in the work, and cheaper methods of distribution than mail become possible.

If you are doing a large-scale mailing, test it on a small quantity of the names first to see whether enough people are likely to want to support your charity to justify mailing the entire list.

Cold mailing issues

1   Buying other people's lists. Many members of the public regard selling mailing lists as an invasion of their privacy and do not like to receive unsolicited mail. These people will contact you from time to time and complain in the most vocal way. Be prepared with your response.

2   It can appear a waste of money. If only 3% of people respond, then 97% will be throwing all that paper away – which is why it is sometimes referred to as 'junk mail'. It is those who reply, not those who do not, who make direct mail an effective fundraising method, but you do have to watch the response rates and mail out costs to ensure that you are being effective. Even if you are, those that are not responding will think you are wasting both your money and the world's resources. Using recycled paper can give the right signals, despite its greater cost.

3   It is expensive. You must ensure that you have the capacity to invest in this form of fundraising which requires a large expenditure commitment, a significant degree of risk and a payback period of several years. If you can't do it properly, then don't do it at all.

Reciprocal mailings

One answer to the low response rates to cold mailings is to undertake reciprocal mailings. The idea is that your best potential donors are those people who have recently given to you (warm mailings); but the next best are those who are giving to similar organisations. These people are likely to be socially concerned and are known to respond to direct mail appeals. They may also be happy to support two similar causes, so if you mail your supporters with an appeal from a similar charity and they mail your supporters with their appeal, you will both gain. And that's how it usually turns out in practice. Typically, response rates can range from 2.5% to 10%. Try to arrange to mail a similar organisation to your own, even though they may be a near competitor. When undertaking this type of activity you will want to devise a simple policy to safeguard your interests and those of your donors.

Looking after your own supporter database

The most valuable resource you have is your own database of donors, members and supporters. Guard it carefully and manage it properly. Keep it up to date by adding all new donor contacts as soon as possible. Change donor details as soon as you are advised of them – for example, a change of address or a death. Check for duplicates regularly as sending a mailing twice to a donor causes aggravation and wastes money. Do not delete people who have 'opted out' of receiving direct marketing materials from you. Hold them on your database with a code that shows they should not be mailed. If you then get their name from another source, you will not risk annoying them by appearing to disregard their instruction.

Keep track of people who are not giving. Just because someone has not responded for a year or two does not mean that they won't respond in the future – but they are less likely to do so. Do not delete them from your list but put them in a separate coded segment in one of your mailings, and examine the results. You would expect the response and average donation to be lower than your most profitable segments, but is it so low that it is no longer worth mailing these names? Or should they be mailed just once a year? Maybe you could try ringing some of your list to see why they have not been giving before you remove them. Or you could try a different tack with them, for example, asking them for a legacy or trying to reactivate their giving with a more hard hitting appeal.

Before setting up a supporter database and using the information you have collected, it is essential to make sure you comply with the Data Protection Act (see Appendix 2).

Managing your data

Your mailings should be planned a year to 18 months ahead. Segment your data records into different groups depending on when they became a supporter, how much and how they gave, and other relevant characteristics. The larger your supporter database, the more you can segment it. Plan your different messages for each segment. For example, what are you going to say to your regular supporters? Are they to be taken for granted and not written to or thanked and otherwise left alone ... or treated just like any other supporter?

A mailing strategy – simple donor pyramid

This is a broad approach followed by many organisations. The idea is that your direct marketing programme will move individual supporters up through this pyramid. Getting the first gift may be done on a continuous basis with cold mailing, advertising or other mass appeals. Once on board the programme will aim at upgrading supporters to the next level of the pyramid. Of course it is not necessarily true that only people who made major donations to you will leave a legacy – any level of donor may do this as well as people who have never donated to you.

Ensure that the mailings are producing the expected results and keeping within budget. Monitor costs. Get competitive quotes for all items of expenditure and make sure your suppliers keep within this. Plan and monitor expected income (maybe based on results from the last comparable mailing). Useful measures are:

- the response rate (the percentage of people mailed who respond)
- the average donation (how much each person gives on average)
- the combination of these two factors, which is the yield (the money received per hundred people mailed).

It is usually better to focus on both response rate and average donations – as you can do different things to improve each. Improving the response rate is part science and part judgement. The science is in the appropriate testing of your mailings. You can test almost any aspect of what you send by sending a slightly different message to a small sample of the total that you are mailing, and then comparing the results. Test your letter, your message, how you personalise it, and test one group against another. Whatever you do, test just one thing at a time, and ensure the group is large enough to give a statistically valid result. Testing is the way you learn from experience and improve your performance over time.

'The Good Mailing Guide'

1   Use emotion in your writing.

2   Include stories about individuals.

3   Ask for money, directly.

4   Use simple language, avoid jargon.

5   Make all written material visually attractive.

6   Portray your beneficiaries as 'doers' rather than as 'victims', not as helpless, but needing your help.

7   Catch the reader's attention immediately, perhaps with a snappy headline.

8   Use someone specific as the signatory – this could be someone well known, your director or chairman, or a frontline worker.

9   Get the timing right.

10   Make the reader give.

11   Appeal to the reader's conscience.

12   Read what you are sending before sending it – would you give in response to your own appeal letter?

This is a list of success factors developed by Oxfam after studying ten years of appeals to supporters.

Getting help

Direct mail is a highly technical fundraising method. You will need to be skilled at:

- writing effective copy
- producing a cost-effective mailing package
- knowing how much to ask for
- planning a mailing programme
- selecting the best lists to rent
- testing (and coding) of the response
- knowing what response rates to expect
- evaluating your performance.

You may not have all (or indeed any) of these skills but you can use:

- professional consultants, who specialise in this medium. Since you are paying for their expertise, it is as well to know precisely what you need, brief them well, and have a contract that sets out precisely what they are expected to do and for how much;
- direct marketing agencies. For the hard pressed, a direct marketing agency will carry out all the necessary functions for a fee. This has the advantage of getting the work off your desk, but it can be expensive;

- freelance help. Designers and copywriters are available freelance, and can be used in conjunction with yourself or with other sources of help and advice;

- fulfilment agencies or mailing houses. The mailing can involve a great deal of work sorting out which letters go to which people and putting everything into the right envelope within a reasonable time. Mailing houses will perform these functions at a much greater speed than you are likely to be able to manage, unless your mailing is quite small. Another advantage of using a mailing house is that they can help you claim a postal discount for bulk mailings;

- other charities with direct mail programmes, who might be prepared to share their knowledge and experience with you.

As with other areas of fundraising the key to direct mail is start small, experiment and build up. You need to constantly analyse response rates and test new ideas before rolling out your mailings to larger groups of donors.

Door drops

Door drops are another method of acquiring new donors. They require a mailing pack similar to the sort that you might prepare for a cold mailing and can be delivered by the Royal Mail, by agencies who specialise in delivering un-addressed mail or by volunteers.

The advantages of this type of cold donor recruitment are that it is cheaper to deliver than mail and can be distributed to large areas of the country quite cost effectively. The disadvantages are that it is not personalised, gets lower response rates and so needs to go to larger volumes to achieve equivalent returns to cold mailing, and has a higher rate of anonymous donations.

14.3 Telephone fundraising

The telephone is now a key fundraising medium. Both incoming and outgoing calls are important for the fundraiser. Incoming calls include enquiries and telephone pledges in response to an appeal. Outward bound telemarketing, which requires some skill, can be used for a whole range of promotional and fundraising activities.

Donation lines

Special response lines for people to call in and make a donation are now commonplace. Donors appreciate being able to make credit (or debit) card donations by telephone in response to an appeal.

You can use a separate number for the response line, which should be answered by someone briefed to receive these calls. Answer machines are not ideal; donors want to speak to a real person. However, if you do need to use one make sure that the message is clear, that donors are told exactly what information to leave and that the answer tapes are long enough to record a number of calls.

If the calls come through a switchboard or receptionist it is important that there is an effective procedure for taking calls, and that the person receiving the call knows what to do. If you spend a good deal of time out of the office, you will want information about people phoning in passed to you quickly.

Premium telephone lines

There are various special lines offered by British Telecom through their Value Call Service. One arrangement shares the revenue between the telephone company and you, the subscriber. The caller pays a premium rate per minute at peak times, and slightly less at other times. The line can be used in conjunction with radio, TV or a mailshot promotion, or to receive donations or give out information.

Other special numbers available give the caller access to you at local rates irrespective of where they call from, and you are charged for this. Or they can allow callers to telephone you at your expense.

Answering services

For some campaigns, you will want to have someone actually answering the phone, but may not have the facilities or staff to do this. One option is to use volunteers. You need to find and brief the volunteers and for large appeals you may want to get additional lines installed. For emergency appeals, you may need to arrange everything in a very short space of time.

Another option is to use a telephone agency, which will have the necessary equipment and trained operators you require. Not only will they answer the phone, but for an additional charge they will deal with any follow up mailings and provide a detailed analysis of the response. This service can be quite expensive, so be sure to get a quote first.

Recruitment and renewals

The telephone can also be used to recruit people to do house-to-house collections, to recruit and keep in touch with people participating in a fundraising event, and so on. It is also an excellent way to get people to renew their membership or increase the value of their committed regular gift.

You may consider using the telephone simply to find out if your supporters have any questions to ask you. Too many telephone calls (and also too many fundraising letters) are concerned with what the charity wants to tell its supporters rather than listening to the supporter's ideas, questions and concerns. Why not simply ring people up to find out if they are happy with what they receive from you and whether there is anything else they would like to know? You may find out some very interesting things about who your supporters are and be able to begin to identify some trends in their behaviour. However, if you are going to do this you must be prepared to listen to their ideas. If they ask you not to ring them again, don't.

Another good use of the telephone is raising money for an emergency. If there is a famine and people are dying, or a spell of bitter weather is giving elderly people hypothermia, then this is a good reason to call your supporters.

What can be done over the phone

In preparation for the World Trade Organisation talks in November 1999, Friends of the Earth developed an integrated telephone and mail campaign in order to communicate some complex and new issues to their supporters. Some supporters were expected to question why Friends of the Earth would be concerned with international trade agreements.

The mailing went out in October 1999, and the phone campaign followed six weeks later, to coincide with the talks themselves. Both were targeted at people already giving to the organisation regularly by standing order asking them to increase the value of their gift.

The appeal was a huge success with both mail and phone elements performing well above their expected targets. The mailing received a total response of 13.5%, over three times what had been budgeted to be received and over four times better than any other upgrade appeal by Friends of the Earth. The phone campaign attained a total response of 33.4%, 30% greater than the budgeted figure. The average upgrade received increased the annual value of supporter's donations by over a third.

The telephone is an expensive way of contacting people so it needs to be used with care. It is unlikely to be a cost effective way of soliciting one-off low value donations (unless they are taken by credit card). However, it comes into its own when you want to develop your donors by moving them from being occasional givers to committed monthly donors, and it can be particularly helpful for negotiating the amount of the donation. Response rates can be over 50% when calling past donors, which is well in excess of normal mailing response rates. However, you will need to send them a letter and form to set up their regular gift, unless you are in a position to offer 'paperless direct debits'. So you would expect around 60% of pledged donations to be converted into actual support at the end of the day.

Getting your message across on the telephone

Successful outbound telephoning needs a good script containing:

- information about the caller and the organisation represented;
- confirmation as to whether it is a good time to talk. For example, if the person being called is about to have a meal they may not wish to stop and talk, so carrying on with the call may cause annoyance. You might also mention how long the call is likely to take;
- reference to previous support or past contact. When calling people who have supported you before, it is important to refer to their past help and thank them;
- a short introduction about the current progress of the organisation and its plans help set the scene for a request for further help;
- a call to action. As with any other form of communication, you should not expect that supporters will necessarily know why you want their support unless you state it explicitly. The call to action must be very direct and clear, and should state precisely what you want them to do. Getting a pledge or a verbal agreement is usually the best you can hope to do over the phone – unless you are seeking a credit card donation or you have a paperless direct debit facility (in which case you can complete the transaction there and then);
- a follow up reminder. You can say that any pledge made over the phone will be followed by a letter or form to sign. This follow up should be done as soon as possible to achieve maximum response.

Deciding who to call is not always easy as your data records may not include your supporter's phone numbers. If you plan to use the telephone, then perhaps you should start including a space on reply coupons or in your promotional literature for the supporter to give you their phone number. There is also then the implication that if they let you have this, they will not mind being called. If you do not have sufficient data records with numbers you may need to look these up. For larger campaigns, there are organisations who can source this information for you; they will also check for anyone who has registered with the Telephone Preference Service not to receive telemarketing calls.

You will need to recruit and train your callers; this is definitely not something just anybody can do. Successful callers will have an easy outgoing confidence that is communicated over the phone. Though many people are used to the phone, put them in a situation where they have to ask a supporter to give, and they become reluctant and tongue-tied.

Using an agency

You may want to take your telephone solicitation out of house by sub-contracting the work to an agency. This can be very helpful for a major telephone campaign. But the use of an agency to solicit funds means that they have to comply with the requirements of the 1992 Charities Act (see box).

Telemarketing and the requirements of the 1992 Charities Act

If you employ an agency to make calls on your behalf, then they are a 'professional fundraiser' under the terms of the 1992 Charities Act. There are a number of requirements:

- a written agreement between the charity and the professional fundraiser in a prescribed form (the Institute of Fundraising has a model form);
- a statement to be given to potential donors informing them as to what proportion of their donation will be used to pay the costs of the fundraiser;
- a cooling off period. When a professional fundraiser uses the telephone to solicit money or to sell goods to raise money for your charity, and people respond with payments, then the professional fundraiser must, within seven days of receipt of the payment, write to people who have given or paid more than £50 giving them the right to cancel. The donor then has seven days to cancel the gift. This only applies to telephone solicitation by a professional fundraiser or commercial participator, and not to funds solicited by the charity's staff or by volunteers, who are not covered by these provisions;
- when a professional fundraiser is used, donors have to be sent a written statement which details what the money is to be spent on and the basis on which the fundraiser will be remunerated.

The agency will need to make a statement about the fact that they are being paid to fundraise for you, and this may antagonise donors if not handled carefully. You will need to be prepared to get involved with the preparation of scripts and be ready to modify them if necessary as the campaign progresses. You will also need to keep in touch with the campaign, visiting the agency to listen to live calls to check that your charity's reputation is being maintained. For a major campaign, carry out tests with an agency. This will incur start-up costs, but will lift much of the burden of the work at this stage from you. If the test looks like being successful, you can then explore the logistics of doing the campaign in-house or recruiting a team of home-based part-time callers.

Whichever way you set about it, you need to make sure of two things: firstly that your supporters are happy to be telephoned and, crucially, have not registered with the Telephone Preference Service; and secondly that it is a cost effective method of fundraising for you.

14.4 Personal solicitation

Meeting and speaking to potential donors face to face is an extremely powerful fundraising technique. There are several forms of personal solicitation that are currently used by charities:

- recruiting committed supporters in the street or from door to door
- talks at public events
- visits to people's homes
- making presentations at private meetings

All these give opportunities for persuasion, questions to be asked and answered, and for reassurance on matters of concern. The degree of personal interaction between the charity and the donor is what sets this apart from other fundraising techniques.

Door to door cold solicitation

This type of face to face fundraising can be daunting as there is usually no known history of support or expressed interest in giving as a reason for the visit. Though this sounds a thoroughly unpromising way of winning supporters, it can work very well in the hands of specially trained fundraisers. The technique is unlike house-to-house collecting, in that you will usually be asking for a regular or high value gift, and so part of the process will need to take place inside the home rather than on the doorstep. However, like a house-to-house collection, there are licensing requirements.

Though some organisations (such as the Karuna Trust) have been doing this type of fundraising for many years, it is now going through a period of quite rapid growth. Individual fundraisers are usually assigned an area and they will visit streets they identify as good prospective sites for their fundraising. They will then call at individual houses, initially leaving information about the charity and making an appointment to return another time once the householder has had an opportunity to consider whether they want to give their support. This type of fundraising can also be carried out on behalf of a group of voluntary organisations.

The fundraisers need to put in a lot of footwork and be prepared for many rejections. However, it can be a very effective method of recruiting committed givers. It is also particularly suitable for getting support for local community projects where donors can see the need and the benefits on their own doorstep. If this technique is of interest, you will either need to train and run your own team (which can take a lot of time and effort) or employ an agency to do it for you.

Street solicitation

This type of face to face fundraising, also known as 'Direct Dialogue', was brought to the UK by Greenpeace from Germany in the late 1990s. Since then it has mushroomed.

The principle is that small groups of trained fundraisers set up on a busy street or in a shopping centre to recruit committed support (usually with a monthly direct debit). Cash is not collected. They wear branded tabards or jackets so that they are clearly recognisable as working on behalf of a particular organisation.

Currently these teams are mostly run by fundraising agencies and the cost is based on the number of new supporters recruited, not the value of the individual gift. This type of recruitment is expensive but can be very cost effective as, in most cases, people are making regular monthly gifts. If you are considering testing this way of recruiting support, contact the Public Fundraising Regulatory Authority, which has been set up by charities actually using this method of fundraising, for advice and information.

Presentations at events

You may have the chance to make a presentation at meetings, conferences or other events. This is an opportunity to speak directly to people about the work of your organisation and its needs. With an experienced speaker, this can also be a good opportunity for raising money. When you are speaking at someone else's event, you may need their approval if you plan to collect money or distribute fundraising literature.

The presentation has to be carefully thought out. Why should that group of people be particularly interested in your work? The answer may be that they are not, but have been attracted by the activity you have organised. If you do not engage their interest, you won't get their support.

Next, you need to work out how you want your audience to respond. You could give out information with donation forms included, carry out a collection at the exits, or write to them afterwards.

Other people's events offer you new audiences, but you can organise your own events for existing and potential supporters. These can be visits, study tours or open days to see your organisation at work, small discussions with an expert speaker so that they can see the problems you are addressing in greater depth, or receptions, perhaps at the home of a well-respected donor and possibly with a guest speaker and some sort of presentation afterwards.

Such events can be excellent for fundraising. You will make your existing donors feel important and give them a better understanding of the issues. This may lead them to give more substantial support or to volunteer.

Warm visits

Warm visiting involves face to face meetings with people who have already supported you or with whom you already have contact. There are two reasons for doing this:

- to talk about your work rather than to specifically ask for money, so as to find out more about their interests and develop a closer relationship with them. This is an investment in the relationship which you hope might lead to more committed giving or a legacy later on;
- as part of a major appeal, when you need to get support and are making a personal presentation on the work of the organisation to a potential new supporter.

How to prepare for visiting a donor

- Have precise information on the individual's past support so that you can thank them and tell them what you have been able to do with their money. Try to locate a particular interest or concern of theirs and show how you are working in that field. In other words, listen first and suggest second.
- Be well briefed about the work of the organisation, so that you can talk about current efforts and future plans in an informed and interesting way. Take photographs or leaflets to show.
- Have some idea of the support you need, and the ways in which they might be able to help you so that if the opportunity arises, you can introduce the idea of further support.
- Know about tax-effective giving – this can be one excuse for being there in the first place – and tell them how their money can be used even more efficiently, by donating it tax-effectively.

You will need to fix an appropriate time and place for the meeting. The charity's offices are often the best place because they give people a more of a feeling for the organisation. Alternatively, some people will feel more comfortable in their own homes. You can go along as well, but the best person to do the actual asking is the person who introduced the potential donor to you, and they need to be properly briefed.

Don't be in too much of a hurry to make the ask; this needs to be correctly timed and may come at a subsequent meeting, after the person's interest has been stimulated and they have had time to consider. Also, listen to what the potential supporter is saying and respond accordingly. Fundraising is not about telling someone what you think they should know; it is about engaging their interest and understanding their needs.

Resources to develop for face to face solicitation

If you are keen to use personal solicitation as a fundraising tool for committed and major gifts or legacies, here are some suggestions for what you will need.

- People who are really good speakers and presenters. You might decide to develop a panel of people who are interested in your organisation and good at speaking at meetings.
- Existing donors who are prepared to speak at meetings to be attended by potential new donors. There is nothing like having people say, 'This organisation is great, and I've given to it' for motivating others to give.
- Volunteers with similar skills for warm visits.
- Good handout material that can be used to illustrate the points you are making. For presentations you may want to use Powerpoint, an overhead projector or a flipchart or even a short video to help get your message across.

All visits should be prepared with care. Rehearse the presentation thoroughly. You should try to predict what questions will come up. Go prepared with photos, brochures, budgets and plans so that you can use these as prompts. Finally, remember to leave some prepared material behind. Most people will not make up their minds immediately, and will be guided or reminded or helped to respond by what you have left with them.

Throughout the meeting, you should give people the opportunity to ask questions. If you are not getting much feel for how the meeting is going, ask some questions yourself. Do they feel it is an important issue? Do they think the project will achieve what it is setting out to do?

At some point you will need to make the request for money. There are different approaches to this. One is to say that you want them to consider helping in one of several ways. A direct approach dispenses with niceties, explains the urgency of the need, and simply asks for money. Always try to ask for a specific amount.

14.5 Advertising for support

Advertising in a newspaper or magazine can be used to promote your cause or to raise money, but it is expensive. You can raise money directly through making an appeal, or indirectly by recruiting members, volunteers or generating enquirers for further information (who you would then approach for support later on). Advertising is extremely successful in raising money at the time of a disaster or when a particular issue has hit the headlines. At times like this your advertisement will reach people when they know that something needs to be done – and you are offering them a way of helping.

There are various ways for you to advertise:

- in the press – taking space in national or local newspapers, through display advertising or small ads (also known as 'off the page' advertising);
- advertising in magazines and journals (general interest or specialist);
- loose inserts in a newspaper or magazine;
- posters (both billboard advertising and smaller posters displayed on notice boards);
- advertising on TV and radio.

Nine questions to ask before you advertise

I find it useful to start work on appeal advertising by thinking of myself as person to person fundraiser, about to set off, ringing the doorbells of potential donors. Like a salesman (for that's what I am), I ask myself these questions:

- Which are the best doorbells to ring?
- How have I identified them?
- What kind of people live behind these doors?
- What's the best time to 'call', remembering the clamour for their attention?
- What's their lifestyle; their attitudes; discretionary income; knowledge of and sympathy for my organisation's work?
- How do I best get a hearing?
- How do I get them to open the door and invite me in?
- What shall I ask them to do and how can I most successfully get them to do it?
- How do I retain their continued interest and practical support?

Not until I have answered these questions am I ready to see how my charity's need can be translated into the 'calls' I'm going to make in printed advertisements. I'm not writing to a mass audience. I'm writing to individuals; to the reader, my press ad (like my mailing), must come as a personal message, telling her or him of a need, so that it evokes a personal reaction and response. But the initial impact needs to be swift, or it will never retain attention.

[*The Printed Fundraiser*, Harold Sumption]

Newspaper advertising

The main problem with press advertising is the high cost, even for a limited amount of space, so messages have to be succinct and eye catching. However, you can select your audience by the known readership of the paper or magazine; you can also predict whether your issue is likely to be given editorial coverage and, if so, whether or not this will be done sympathetically.

The most you can hope for (except in exceptional circumstances) is that a press advert will give a 3:1 revenue to cost ratio. Most organisations will not achieve anything like this, and many find that the returns are substantially lower than the costs. It may be that what you can achieve with advertising would also be achieved more cheaply with effective and well-targeted PR.

How big a space should you use?

Space size	Responses
1/4 page	48
1/2 page	71
3/4 page	87
full page	100
Double page	141

This table illustrates what research and practical experience has shown about the disproportionate effect of using small spaces in advertising. The responses are those you would expect to receive indexed against a full page. You should bear in mind that you may be able to get a larger space for a greater discount and thus counter the advantage of taking a smaller space.

[Commonsense Direct Marketing]

Opportunistic advertising

The most exciting aspect of advertising is its flexibility. You can place an advertisement almost immediately, so if a disaster or some other high profile event happens one day, you could be appealing for help the next morning.

What might be classed as a disaster? This is not necessarily a serious emergency, but what your public is being told is serious by newspapers and other news media. A famine overseas is an obvious example, or the domestic disasters that occur from time to time, such as a major oil spill. Then there are the regular 'disasters' that are perceived or stage managed, such as the plight of homeless people in the winter highlighted by appeals run by Crisis or Shelter around Christmas, when the weather is getting cold and public sympathy is high. Timing is everything, and one estimate is that 30% of your response is likely to come just from getting this right.

Acquisition advertising

This is all about finding new supporters who can be put on your mailing list and profitably appealed to at a later date. For example The Refugee Council took full page adverts in the papers to invite donations to support destitute asylum seekers in this country. Very little surplus was made over the costs of the advertising yet hundreds of new donors gave support. Many will go on to give more substantial sums on a regular basis. Beyond this, the space allowed the organisation the opportunity to talk about its work at a time it badly wanted to raise the profile of the issue of refugees.

Decide before you start how much you can spend to recruit a new supporter. Some organisations are happy if they can find new supporters for £50 each, although in the end it depends on how much you can expect to raise from each supporter in the longer term.

Awareness advertising

If no one knows much about you or if you want to launch a new campaign, you may need to build awareness first, rather than immediately try to raise money or recruit supporters. Awareness advertising is expensive and difficult to measure, and it often demands the use of very large spaces with the advertising continuing over a period of time.

Although this approach is often used by large companies, it may not be the best way of using limited charitable funds. It may be that the effective use of PR will buy a good deal more awareness than any amount of advertising. However, one advantage of paying for the space is you can control both the timing and content of the message.

Loose inserts

One of the main problems with buying space in newspapers is the size constraint. To buy a 20 cm space across two columns in a national broadsheet may cost over £4,000, so the space you will be able to afford is very limited. Loose inserts, like the illustration for WWF UK on the right, can address this problem. Depending on the publication, anything from a small leaflet to a Christmas gift catalogue can be inserted or bound into a publication.

There are four important differences between an insert and an advertisement.

- There is much more space available to you and you can even include an envelope with the insert, although there may be restrictions on the weight, size or shape of the insert imposed by the publisher, and the print cost will vary with the size of the insert. This makes inserts an ideal medium to describe your work and set out the different ways of supporting your organisation. Inserts can work extremely well for membership recruitment, campaigns for committed giving such as child and community sponsorship schemes, and those appeals that demand space if they are to be promoted effectively.
- The cost per recipient is much higher, but inserts can be very cost-effective because of the combination of the space available to you, cost and value for money factors, and the ability to include a response mechanism as part of the printed insert.
- Inserts take time to arrange and produce so, unlike adverts, cannot easily be produced to take advantage of topical events.
- They can be easily detached from the publication, without damaging it; on the other hand, they can also fall out and get lost, or thrown away.

Inserts also provide excellent opportunities for testing the message or format of an appeal.

Evaluating the results

You should always try to evaluate the effectiveness of any advertising you pay for by using a coded coupon, special reply address or phone number in the advertisement or insert. The coding should be done for the campaign as a whole, and for each separate promotion within it. This is the only way you can find out which medium works best for you. Results can then be measured in terms of:

- income raised per £ of media cost
- cost per new donor recruited.

In the case of awareness advertising, you can do research before and after to measure any increased awareness generated by the campaign – this is expensive, so is only really viable for major campaigns by large charities.

Posters

Posters fit least well into the fundraising area, largely because they don't allow for an immediate response, but they are nonetheless a useful promotional medium. They can range from the huge 96 sheet hoardings visible on main roads right down to the smaller posters and handbills used in windows and on notice boards.

Commercial posters

Posters are an extremely potent communications medium. Their impact depends on the size of the image and the extent of the coverage, but naturally it requires a great deal of both to get a message across, and this is expensive. Charities can use the medium in small bursts to highlight a special week or the launch of a campaign, either nationally or in a chosen area or, like political parties at election time, they can rent a site for a day to promote a poster which will generate controversy and media coverage.

It is also important to understand what posters cannot do. Posters cannot be used in rural areas – most sites being in towns and cities. They do not allow for any direct response, except via a phone number. In any event, the time for which people see a poster, either in a car or walking around a town, is extremely short and in neither case are they particularly well-placed to respond to your appeal. Thus, at best, posters can only act as an awareness medium to support other activities.

Mini-posters and handbills

In a different league from the commercial poster industry are the small posters or handbills which are used to publicise almost anything locally. These are attractive for fundraising, since they can be printed cheaply and displayed free. One commonly used idea is to print a poster as a part of one of your leaflets for example, so the leaflet folds out to become a poster

Depending on what you are promoting, these mini-posters can be targeted at whoever you want. They can be put in windows, in local shops, on library notice boards, in community centres, in schools, or anywhere you feel you can reach your target audience. Volunteers can distribute thousands of posters and leaflets and create a highly visible campaign at little cost.

Advertising on TV

Television advertising is very expensive, so it is important to identify realistic objectives for any advertisement. If you simply wish to promote a message you should note the Independent Television Commission rules on what you are allowed to say. Alternatively you may want to advertise activities going on in the regions or around the country. The Children's Society and Christian Aid have both used TV advertising to support their national fundraising weeks. This can give your volunteers moral support and make the public aware in advance of a flag day or house-to-house collection. Direct response advertising on TV (DRTV) is much more widely used. This differs from the classic commercial in that it invites donors to make a donation by phone with a credit card. The other way this is being used is to recruit committed donors on to low value monthly gifts by direct debit. Both Oxfam and the National Canine Defence League have been very successful in doing this.

Air time can be bought in a range of ways. Individual spots can be purchased, but are extremely expensive at peak times. The evidence suggests that off-peak times such as afternoons and late at night are better for charity advertising. In this case, packages of spots might be purchased at a discount.

The choice of media depends on your objective: if it is to get a message across to a national audience then the independent network, Channel 4, breakfast TV, or a satellite or cable channel can be used. If you are a local charity or want to test your commercial in one region, then use the appropriate regional TV station.

Getting the message right can be difficult. If it has little impact, you risk wasting the chance to bring your charity to the attention of millions. But if you attempt to make it too strong and emotive, you risk having the advertisement turned down by the broadcasters or the regulators. It is advisable to check with the appropriate authority on what is acceptable before committing to too much expense.

TV commercials are expensive to produce, costing anything from £15,000 upwards, depending upon whether you do the shooting in a studio or on location. To cut down on costs, you can try asking the professionals to donate their services free, use existing film or slide based material, use a personality (preferably in a studio), find a partner to share the cost, or get the advertisement sponsored.

Advertising on radio

Advertising on radio has the advantage that it is much cheaper than television, and can be tailored to a local audience. Radio time is bought in exactly the same way as TV time. National packages are available, but radio can be especially useful for supporting local or regional events. It would be quite normal for an advertising agency to place adverts with a dozen or so radio stations to cover one part of the country. For example, a concert, shops or a charity week can be promoted on local radio stations in the catchment area of the audience. This information does not require any visual treatment.

The creative possibilities with radio are considerable, but will require the help of professionals. Ask your local radio station whether they can help prepare your commercial. Radio lends itself well to competitions, celebrity voices and to repetition. You can expect well-known voices to give their time free, if properly approached. The cost of production may be from hundreds of pounds to a few thousand. If you have to distribute tapes widely, this will be an additional cost.

Advertising issues

1 Seeing it through other people's eyes. In fundraising, it is necessary to illustrate the cause in some way. Images of the beneficiary and their needs are among the most powerful means of generating a response. But what effect might this have on the beneficiaries themselves or on public attitudes towards the cause? Organisations dealing with the problems of disability use much less harrowing pictures, especially when they are controlled by the people with disabilities. Many opt for positive and optimistic images.

2 Free or fee? A number of campaigns have been developed using free space whenever it becomes available. The disadvantage is that you have no control over the intensity or timing of your campaign.

Once you have decided to use advertising, there are two key decisions to take: how to design and produce your advertising and how to place it. You can do both, but you will never be able to purchase media as cheaply as a media buyer or an advertising agency. Developing a creative approach and the production have traditionally been the function of advertising agencies.

So unless you are conducting a small scale local campaign you are quite likely to need the input of an agency and must budget for this.

Television and radio appeals

As well as paying for advertising there are opportunities for free coverage of one sort or another. The opportunities for free appeals are limited. However, you can use TV to get your message across in ways other than a direct appeal and these can, if well coordinated, enhance your other fundraising work. The main opportunities for using TV are:

- The Lifeline appeal
- Community Service Announcements
- Editorial appeals.

If you do get an appeal slot, Broadcasting Support Services can supply you with a copy of the Charter and Recommendations of the Broadcasting Appeals Consortium. In addition, you should be aware that if you use professional fundraisers in the course of the appeal, there are specific requirement concerning the donor's right to cancel.

Strategy for broadcast appeals

	Large national charity	Small national charity	Local charity
Type of appeal			
Lifeline TV appeal	✗	✓	✗
Editorial TV	✓	✓	✓
Public Service Announcement	✓	✓	✗
Community Action programming	✓	✓	✓
Telethons	✓	✓	✓
Editorial radio	✓	✓	✓
Radio 4 appeal	✗	✓	✗
TV adverts	✓	✗	✗
Radio adverts	✓	✓	✓

The Lifeline appeal

Lifeline is the name used for BBC TV appeals, but the mechanisms are similar for ITV appeals. To get an appeal you must apply either to the BBC or the Independent Television Commission. Both are advised by the Central Appeals Advisory Committee about which appeals should be given air time. Appeals are allocated TV time on monthly slots, usually on Sundays. There are opportunities for appeals UK-wide as well as nationally in Scotland, Northern Ireland and Wales.

You are allowed to apply once every two years (every three years after a successful application) to the BBC and to the ITC, but you can never guarantee that you will be granted a slot. You only have to fill in a simple form, so if you feel that your charity has significant public interest and appeal, why not apply every two years? If you are successful, the publicity and the financial support generated can be considerable, although the sums raised can vary wildly. In 1999 money raised ranged from below £725 up to £170,000.

If you obtain an appeal slot, you need to think about how to make the most of it. The first step should be to meet the producer allocated to you by the broadcasters. You will want to discuss with them the general approach to the appeal, the presenter, and how the script will be developed. Charities are not expected to have all the required broadcasting skills, so broadcasters offer these services. You may want to develop your script in-house, based on your more intimate knowledge of the organisation and its work.

An important decision is who will be the presenter. Actors are popular, as they can bring most scripts alive. The person should also be credible to the audience perhaps through some existing connection with your charity or cause, or because they have the right style. The broadcasters will be able to suggest possible names to you and help you approach them. The actual production of the appeal will be organised by the broadcasters, who will provide you with a producer with the appropriate skills. All that remains for you, the fundraiser, to do is to ensure that you have enough staff, or preferably volunteers, who will be able to handle the donations and enquiries that arise.

Community Service Announcements

CSV Media, part of the organisation Community Service Volunteers works with charities and other voluntary organisations helping them to produce appeals and campaigns on regional TV, local radio, and the BBC's Ceefax pages. These are known as Community Service Announcements (CSAs). They are an extremely good way of recruiting volunteers and they are free.

CSV Media also provide action desks at local BBC and independent radio stations and to regional television stations. Contact CSV Media direct or your local independent TV or radio station for more information.

Community action programmes

A number of TV and radio stations broadcast community action programmes. These are short programmes covering the work of voluntary organisations, and are not appeals for money. Each station has its own format. Some organise weekly or monthly programmes, each of which covers a specific local issue.

These programmes generally do not focus on one organisation. Opportunities lie in the chance to get the issues you are dealing with on air, to help in the research for the programme, to get coverage for your work, to produce or be included in the printed material that is made available to responders, and in providing volunteers to deal with enquiries.

Other opportunities exist where there is a series of programmes on a particular theme which relates to your work. These are often backed up with materials and include contact points, and these are sent to responders and distributed in the community – to schools, churches and so on. One charity, for example, was invited to produce a guide to services for people who had suffered sexual abuse.

In September 2000, the Media Trust launched the Community Channel on Sky Digital. This is a specialist channel for the voluntary sector putting out programming produced by the charities themselves. Present viewing figures are low and restricted to those with access to the relevant broadcasting formats. But there are hopes that this channel will establish itself and gain an audience over the next few years.

Editorial appeals

Each year, especially at Christmas, some TV magazine and news programmes feature some sort of appeal. Usually they do this only once a year and they always plan well ahead. Blue Peter is the best known example, supporting charities that appeal to children. In their case money is rarely sought – stamps, clothes and other convertible items being the usual object of the appeal. Local and regional news programmes have similar appeals.

To get your charity featured, you must make yourselves known to the producers of the programmes, and in the first instance to their researchers. This should be done at least six months in advance, and preferably well before then. If you can create a link between the audience and the appeal, you are more likely to be successful.

Special fundraising telethons

Telethons were a feature of the 1980s and 1990s and look set to continue to raise relatively large sums. They are to an extent a counterbalance to the pulling power of the large charities, as most of the proceeds are distributed to smaller and local charities.

- The BBC Children in Need appeal began appearing annually as a TV and radio appeal in 1980, and consistently raises over £20 million annually for children's charities.
- This was followed in some style by Live Aid in 1984, which was run as a one-off to raise money for famine relief in Africa.

- Comic Relief has been run every other year from 1986 by Charity Projects, and raised £35 million in 1999 for development projects in Africa and selected causes in the UK.

There are opportunities for charities to be featured as part of the telethon broadcasting, but the main chance is to apply for and get a donation of money after the event from Children in Need and Comic Relief (see chapter 6 on grant-making trusts).

Radio appeals

Radio must surely rate as the most under-exploited fundraising medium, as it holds many opportunities for the imaginative and energetic fundraiser. Possibilities include:

- the Radio 4 Appeal;
- Community Service Announcements. The procedure is the same as for television;
- paid advertising (see earlier in this section);
- editorial coverage. Nationally there are opportunities in programmes such as *You and Yours*; locally, news and chat show programmes present the best opportunities;
- phone-ins. It is always possible to phone in to a chat programme, or to get your supporters to do so, to express a point of view, promote an activity or make a request for support.

The Radio 4 Appeal (previously known as The Week's Good Cause)

Each week Radio 4 dedicates a slot on Sunday mornings to a charitable appeal. The procedures for getting an appeal are identical to that described for the Lifeline Appeal (see above). You can never guarantee that you will get a slot, but as for Lifeline appeals on TV, there is nothing to be lost, and you should consider applying every two years.

The estimated average donation for these radio appeals is £33.87. However, in 1999 approximately 60% of the appeals broadcast raised less than £10,000.

14.6 Fundraising on the internet

Since the late 1990s the internet has developed rapidly as a widely used medium for communication. There are few fundraisers who are not aware of it, but its potential for fundraising has not yet been properly realised. Whether the internet becomes a serious medium for fundraising will depend upon how fundraisers decide to use it, but will be helped by:

- the continuing growth in the number of households with computers and modems;
- the number of people signed up to an Internet Service Provider (ISP);
- the growing availability of cheaper, faster telephone lines;
- the growth of internet access via TVs and mobile phones.

The internet is not a temporary craze and will most likely become an important medium for fundraising. Three issues will determine exactly how useful the internet will be to fundraisers.

The first is the development of secure payment systems. The obvious way of transferring money over the internet is to use a credit card. However, the opportunity for fraud is considerable – although this is true for other fundraising methods as well. If charities encourage members of the public to commit their credit card details to the internet, and if that information gets picked up by unauthorised users, then everyone loses. To counter this risk, there are systems of encryption available. You should definitely not consider asking for credit card details unless you can guarantee that these will be sent to a secure server and that you will be able to collect the details equally securely. There are also many new developments in ways of making payments that can be used on the internet – for example, paperless direct debits, where payments can be set up from a donor's bank without the need for their signature.

The second is the development of internet banking, which is giving people greater confidence in internet security. In fact keeping an eye on what banks, utilities and organisations like Charities Aid Foundation and NCVO are doing in this area can also help you keep abreast of the possibilities of this medium for fundraising.

Thirdly, there is the growth of on-line shopping. If people are routinely shopping on-line, it is a simple step either to buying charity goods on line or making donations.

Anoraks or donors?

2.35 million people in the UK have used the internet in the last 12 months (2000/2001)

80% were ABC1s

35% earned more than £25,000 pa

34% were between 25 and 34 years old

33% were between 35 and 55 years old

Possible uses of the internet

For fundraisers, the internet presents a number of opportunities with others undoubtedly emerging in the future.

- It is an ideal medium to explain the details of your work to those who are interested. The number of charity websites is growing and many take the opportunity of the ease of updating information to publish news about their latest campaigns on their website. The medium lends itself not only to providing this sort of information, but to linking it with all other aspects of the organisation's work, such as the recruitment of new members, or encouraging people to attend events.

- For those organising events, the internet provides special opportunities. One US charity has organised a silent auction. Bidders send in bids for donated items and within a given period, the bids accumulate. At the end of the period, the highest bidder wins the item they wanted. Comic Relief use the internet to publicise their Red Nose Days and also take donations – during their 1999 appeal almost £500,000 was raised through the internet.

- There are now opportunities to build closer personal links with supporters. With their co-operation, supporters can receive the most up to date information about you tailored to their interests whenever they log on to your site.

For organisations looking for more direct financial support there are a number of methods that can be used.

- *Simple appeals*. Many organisations now put appeals or opportunities to donate on their website as well as through more traditional channels, such as mail. However, more sophisticated ways of getting donations are being tested by larger charities such as the NSPCC. As part of their Full Stop campaign they set up a donate-4-free website with the involvement of their website sponsors. All people had to do was click on the donate-4-free button and a donation would be made for them.

- *Printed appeals*. Many internet users will be able to print the contents of screens that they have downloaded from the internet. This can then be used to solicit support. For example, the screen becomes a donation form, a membership form, or a standing order form, which can then be filled in with the relevant information and printed out to become a fully completed pledge form. The drawback of this is that it still requires to be put into the post – and so still has many of the problems of direct mail – requiring an envelope, a stamp and a trip to the post box.
- *E-mail appeals*. As the number of your supporters with access to the internet grows you can collect their e-mail addresses and send donation appeals to them. Oxfam now regularly e-mails 20,000 of their supporters.
- *Information provision*. The internet can be a very cost effective way to supply information to your donors. You could develop an e-mail newsletter to send out to your donors.
- *On-line shopping*. Some charities who trade through catalogues are now putting these on line to sell directly. Again, the main issue here is making the customer feel happy about paying by credit card online.
- *Credit card giving*. Undoubtedly the way of the future lies in being able to commit support immediately over the internet. There are still debates about security but this is changing.

Getting onto the internet

The first step is to ensure that your organisation is equipped to get connected. For the smallest of organisations, this may simply involve finding a volunteer who is already connected. The equipment required is not sophisticated and works with most computers. You need a modem which is either built into the computer already, or can be bought separately. Connection to the internet is carried out through one of the many Internet Service Providers (ISPs). Read one of the many internet magazines to compare what is on offer, or ask other organisations for recommendations. You may also need an extra phone line if you are likely to be using the internet a lot. With this simple equipment you are in a position to access other people's websites and send and receive e-mail messages.

The next step is to create your own website, which can be hosted by your ISP. Most internet accounts come with a certain amount of web space for this, which will probably be enough if you are just starting out. You will need a domain name, which can be purchased through your ISP. Try to choose something meaningful and memorable, although you may find some of your best ideas are already taken.

Each page of your site is a screenful of data which can then be visited by anyone else on the internet. You can have just one page with a small announcement of your existence and work; or you could consider a complex of pages linking your work, your services to clients and your fundraising requests.

news take action donate shop get involved search contact
About Oxfam Emergencies Development Campaigns Policy Fair Trade Publications Kids&sc

Other ways to give

Make a secure online donation

Leave a legacy to Oxfam

You and your company

Where your money goes

I want to study more because it might help me to get a job. One day I would like to be a teacher.

Shaheena Akhter, schoolgirl, Bangladesh

For just **£15** you could pay for five children like Shaheena to go to school for a year.

Please give today.
Your money will be used where it is most needed.

 Simply tick the Gift Aid box on the secure online donation form to make your gift stretch even further. Your money will be used where it is most needed

Photograph: Shafiqul Alam/Oxfam

Oxfam
Visa
card

About Oxfam . Emergencies . Development . Campaigns
Policy . Fair Trade . Shop . Publications . Kids&schools

An Oxfam web page.

Visit a range of other sites to see how they work and note the good features that you would like to copy and the bad ones – like pictures that take forever to download or text that disappears off the edge of the screen – to avoid. The RNIB can supply information about designing accessible websites for people with a visual impairment. It is not difficult, and can make all the difference to the way your organisation is perceived.

To create your site, you can either get an individual to do the programming involved, or go to a specialist organisation. Before commissioning anyone, make sure you agree a contract which stipulates exactly what you will get for your money and who will have copyright in the design and content of your site – this should be you! Think about who is going to do the updating, too. There is no point in paying to have a beautiful site created if you are not going to be able to keep it up-to-date.

Finally, make sure that people browsing the internet can find you. A good designer will ensure that your site is registered with the main search engines. You could also look for other sites to link to, or consider joining an umbrella site such as One World.

Resources and further information

See also general lists at the end of the book.

Organisations

BBC Appeals Office
Room 214
Henry Wood House
3 & 6 Langham Place
London W1A 1AA
www.bbc.co.uk/info/bbc/app/index.
html
Tel. 020 7765 4595

Broadcasting Support Services
BSS London
Union House
Shepherd's Bush Green
London W12 8UA
www.bss.org.uk
Tel. 020 8735 5000

**BT Value Call (Premium Rate)
  Service**
Freephone 0808 100 1293

CSV Media
Tel. 020 7278 6601
e-mail information@csv.org.uk

Data Protection Commissioner
Wycliffe House
Water Lane
Wilmslow
Cheshire SK9 5AF
www.dataprotection.gov.uk
Tel. 01625 545745

Fundraising UK Ltd
(website for charity fundraisers)
www.fundraising.co.uk

ITC Appeals Office
70 Brompton Road
London SW3 1EY

Mailing Preference Service
Freepost 22
London W1E 7EZ
Tel. 020 7766 420
e-mail mps@dma.org.uk
A service provided by the Direct
Marketing Association, who also run
the Telephone Preference Service (see
below).

Media Trust
3–7 Euston Centre
Regent's Place
London NW1 3JG
www.mediatrust.org
Tel. 020 7874 7604

Occam Direct Marketing Ltd
Tel. 01761 233844
Run Reciprocate co-ordinating
reciprocal mailings for their clients.

**Public Fundraising Regulatory
  Authority (PFRA)**
Set up in 2000 by charities involved in
face to face fundraising.
At the time of publication PFRA can be
contacted through ICFM:
pfra@icfm.co.uk

Royal Mail Mailsort Services
Royal Mail Sales Centre
Tel. 0845 7 950950
This will give you discounts for
mailings of 4,000 or more.
Mailsort 1 – aims to deliver the next
working day
Mailsort 2 – aims to deliver within 3
working days
Mailsort 3 – aims to deliver within 7
working days

Telephone Preference Service
5th floor
Haymarket House
1 Oxendon Street
London SW1Y 4EE
www.tps-online.org.uk
Tel. 020 7766 4420
e-mail tps@dma.org.uk

Publications

The following publications are available from the Directory of Social Change.
Prices were correct at the time of writing, but may be subject to change.

Asking Properly, George Smith, White Lion Press 1997, £20

Building a Fundraising Database Using your PC, 2nd edition, Peter Flory,
DSC/CAF 2001, £12.95

Data Protection, 2nd edition, Paul Ticher, DSC 2002, £14.95

Friends for Life, Ken Burnett, White Lion Press 1997, £20

Other publications

Commonsense Direct Marketing, Drayton Bird, Kogan Page 2000, £22.50

Institute of Fundraising Code of Practice on Fundraising on the Internet

Institute of Fundraising Code of Practice on Reciprocal Charity Mailings

Institute of Fundraising Code of Practice on Personal Solicitation of Committed
Gifts

15 GETTING YOUR MESSAGE ACROSS

This chapter deals with how to put together materials (funding applications, appeal letters, annual reports, leaflets) that can be used to communicate a fundraising message. This is followed by a section on how Public Relations can be used to support fundraising work.

Details of organisations and publications referred to in this chapter are on p. 325.

15.1 Applying to potential funders

Writing a good letter or application is one of the most important fundraising skills. The difference between a good and a bad application can be the difference between success and failure. Your application needs to communicate the needs of your organisation to potential supporters and will usually be the basis for the funder deciding whether or not to make a grant. More detailed advice can be found in *Writing Better Fundraising Applications*.

Planning your application

How you put together your proposal depends on who you are applying to; what their priorities and interests are; their procedure for selecting and assessing grant applications; what you need to say about your organisation; what you propose to do with the funds; and when you will be submitting the application. There are several factors to consider at this stage.

- *Application forms*. Does the donor require applications to be submitted in a standard format, or is there an application form? If so, you should comply with it. Increasingly, you may be offered the opportunity to apply by e-mail, or download the application form from a website (particularly for Lottery applications).
- *Application dates*. Most donors work to a grants cycle. For central and local government this is an annual cycle, and applications have to be submitted in the early autumn for the grant year beginning the following April. For many foundations, grants are decided at quarterly meetings,

and they may have a long list of applications to consider. You can't just send off an application and assume you will get the money when you need it. You have to fit your fundraising into their grant-making timetable, and this means planning ahead.

- *How many donors you plan to approach*. Even if you are sending the same proposal to a large number of donors, you should still try to make it personal to each – for example by having a standard proposal accompanied by a personalised covering letter. This can include reference to any previous contact, how the project particularly fits within the donor's guidelines and current interests and (if relevant) whether and how the donor will benefit from the association (this is particularly important to companies – see chapter 8).

- *The funder's potential for giving*. Large funders, including major trusts and government funding programmes, will expect quite a lot of detail. They are looking not just for good ideas, but for evidence of need and ability to deliver. Those who will make less significant donations, which includes smaller trusts and most companies, simply will not have the time to read a long application. They will want something clear and to the point – so a page or two is likely to be enough. You should try to include all the important points in your letter. If they do need any more information, they can ask for it.

- *The likelihood of success*. Fundraising is time consuming so it's best to concentrate on a few applications which you think stand a greater chance of success rather than scattering your efforts widely.

Targeting your proposal

Who you send your proposal to will depend on a number of issues.

- *Urgency*. If you need the money urgently, your best chance may be to approach those who have already supported you. You have already convinced them that your organisation is worthwhile, and they may be willing to support you again. However, first check any conditions they have on how long you need to wait before applying again.

- *Scale of need*. If you require a large sum of money, you can either apply for a few large grants from donors interested in your sort of work (or who have already supported you), or you can mount a wider appeal to a larger number of donors.

- *How many donors to approach*. Funders may want to know how many other people have been asked and who has already agreed to give. Again, careful targeting of a few is more effective than a more general mailing. You can use an early, generous donation to set an example to other donors. If you hope to obtain government support, it is usually best to secure this first, so you can tell other funders about it.

- *Type of project.* New projects and new initiatives are more likely to be of greater interest than simply contributing to the running costs of the organisation or providing a basic service. Try to construct the proposal to make your work appear new and exciting, showing that you are addressing matters of current concern in a fresh and innovative way. This is often simply a matter of presentation.
- *A personalised approach.* As mentioned in the previous section on planning, try to personalise the approach as much as you can, referring to previous contact and support.

Content

Decide what you are going to ask for funds for – strategic development, capital costs, a specific piece of expenditure or a particular project. Read or re-read chapter 2, section 2.3 *Making your case*, before you go any further. Once you have established what you want the funds for, there are other points you need to consider:

- the aims and objectives of the project;
- the problem or need that is to be met;
- the urgency of the need, and whether there are consequences if nothing is done;
- the working methods to be used to meet your aims;
- why the method you have selected is the best or the most appropriate or the most cost-effective;
- the expected outcomes and achievements of the project;
- what it is about your organisation that makes it the most appropriate to run the scheme;
- if the work is innovative, what you will do to disseminate the experience gained from the project so that others can benefit;
- how you plan to monitor and evaluate the project;
- a clear budget for the work, which justifies all the expenditure;
- when the funding stops, showing what will happen in the future: will the project become self sustaining? Find alternative funding? Or finish?
- the other grants that can be (or have been) mobilised to add to the sum being requested from that particular donor;
- when the money is needed;
- any collaboration with other organisations and agencies;
- how you will bring in additional skills and resources, use volunteers and work with local community groups;
- your plans beyond the project, and how you will build on and develop your work during this next phase (which should at least be considered, even if you have no firm plans at this stage).

Broad checklist for a proposal

1   Have you got a strategy for the immediate project?
2   Have you planned ahead for when the funding ends?
3   Have you picked the right project for that funder and tailored your application to address their particular interests and priorities?
4   Have you done enough to establish your credibility and included a clear statement of your charity's functions and objectives?
5   Have you prepared a realistic budget and included a set of your most recent accounts?
6   Have you been specific about what you need?
7   Have you set an initial target for what you need to raise to start the project?
8   Is your proposal clear, concise and factual?
9   Have you included pictures illustrating the project or the problem you want to address?
10 Is it addressed to the right person?

How much to ask for

Do some research to find out how much each donor usually gives. This may well be less than you need. In this case you will need to approach a number of donors, asking each to contribute part of the total. There are different ways of doing this. You can write to several sources, and ask each to contribute a share of the total (an appropriate proportion depending on their size). You can break down the project into separate components; each element might then become the subject of an application to a particular donor, and in each application you can highlight the particular importance of what you are asking for – as well as the value of the project as a whole.

Then you must decide on your strategy. Do you approach all your prospective donors at the same time? Or do you go to one first, hoping to gain their support before approaching the others? If you have a funder with whom you have worked closely in the past and who is prepared to make a commitment to support the project, their support might encourage others. However, if you have to wait to get commitment from one funder before approaching others, this can delay your funding process.

Whatever you decide, it is important to have a plan and make clear to everyone how you propose to raise the money you need.

Structure

When writing up your proposal, you should consider the following aspects.

- *Length*. The application length will vary depending on the funder being approached. For a major project (such as a new building) you will probably produce a long, detailed proposal. But you should also prepare an executive summary or a two-page covering letter which sets out the key points. For less complicated projects, keep the length to a minimum. This will make it much easier for the donor, who is probably receiving a steady stream of proposals. A page for a company, or two pages for a trust will normally be sufficient. You can attach more detailed information if you feel that it will be of interest.

- *The key points*. At the heart of your proposal, you will describe the needs you are trying to address, the aims of your project, and how you will achieve them. Include as much detail as is necessary for a person who is not knowledgeable in your area. Also show how you expect to measure the success of the project. Make sure you address the critical questions of accountability, equal opportunities and user involvement.

- *Credibility*. If the funder has had no previous contact with your organisation, they will want to be reassured that they can entrust their money to you. This can be done in a number of ways: providing CVs of key people; listing the names of well-connected committee members or patrons; mentioning the support you have previously received from other major donors or government bodies; providing evidence of other projects you have successfully developed; copies of good press coverage; independent evaluation of previous work; positive feedback from users, experts or others.

- *Recognition of the importance of the problem*. If the problem is not widely recognised, refer to authoritative reports or obtain endorsements from prominent people.

- *The budget*. Your budget will always be carefully scrutinised by potential funders. It needs to be clear, complete and accurate. Donors are not interested in the details of your stationery or postage bill, but will want to know your major areas of expenditure and income. You should identify capital or other one-off costs, salaries, overheads and any other major operational costs. Similarly, income estimates will show the money you expect to generate from the project itself or through fundraising, both during the lifetime of the requested grant and beyond. You should always attach your organisation's audited accounts for the latest year for which they are available.

Getting the budget right

There is a tendency to undercost proposals. If you do this, you will not raise the money you need to run your project effectively. So you should ensure that:

- every item that you expect to have to pay for is included;
- each item has a realistic cost;
- inflation is accounted for. Different funders will have different systems for dealing with this, but you don't want to find that the price of something has shot up just when you need to purchase it;
- administrative overheads associated with the project are put in where possible. The organisation as a whole functions to make the projects happen and the cost of running the organisation has to be paid for;
- publicity costs are included.
- Language and jargon. Many proposals are badly written and boring to read. The application is a selling document – selling the idea of supporting your project to a potential donor. Avoid long sentences, long paragraphs, meaningless words, jargon (which means something to you but nothing to the reader) and waffle. Use short words, short sentences, short paragraphs, bullet points, bold text to highlight key features, headings and subheads to indicate the different parts of the application. Get someone else to read what you have written before you send it off – ideally this will be someone who knows little about your work, as they will then be in a position of most of the people you will be sending your application to. They can challenge your assumptions and ask for explanations where things seem unclear.
- Facts and figures. Back up any claims about the extent of the need and the effectiveness of your methods with facts and figures. Everything may be 'desperate', 'urgent', 'important', 'unique'; but you need to prove this. Include just a few selected facts and figures in your proposal – you can also provide a wealth of detail in a background paper attached as an appendix to the application.
- The human story. Include short case studies and examples of how people have been helped and what they have gone on to achieve as a result of your help. This demonstrates that you are effective in helping people – which is what most donors are interested in supporting. Also, if you can, include pictures or photographs to illustrate the story you are telling.
- Presentation. Presentation can make a difference. Different standards and expectations apply to different donors. For example, a sponsorship proposal directed at the marketing director of a major company may well need to look different from an application to a national foundation. Government agencies and international donors have their own standards and preferred formats. Tailor your style of communication to your audience.

Making the application

To be successful you need to know as much as possible about the donor you are approaching. For example:

- what constraints are imposed by the donor (there is no point applying for something that they cannot or will not support);
- the typical size of the grants they award. Some funders make grants at two or three levels: large grants to major initiatives; medium-sized grants to national organisations or to projects they are especially interested in; and much smaller grants for local initiatives;
- the funder's interests and what they have supported in the past;
- who to write to (their name and job title), who makes the decisions and who they are advised by (so you can plan any lobbying);
- whether the funder expects any recognition or benefit for their support;
- their decision-making cycle and the best time to submit an application.

Research all the donors you plan to approach and keep this information on record. Suggest a meeting, or other ways to bring your work to the attention of the donor, such as inviting them to visit your project. Contact key advisers or trustees of the donor organisation (where you have good contacts) to tell them about your proposal. Above all remember that sending a completely inappropriate application is a waste of everyone's time – so read any guidelines before applying. Also if you have their telephone number phone them to check whether you are applying at the right time, and if they still have funds available.

Following up a successful application

Your work does not stop once a funder has offered you a grant or sponsored your project. You need to check that all the conditions of the grant are noted. You will also need to fulfil any particular requirements of the funder and keep in touch. This might take the form of:

- *benefits*. Providing the benefits you have offered – for example with company sponsorship giving clear recognition of their support;
- *regular reports and feedback*. Whether this is a condition of the funding or not, you should keep your funder informed about how your project is progressing. This should include financial information, a narrative report and any technical details. This is important if you wish to apply to the funder again. Above all never forget that you are accountable for how the funder's money is spent and they will want to know exactly how it is being spent;
- *invitations to events and receptions*. This includes events organised specifically for the project they have supported, such as an opening ceremony for a building or a reception for an exhibition. Or you may want to

organise a small reception specially for your funders, so that you can develop your relationship with them and get them more involved with other areas of your work.

Don't forget to thank your funders and acknowledge their support in appropriate ways, for example in your annual report.

15.2 Writing an appeal letter to supporters

The bulk of your supporter base will hear from you most often by letter. Letter-writing is not just a question of raising money. All letters to your supporters are important whether the recipient responds or not. Letters create an awareness and can help build a relationship. This is important, particularly when a large proportion of the recipients will not respond.

Direct mail appeals should aim to raise money at a cost ratio of 10:1 from a warm list, meaning that you should be raising £10 for every £1 you spend. If you get the communication right, this fundraising technique can be one of the best sources of continuing income – see chapter 14 *Direct marketing* for more information on direct mail.

Grabbing attention

'This Valentine's Day 500 people will die of a broken heart'

[The British Heart Foundation communicating a powerful statistic about the numbers of people dying from heart disease on a day when a lot of people are thinking about their loved ones.]

'Do you really need 50p more than he does? ...
... 50p a day won't get you very far. But use it to sponsor a child in need, and it could go a lot further than you ever thought possible. Just £15 a month helps us provide clean water, health care, basic education, seeds and tools for growing food ... all things that could make life better, not just for one child, but for everyone in the community.'

[ActionAid showing how much can be done for so little.]

'You hold in your hand an instrument of torture ...
... it can also be an instrument of change.'

[An Amnesty International UK member recruitment mailing pack featuring a pen, which can be used by a torturer to do harm, but also by a supporter to commit financial support.]

There are several elements of an appeal letter to consider: the salutation, the entry, the appeal itself, the call to action, the signatory and postscript.

1 The salutation

The salutation (Dear …) should be made as personal as possible. When writing a small number of personal letters, you can top and tail them by hand. For larger volumes of correspondence, it is probably better to mail merge all the elements you wish to personalise. Then for the biggest mailings you will need to look at laser printing the personal information.

2 The entry

You need to grab the reader's attention immediately. If you don't, they may not get beyond the first paragraph. A letter from a respected celebrity or an impactful statement may make people read on; an intensely emotional opening to the letter can also work well.

3 The appeal message

Having gained the reader's attention, you must hold it. One way of doing this is to write in a simple straightforward way, clearly laid out with short words and sentences and a variety of paragraph sizes. Key ideas should be underlined, indented or highlighted. In terms of content, you need to:

- state the problem
- show how you can help resolve it
- demonstrate your credibility by showing what you have achieved in the past and others who have helped you
- indicate how much you expect the donor to give and what this will achieve
- make the call to action clearly.

4 The call to action

The call to action is crucial, and where many, otherwise well-written, appeal letters fail. People can be reluctant to ask precisely and directly for what they want, yet that is exactly what is required. Start flagging up the call to action early on in the letter. Repeat it throughout the letter and make it absolutely plain near the end. It should consist of:

- what you want
- how much you want them to give
- the payment mechanism (cheque, credit card, direct debit)
- when – how soon you need it (usually immediately, to create a sense of urgency)
- who to send it to (a personal name to reply to will always be better than an anonymous department)

The call to action

There's a bigger picture out there ... and you can be part of it!

- If you love art, it's the best £27 you'll spend all year ... become a member of the National Art Collections Fund (The Art Fund) and you'll not only be a patron of the arts, you'll also see the art you love for free.

[The National Art Collections Fund]

Help them build a future free from hunger and disease ...
... for just £2 a month.

- People in the Third World don't want to live on handouts. All they want is the opportunity to work themselves out of poverty – and the chance to live dignified and independent lives. Your £2 a month will help these people in their daily struggle to help themselves.

[Oxfam]

Your next decision could affect a child for the rest of their life.

- When you sponsor a child through ActionAid, 90% of your money is spent directly on our development work. We work closely with people, providing long-term solutions to poverty – and so creating a situation in which people can begin to support themselves. In return for your help, you'll gain a valuable insight into the lives and needs of poor communities in the developing world. And, of course, you'll know you've played your part in improving the life of a child and the lives of everyone in the community.

[ActionAid]

Each of these examples illustrates a direct call to action. What the charity wants the donor to do is clearly spelt out. The text is simple and direct. The examples show how you can write good copy to appeal to your donors – showing the benefits that will be obtained by responding, confronting prejudices, and illustrating the cause in an attractive way.

5 The signatory

Picking the right person to be the signatory of the letter can make a huge difference to its impact. You may decide it should be your director, one of your trustees or, if you are a medical charity, it may be some kind of expert such as Macmillan nurse or a research scientist.

6 The postscript

Save an important idea for the PS. This is one of the most read parts of the letter so use it for your final argument to clinch their support or reinforce the message. This can be produced in a printed typeface or a reproduction of the same handwriting used for the signature.

15.3 Using printed materials for fundraising
Getting the most out of your annual report

Every organisation has to produce an annual report and this can be extremely useful in supporting your fundraising programme. It is an opportunity to promote your strengths, highlight the importance of the need, demonstrate your effectiveness, celebrate your achievements – and also raise money both directly and indirectly.

Eight reasons for producing a good annual report

1   A good annual report explains your organisation to the outside world. It tells the story of your aims, achievements, commitment and style of working.

2   A good annual report reports back to donors and others. A bad one can destroy a donor's confidence.

3   A good annual report is your sales brochure ...

4   A good annual report encourages staff and volunteers, giving them pride in their employer and their work.

5   A good annual report motivates and attracts ... whereas a bad one will put people off.

6   A good annual report gives a clear picture of sound stewardship, showing good use of your supporters' money.

7   A good annual report can directly solicit involvement and raise money.

8   A good annual report reinforces public trust and gives credibility to the organisation and the voluntary sector as a whole. A bad one can destroy credibility for all voluntary organisations.

[*How to produce inspiring annual reports* Ken Burnett and Karin Weatherup]

An annual report and accounts are a legal and fundraising necessity. All your major funders will want to see them, as will the Charity Commission, Companies House or whoever you report to. Look on it as a useful promotional opportunity rather than a chore. Here are a few important points:

- **do** use illustrations and photographs liberally. They can often convey more than the printed word;
- **do** list major donors. This recognition (and you will be sending them a copy) will encourage them to think about giving a repeat donation, and encourage prospective donors (who could get a copy of the report with your appeal letter) to give;

- **don't** put your lists of supporters and committee members at the beginning. You are also writing the annual report to create interest in your organisation and long lists of names can be off-putting;
- **don't** forget to include some sort of response mechanism: a form to fill in to send a donation or ask for more information, a phone number to call or website to visit. There is no point in provoking a reaction if your reader then has no easy means of contacting you.

Many of the standard fundraising techniques also apply to your annual report. Be positive and communicate a sense of enthusiasm and achievement. You have more space than an appeal letter so you can use a range of techniques to get your message across. For example, why not try to include the following?

- *Drama*. Voluntary organisations revolve around dramatic issues – the fight against disease, giving children a chance in life, protecting the environment from destruction or whatever – but so many annual reports are dry! Tell some good stories about what you have done.
- *Human interest*. Include case studies, interviews, profiles, testimonials or quotes to make your organisation more real.
- *Support*. Show how much people value your work, either through messages they have sent or endorsements they have given.
- *Boxes alongside the text*. Annual reports can look like a really daunting read. Try to break up the text with boxes which have facts, quotes, snippets of information, key points or other simple points.

You will have your own ideas as well, but above all remember that annual reports should be attractive and easy to read, even if some of the content may sometimes be challenging or even shocking.

Producing effective printed materials

Your annual report will be only one of a range of printed materials that you can use to promote your organisation and your cause. Creating effective fundraising and publicity leaflets and other literature is one of the fundraiser's most important tasks. Good fundraising ideas can be destroyed by poorly prepared or badly presented material. Good writing skills are vital, as well as a basic understanding of design and production processes.

The process of creating printed material usually follows a similar path. The stages include:

- conceptualisation or visualisation, which may include producing a dummy or sample copy
- setting aside a budget

- copywriting and gathering together of photographs and other visual material
- design
- print and production
- distribution.

You may decide to take on some of these elements yourself but it is likely that others will be done by outside suppliers and each stage might be produced by someone different. The more people that are involved the more things there are that can go wrong. There is also a greater risk of losing or watering down the original concept.

You need to decide who does what. Many people, even in a small organisation, feel they can write effectively. However, you need specific writing skills to present a good, clear, logical case and to express your ideas forcefully. This may require outside help. If you decide to use promotional consultants and designers, they may have the skills you need, but you have to brief them properly and be confident that they can produce what you need within the budget you have.

Anna's memories will always be with her. With your lasting gift, so will we.

The Medical Foundation for the Care of Victims of Torture has produced a simple leaflet about leaving them a legacy. The leaflet first states the need for the organisation with a case study, followed by how to go about leaving a legacy and wording for particular types of gifts. It also includes a form on which responders can declare how they will be helping or ask for a more detailed will making guide from the organisation.

Some general principles of effective communication

You must be clear about what you are trying to achieve. Write down the objectives of each piece of communication, and include this in the brief to the writer and designer (if you are not doing it all yourself). Who is your target audience: volunteers and supporters, funders, professionals and others interested in the cause, other stakeholders (name them), or the general public? What are you aiming to do: increase awareness, communicate information (if so, what?) or raise money?

Decide on your primary audience and your objectives and concentrate on these. Other things will follow (such as raising awareness). But make sure that the primary purpose is clear and the main message comes across.

Then identify who you expect to read the material and think about what tone is needed to appeal to them. If they are readers of a magazine or on a particular mailing list, you should know something about them and their interests. You also need to see if they have had any previous contact with you or knowledge about your work. You expect your past donors be fairly knowledgeable, and you will write differently to them than to those who know little or nothing about you. Try to get a picture of who your existing donors are: their age, sex, interests, preferences and degree of commitment to the organisation. Once you have this picture in mind, you will be able to tailor your message to reach them more effectively.

Keep to your budget. You may have limited space (in an advertisement, for example) to get your message across. Print and postage bills on a mailing can be high. If you want to include photographs are these already available or will they need to be taken?

Ten suggestions for writers

1   Get to know your audience.
2   Use simple, direct and everyday language.
3   State your proposition boldly and clearly.
4   Feature real, identifiable cases and people.
5   Communicate the need.
6   State clearly what the reader's support will enable you to achieve.
7   Remember that cleverness rarely pays.
8   Avoid seeming too professional.
9   Remove any unnecessary detail.
10   Give a clear course of action.

[Ken Burnett, a communications consultant, gives this advice to his staff and clients]

Set a clear deadline for when you need the finished product, especially if it is going to be mailed or presented at an AGM. Things take longer than you think, so give yourself room for slippage and make sure that everyone involved sticks as close to their deadlines as possible.

Concept

You need to create a theme or style for your material and approach and you need headlines or slogans. These ideas can be generated through brain-storming the project. Gather a number of interested people together in a room, identify the object of the exercise and the rules of the brain-storming process, then get everyone to contribute as many ideas as possible, however unusual. A refinement process follows to select one of the suggestions or develop the approach out of several ideas. Out of this will come the general strategy which will in turn generate the actual copy.

At this stage, you will need a designer to produce roughs. If you don't like the rough design, ask for a new approach before too much time has been spent. Backtracking later on will cost money and you may miss your deadlines. The visualisation need be no more than the front cover for a leaflet and a sample page – enough to give you an idea of how it will feel and look.

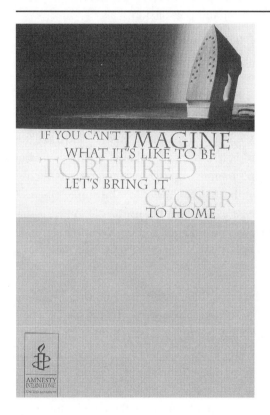

A hard-hitting Amnesty International UK insert asking people to become members of the organisation.

Copywriting

Not everybody can write well. A good copywriter makes ideas come alive. However, small organisations cannot always afford to hire copywriters, so fundraisers usually have to write their own materials. Courses to help you are available through the Directory of Social Change and other organisations. Funding may be available for small voluntary organisations through the Paul Hamlyn Foundation.

When hiring an outside consultant, always look at their portfolio to see what they have done for similar organisations. Brief them clearly about what you are trying to say and why and who your target audience is. Some will have an instinctive understanding of your work others will not. Good copywriters are expensive so if you do not have the budget you might try to get one to volunteer their services. Or get a good local journalist to help.

Good copy needs a clear structure. The acronym AIDA is useful here. This describes the process of communication and persuasion:

- Attention: attract the reader's attention
- Interest: if you don't identify a reason for the reader to be personally interested, you will lose them
- Desire: to support your cause
- Action: the practical steps they will take to deliver this support.

Headlines, pictures or strong ideas all create a visual impact to attract the reader's immediate attention. Grab their interest by showing why you exist and the needs you are serving. Don't imagine that your supporters will continue to support you without a continuing reminder of the importance of what you are doing, or the human cost of ignoring the problem. You can generate desire by showing that things can be changed if they give their support. Action demands that you tell them what you want them to do and what sort of gift they are expected to make.

Keep everything simple and understandable. Avoid jargon. Organisations tend to develop shorthand ways of describing their work. This is useful when talking to colleagues, but can be meaningless to outsiders. Find someone outside your organisation to read your first draft. Ask them what they have and have not understood. You may have to agree the copy with other people in your organisation. Most people's reaction to checking someone else's text is to look for typographic errors and false statements, and then add their own thoughts, leaving accurate but heavily qualified text that loses all its punch and impact. Accept their comments, but remember that effective text cannot be written by a committee. They may have skills in providing the service or in running the organisation; yours are in fundraising and communication.

The KISS principle

An important principle is that of simplicity. KISS is the acronym often used to remind us of this:

Keep
It
Simple
Stupid!

Design

Design gives the printed piece its character. Good designers can lift the central idea from a piece of text and make it infinitely more compelling. The elements of this include the copy, the headlines and sub-heads, the photographs and illustrations used, as well as the design style. Other areas for consideration here are the use of space, number of colours (the usual options are one, two or four-colour printing), the quality of the paper and whether to use recycled or wood-free paper, the use of text reversed out so that it appears in white, and blocks of the page overlaid with a tint of the colour. When deciding all these, you should bear in mind that if the finished product seems too 'glossy', this can create an impression that you are spending too much of their donation on these materials – which can discourage people from giving. Conversely, if the finished product looks shoddy, then this can reflect on your competence.

You may already have a house design style, including the use of logos. If you do – and consistency is important – ensure that the designer is clearly briefed about this.

Remember also that your readers may not all have perfect eyesight. The RNIB can supply guidelines for making printed materials more legible to people with a visual impairment. Much of it is commonsense, and relates to the size of the type and the use of coloured backgrounds. Make sure you brief the designer on how far their ideas should be constrained by considerations of this kind.

Illustrations can take many forms and help bring a design to life. Photographs are the easiest to use – but not if they do not make a point or are of poor quality. Photos should always be captioned, as captions are among the most read parts of any publication (and remember to credit the photographer). The best photos are those that involve people doing things, rather than pieces of equipment, buildings or committee members posing for the camera. Illustrations, diagrams, plans and visualisations are a good alternative, especially for things that cannot yet be photographed (such as a building you are planning to put up).

Recycle this paper today ♺

An eye catching Greenpeace insert using the concept of recycling to promote giving

A good designer will integrate all these elements for you. If you are using an outside designer, get a firm quote for the design cost before agreeing to proceed. Beware of how much the cost of corrections can add to your final bill. One way of saving money over a period of time is to design newsletters, handbills and leaflets that are produced regularly in a similar format in-house to a pre-designed format created for you by a professional designer.

5 simple steps to take action

1 **GET** angry at what companies, governments and individuals are doing to your world.

2 **RECYCLE** this paper by using it to join Greenpeace now and help stop the destruction.

3 **USE** the form inside to give your support whether by Direct Debit, card or cheque.

4 **SEND** it back to us today. The sooner you do it, the sooner we make a difference.

5 **IF** you have any doubts, read on. Then follow steps 1-4. After all, if people like you won't help Greenpeace, who will?

GREENPEACE

Printing

The final stage is getting the finished material into print. Ask around to get recommendations for printers from colleagues in other organisations, or perhaps you have good local contacts through your staff or volunteers. If you are using outside printers get three quotes to get the best price possible – it is surprising how much prices vary, even on the most tightly defined jobs. You should even ask printers you deal with regularly to quote for new jobs. This does not demonstrate mistrust, but is good business practice.

Getting quotes

When asking for a quote, you need to be clear about the following points.

For dealing with designers:

- establish the date you will supply text and instructions to the designer and the date you expect to receive the completed job
- sample visuals needed
- format, size and price guidelines for the job
- copywriting (who will do it, and when the final copy is needed)
- how copy will be supplied (on disk if you can)
- photographs needed (what is required and by when, who will commission the photos and when they are needed)
- illustrations needed (what is required, by when and who will commission them)
- who is responsible for proof reading the text and the checking the design proofs.

For dealing with printers:

- date that the completed artwork will be sent to the printer, and date required for receipt of completed job;
- paper size and number of pages – printers use standard size sheets of paper, so the less the wastage, the more economic the format of your job;
- print quantity – the more you print the cheaper each one becomes. Short runs are particularly expensive but so is producing extra copies you do not need;
- paper quality – it usually pays to print on stock paper used by the printer which is bought in bulk; and colour of the paper – tinted paper is more expensive than white paper;
- number of print colours (one, two or four). One colour can look dull. Four colour, which uses a mix of four inks to create the effect of the full range of colours, is expensive, and the use of special inks (such as silver or gold) can also involve substantial additional cost. Two-colour offers plenty of scope for creative design and is reasonably cheap – bear in mind that you don't have to use black as one of the colours;

- photographs and halftone illustrations (this can add to the cost, but increase the effectiveness of the communication). Will these be supplied as scans on disk or will the printer have to scan them?
- what kind of proofs you want to see and how long do you have to agree the proofs?
- folding – complicated folds will usually be more expensive than simple folding; scoring or perforation can also add to the cost;
- packing and delivery (the price usually includes delivery to one address).

15.4 Public Relations and dealing with the media

Effective Public Relations (PR) is an essential ingredient of successful fundraising for two main reasons. First, it draws the public's attention to the cause or the need. Without this attention and understanding, the task of the fundraiser becomes much more difficult. If your meeting with the head of a local company coincides with positive articles in the press about your organisation's work, you will immediately be taken more seriously.

Some tips on PR

- Keep a list of sympathetic media people to send promotional material to.
- Make friends with journalists, including those on local papers and radio, keeping them in touch with what your organisation is doing.
- Publicise your organisation's achievements both in its work and its fundraising (such as the receipt of a substantial grant or donation, or support from a government body or from an important company) by sending out a press release. Follow this up with a phone call to encourage interest.
- Use beneficiaries to talk about the work of your organisation, either through interviews or through quotes in press releases.
- Issue a press release when the annual report comes out or when research is published on the cause. Try to get a feature written about it to coincide with publication, or make it newsworthy so that journalists will want to cover it.
- Stage a special event to generate PR, especially one that illustrates the need or demonstrates the support that your cause is attracting, for example, delivering a petition signed by supporters to the Houses of Parliament when an issue of concern to your organisation is to be debated.

PR can also help position your organisation in relation to other organisations in the same field. 'Why do we need so many charities, all apparently researching the same diseases? Shouldn't they all combine?' can often be a natural response from the public. Good PR can identify the special importance of your work and its particular ethos and contribution, get this recognised by the public and help eliminate an important barrier to public generosity.

News releases and press conferences

When you have something new to report a news release to a selected list of newspapers, radio stations and TV channels is one of the most effective ways of publicising it. This can be in response to a recent development in your work, a major donation received, a new publication produced or research completed, a celebrity supporter joining your ranks, or some form of stunt designed specifically to highlight your work or generate publicity.

An effective news release answers the questions who, what, when, where, and why. To be effective at a local level, it should have a clear local angle. Write it in the form of a short article, so that editors can use it verbatim, if they wish. Some might be really interested in the story and want more background information, which you can include separately. Picture editors appreciate photos.

If the event is of real interest, you might consider holding a press conference where you invite the press to come and hear a story directly, but expect to be closely questioned on the project and your organisation. The timing of a press conference is critical. Its proximity to other important news stories can make or break yours, though you may have relatively little control over this. For example if there is a major political development or financial scandal, there will be little room in the newspaper for other news breaking at the same time. You also need to know the schedules and deadlines that journalists are working to.

Location is important. An interesting venue can add to the feel of the story – for example launching a campaign on genetically modified foods in the middle of a field. The venue should also be easily accessible to journalists. You might want to hold a press conference at an event which is guaranteed to get good coverage itself – such as a national conference.

One way of making the press conference go with a swing is to announce that it will be given by some well-known people, renowned either for their entertainment value or for their serious interest. An actress or celebrity will often use pithy words for journalists or be well rehearsed in the photo call for photographers. Similarly, reporters will know that senior figures at press conferences can usually be drawn on the issues.

If you are using a celebrity, having a conference chaired by a senior person from your organisation will help control the questions and steer them away from the celebrity who might not know the answer. To get your message across with no deviation or hesitation, there is nothing quite like a dry run first. If you can't manage this, you will have to give the spokesperson a full briefing. See section 12.5 for more on working with patrons and celebrities.

For those who cannot get to the conference, put together a briefing pack. Some of the fullest coverage from a press conference comes from journalists who have not even attended. But you might never have got this coverage without having organised the conference in the first place.

Photocalls and events

The media are always attracted to the unusual, the famous and the picturesque. A photograph to illustrate your cause or an element of it in an unusual setting may well be just what you need to get media coverage. For example the organisation Volunteer Reading Help and Southern Water publicised their relationship with a photocall with the swimmer Duncan Goodhew, who is also dyslexic, reading to a seven year old girl underwater in a swimming pool! This puts the work of the organisation in an unusual setting which ties in with their sponsor and the celebrity.

The challenge with these sort of activities is not just to organise them successfully, but also to select an activity that is relevant to your work so that any publicity can be linked to it. Needless to say, don't encourage dangerous stunts. If anything goes wrong, your organisation will receive the blame, whether it was your fault or not.

Letters in the press

One of the most helpful ways of creating a positive climate of opinion about your organisation and its work is to write letters to the newspapers. This can be done by staff, or better still by volunteer supporters. Local organisations should target local newspapers to spread the word quite widely for little cost. Letters should be topical. If they are linked to a local event or signed by a well-known local personality, they are more likely to be published.

A letter of thanks for local help after a flag day or other event can give you the opportunity to show how successful the event was, how efficiently the money was raised, and how well it is going to be spent. Answering letters that others have written to the press is another opportunity. You can also use local radio phone-in programmes where you or a volunteer can ring in to make a point, announce a development or even appeal for support.

Damage limitation

If a negative story about your organisation is featured in the media, it is important to act quickly and in a constructive way. The first people to contact are your key donors. They need to be reassured that what they have read is not true; and they need to be given the facts. Next you should reply to the offending article as swiftly as possible. Though the damage may already have been done, it can be mitigated by an article or letter in reply. Then you should issue a statement to other newspapers and to your own staff and trustees setting out the facts of the matter.

You may get advance warning of media interest. If so, establish the facts; identify a spokesperson to put a rational and consistent case to the media; or consider inviting the senior management of the newspaper or the television station to withdraw the offending article.

If the bad coverage has a substantial element of truth, you are in less defensible position and need a different approach. Accept responsibility for the situation, identify the immediate action already taken to remedy it and invite the newspaper to do a follow up article in a more positive vein, which can help rehabilitate the organisation.

In all these situations there are a number of useful guidelines:

- ensure that the staff of your organisation do not speak to the media unless they are specifically authorised to. There is nothing so damaging as the leaked report or an inept interview from a well-meaning staff member;
- make sure that you establish the facts at an early stage and that these are accurate. Then make them well-known;
- make sure that your internal communication systems are working well, that you can get any new twists of the story across to colleagues speedily, and that trustees and supporters are kept informed;
- if you haven't already got one, draft an emergency plan in which you anticipate the possible disasters that could happen and allocate responsibilities accordingly.

PR and campaigning

For campaigning organisations, PR is a major tool helping them to achieve their aims. It has important implications for fundraising. Sometimes campaigning and fundraising are seen as separate activities that require different people and skills. However, if the campaign is an intrinsic part of the organisation's reason for existing, when the campaign gets good coverage, good fundraising results may follow.

Most not-for-profit organisations do not see campaigning as a major part of their work, but many need to campaign on particular issues from time to time or seek to set themselves up as the experts in a particular area. This creates an interesting opportunity, since the media will often turn to the organisation when they need informed comment on an issue.

Try to get your organisation regularly mentioned in the media by:

- issuing news releases;
- setting up events and stunts which will attract publicity. Better still, use these same skills to set up interesting fundraising events that the media will want to cover;
- holding press conferences;
- writing to the letters page of newspapers and magazines.

Timing is all important in media work, not only because of their deadlines, but also your need for coverage to enhance your fundraising. Media exposure should happen just before you launch a major fundraising initiative and be targeted towards the people you are approaching for support – in whatever form you can obtain it.

Integrating fundraising and PR

Your public relations should be integrated with your fundraising so the PR maximises your fundraising potential, and vice versa. Ideally if someone has a specific PR role, they should be asked to produce plans to show how they can best support the fundraising needs, at the same time as meeting the PR objectives of the organisation.

In small organisations, PR is unlikely to be a separate function, and will probably be carried out by a senior member of staff (or even a committee member). However, everyone should be encouraged to recognise the importance of good PR in generating extra funds for the organisation.

One option is to appoint a public relations agency. Some work mainly with the non-profit sector, or you could use a commercial agency interested in your cause and willing to take you on as a client at a reduced fee. The Media Trust has a brokerage service linking voluntary organisations with media companies who will undertake pro bono work or charge lower fees for this type of client. Any agency you use needs to be briefed well if they are to present your work appropriately. You can monitor the results of your PR through the use of a press cutting agency. This will show you whether you are getting your money's worth.

Resources and further information

See also general lists at the end of the book.

Organisations

Paul Hamlyn Foundation
18 Queen Anne's Gate
London SW1H 9AA
www.phf.org.uk
Tel. 020 7227 3500
Fax 020 7227 0601
e-mail information@phf.org.uk
Produces a guide to skills training in
publishing.

RNIB
(for print guidelines)
224 Great Portland Street
London W1N 6AA
Tel. 020 7388 1266

Voluntary Sector Publishers' Forum
c/o Publications department
NCVO
Regent's Wharf
8 All Saints Street
London N1 9RL
www.ncvo-vol.org.uk
Tel. 020 7713 6161
e-mail ncvo@ncvo-vol.org.uk
Produces a newsletter and organises
conferences for members on
publishing-related issues.

Publications

The following publications are available from the Directory of Social Change.
Prices were correct at the time of writing, but may be subject to change.

The DIY Guide to Charity Newsletters, Chris Wells, DSC 1996, £10.95

The DIY Guide to Public Relations 2nd edition, Moi Ali, DSC 1999, £12.50

How to Produce Inspiring Annual Reports, Ken Burnett and Karin Weatherup,
DSC 2000, £12.50

Writing Better Fundraising Applications 3rd edition, Michael Norton and Mike
Eastwood, DSC 2002, £14.95

Writing for Change, fahamu 2000, CD ROM £20

16 FUNDRAISING WITH VOLUNTEERS

Volunteers can be an extremely useful resource. The National Centre for Volunteering estimated the value of formal volunteering (which is defined as any voluntary activity undertaken through or for an organisation or a group) as being worth £40 billion in 1998. This chapter looks at ways volunteers can contribute to fundraising.

Details of organisations and publications referred to in this chapter are on p. 335.

16.1 Working with trustees and management committee members

Some organisations are run entirely by volunteers, and do not employ paid staff. Some – like the Samaritans – use volunteers to carry out the service delivery, but use paid staff for administration, coordination and fundraising. The Citizen's Advice Bureaux, on the other hand, use both volunteers and paid staff for advice giving. Many others use volunteers on an *ad hoc* basis, or to bring in extra expertise. But whatever the structure of your organisation, you will have at least one important set of volunteers: your trustees or management committee members.

Your management committee is a key element in the fundraising process. The ideal is to have a balanced, well-briefed, motivated and forward-thinking team of people who can provide energy and direction. One of the main roles of the management committee is to ensure that you have sufficient resources to carry out your current work and your development plans. This means having a strategic view of the organisation's fundraising potential, and ensuring there is sufficient expertise and administrative support within the organisation to raise the money that is needed. So for the fundraiser, it is vital to get people onto the management committee, or fundraising sub-committee if there is one, who will ask the right questions, think long-term, advise on crucial issues, suggest useful contacts, and bring clear thinking to the fundraising.

But what if your management committee does not or cannot do this? Depending on the size of your organisation and the amount of contact you have with the committee, there are several steps you or your director or other staff members can take.

- Identify the potential contribution that an effective management committee can make to the running of the organisation and to the fundraising.
- Discuss this potential with individual members who recognise the problem and want to help sort it out.
- Undertake an 'audit' of the skills, experience and expertise that you would like amongst your committee members.
- Identify and approach appropriate new people who may be willing to bring these skills and expertise onto your committee.
- You can then draw up a plan for reforming the committee, replacing those who have lost interest and setting a new agenda for the committee, and allocating roles and responsibilities to individual members.

Getting the most from your management committee

Collecting a group of skilled and experienced people is only the first stage. You need to get the most out of this group and ensure their continuing interest and involvement. Voluntary organisations often assume that committee members and trustees instinctively know what is expected of them or hope they will create a fulfilling role for themselves. But it is much better to spell things out from the start so that everybody is clear about the expectations. Here are a few ideas.

- Give each new person a proper induction. Show them the work of the organisation and introduce them to some of the beneficiaries, so that they understand the impact the organisation has. Introduce them to members of staff so they understand who does what, and give them leaflets about the work of the organisation.
- Discuss with each person exactly what they might contribute. It is better to ask for specific contributions and commitments rather than help as required, and for something significant for a limited period of time.
- Agree matters like regular attendance at meetings, remuneration of expenses and training or attendance at conferences.
- Review their contribution (as a group if everything is going well, or individually if it isn't) on an annual basis.
- Find ways of keeping them motivated by continuing to impress on them the importance of the organisation's work, showing them its successes and achievements, involving them in discussing matters of current interest or concern, and continuing to expose them to your front line work.

16.2 Recruiting and using volunteers

Volunteers are frequently used to raise money for an organisation – to run charity shops, organise local fundraising activities, and to act as support groups. There are a range of fundraising tasks which could not be carried out without them – either because the organisation would not have sufficient time or the capacity to do certain types of fundraising in the first place, or because if volunteers were not being used, the money could not be raised cost effectively. Volunteers can also assist fundraisers by providing administrative support and back up.

Volunteers can therefore be useful to fundraising in all sorts of ways, and volunteer management means more than just finding the people to do the work. In order to get the best out of your volunteers, they need to be chosen well, placed with imagination, given satisfying work to do which matches their skills and interests, and managed with skill. They are not simply there to be deployed as cheap labour in the worst jobs. Rather, they can add hugely to the resources available to you, enabling you to do more with less and to do it better.

The economic value of volunteering

Volunteering has an economic value, which the National Centre for Volunteering has tried to estimate.

- The economic value of volunteering measured in terms of its wage value is £40 billion a year. This is calculated by using an hourly rate of £9.13 (based on average earnings in 1997) to multiply the total hours worked, as indicated by the 1997 national survey of voluntary activity. The figure of £40 billion is a significant increase on £25 billion in 1993, probably a result of a large increase in hours contributed by active volunteers despite a fall in the actual numbers of people volunteering.
- Men and women make a similar economic contribution through their formal voluntary work. Whilst men are slightly less likely than women to volunteer, they contribute slightly more hours.
- All age groups make a contribution. People in the older age groups (65 to 74) are less likely to volunteer than those in the middle age ranges (from 25 up to 54), but contribute more hours to volunteering.

Alongside the value of volunteering, there is a cost in using this pool of 'free labour'. This includes the cost of recruitment, induction, support and training, and the payment of out-of-pocket expenses and project costs.

[Figures taken from NCV 1997 *National Survey of Volunteering*]

If you use volunteers, you can also take advantage of this fact to support your fundraising case.

- You can show the numbers of volunteers and the amount of volunteer time you are mobilising. This shows that other people share an enthusiasm for what you are doing, as well as your own good sense in mobilising people's time for your cause.
- You can illustrate the value of the volunteering to your organisation by estimating the value of the time put in or the work done by the volunteers – for instance, you can multiply the number of volunteer hours by the average wage.
- In your annual report you can show the value of the volunteering and how this enhances the service you are providing and makes it more cost-effective.

Types of work that volunteers can do

1 Membership of committees

Quite a bit of fundraising work can be done or overseen by committees. These normally consist of volunteers, many of whom will also get involved in other aspects of the organisation's work. Different organisations use different committees (some use none at all). There are a number of different models for fundraising committees.

- A fundraising strategy committee will usually report to the management committee. It monitors and develops the fundraising across the organisation, but is purely supervisory. This group will not actually raise money.
- A fundraising advisory committee is a looser grouping. It consists of a wide range of people, chosen for their occupation or experience. It can be a useful source of ideas and a means of getting new ideas taken up by the organisation.
- An event committee can be crucial when fundraising events are being organised. It is likely to be an *ad hoc* group specifically created to organise a ball, film première or other activity (see chapter 12, section 12.2 for more on events).
- A campaign committee is most effective where individuals are recruited specifically to help raise large amounts of money for a major appeal. Members are chosen because of their ability to give substantial donations themselves and for their willingness to ask others to give (the rich, important philanthropists, leaders of industry and commerce, and those in charge of government programmes). Meetings are rare, and the role of the chair in leading the group and ensuring that the money is raised is crucial (see chapter 13 for more on capital and big gift campaigns).

- Local committees are groups of local representatives of your organisation. They should be activists and be prepared to get involved in any activity that is needed, including fundraising, public speaking and media work.

The role of any committee must be clearly thought through. Starting with the right brief is the key to recruiting the right people.

2 Administration

The administrative office of a charity is usually an extremely busy place, where there is more work to be done than people can cope with. There are all sorts of ways in which volunteers can help:

- addressing and stuffing the envelopes for an appeal letter;
- dealing with the response to appeals – banking the proceeds, sending thank you letters, and putting the names of those who responded on to the database;
- helping with membership renewals in writing or on the telephone;
- answering the telephone;
- editing newsletters;
- research;
- organising public meetings.

Volunteer jobs should match the skills of the volunteers you are using. Also they will need supervision and support if you are to get the most out of using volunteers.

3 Fundraising

Volunteers can raise money (and other support) in various ways:

- house-to-house and street collections;
- organising a fundraising event, such as a sponsored walk, where a team of volunteers can be entirely responsible for running the event;
- getting gifts in kind or brochure advertising;
- selling raffle tickets or Christmas cards.

Much of this fundraising work can be done largely unsupervised. Many people get a real satisfaction out of this sort of work, doing something useful in their spare time and working with a group of like-minded people. Inevitably, they will be representing the charity and people will ask them about what the organisation is doing. It is important that they understand what the organisation is doing and share its values: in a sense they are acting as your ambassadors. Some sort of induction is helpful, so that they can be briefed about the organisation's work and meet some of the staff and beneficiaries.

Who volunteers?

Many different types of people volunteer for all sorts of reasons. You may find that they are those people with least time on their hands.

- People who have a particular connection with the cause may be willing to volunteer out of a sense of commitment.
- Recently retired people may have time on their hands, and be willing to do something useful and challenging. There are a number of schemes which promote senior volunteering and which act as a link between the volunteer and the organisations looking for volunteers. The best known are REACH (the Retired Executives Action Clearing House, which is an independent charity) and RSVP (Retired and Senior Volunteer Programme, run by Community Service Volunteers).
- Employees. Employees in the Community, which is part of Business in the Community, promotes and supports employee volunteering. Many companies encourage their staff to volunteer. A few offer time off during the working week, but most expect the volunteering to be done in the evenings or at weekends. Some have a grants scheme, which entitles employees to receive a small grant for the organisation they are volunteering with.
- Professional skills volunteering. Lawyers, accountants, surveyors and others are encouraged to volunteer by their professional associations, using their special skills for the benefit of a community or charitable organisation. Many lawyers work with law centres and citizen's advice bureaux, for example. Lawyers in the Community, which is a scheme run by Employees in the Community, encourages lawyers to become trustees and committee members.
- Unemployed young people including recent school-leavers and graduates yet to get their first job might be persuaded to volunteer just to keep active. You can tell them that they will develop new skills and this can improve their job prospects. The New Deal for the long-term unemployed has a Voluntary Option where young people can work with a voluntary organisation as a route back to employment. Some of the leading charities receive a steady flow of requests to volunteer from recent graduates seeking a career in the voluntary sector. They hope that voluntary work will be a gateway into a paid job, and this can be the case.
- People between jobs. The expectation of lifetime employment no longer exists for most people, and temporary unemployment or part-time work are features of modern life. People between jobs need to maintain their confidence and keep their skills; people with part-time work may have time to spare; women with children growing up may find they have time

available and want to start thinking about a second career. All these groups are potential volunteers, who see volunteering as providing something useful for themselves.

- Young people at school and college or in youth organisations. There is the National Centre for Student Volunteering (SCADU) and the National Federation of Youth Action Agencies, and schemes such as Changemakers encourage young people to become involved and develop social enterprise skills as an important part of their informal education. The Rank Foundation runs a 'Gap' scheme which provides for young people to work with charitable projects that the foundation is already supporting – during a gap year after school and before work or further education, or while unemployed.

- Some people will just arrive on your doorstep or ring up asking to volunteer. They probably share an enthusiasm for what you are doing and want to help.

If you need help with something that sounds interesting, then just ask. If you ask enthusiastically, then you may find that people are prepared to help out. Remember that if you do not ask people will not know that you need help.

Volunteer recruitment and selection

The recruitment and selection of your volunteers is an important task. As with a paid member of staff, there should be a proper job description, and the volunteers should be selected according to their ability to do that job. You need to decide your policy on remuneration – whether you are going to offer to reimburse out-of-pocket expenses or even give some sort of honorarium or allowance. There are two important points to consider.

- *Equal opportunities*. If you don't offer expenses, or if you put pressure on volunteers not to claim expenses, then this could have equal opportunities implications. You may also want to actively encourage the participation of certain groups of people as volunteers, such as young people, the unemployed, black and ethnic minority people, disabled people, elderly people, and you might develop ideas for actively recruiting from such groups.

- *Unemployment benefit*. If you recruit unemployed people for voluntary work, you will need to adhere to DSS requirements; otherwise the volunteer may lose benefit. These requirements relate to availability of work, the level of any remuneration received and whether there is any liability to pay National Insurance. With the introduction of the Jobseekers Allowance, the requirements have been relaxed in an attempt to encourage volunteering by unemployed people. Details are available from the local Job Centre or contact your local Volunteer Bureau or the National Centre for Volunteering.

1 Recruiting people locally

Where you need a number of volunteers in one place – perhaps to help in the office or help out on a fundraising event – a range of recruitment opportunities exist. People occasionally turn up at your office or telephone you for information. If they seem interested, then you could ask them directly if they would like to help as a volunteer.

Your publicity leaflets – or an article in your newsletter which asks for support – may offer the option of giving support in time as well as in cash.

Public meetings and other speaking engagements, including your organisation's annual general meeting, are opportunities to make your need for volunteers known. Those attending might offer, or know someone who might be interested.

Your local Volunteer Bureau will keep a list of people looking for volunteering work, and may have someone who is ideal for you. The TimeBank Campaign aims to recruit volunteers and passes names on to local Volunteer Bureaux. Also various websites are being developed, including DoIt which is part of YouthNet.

You might try to get a feature article on your organisation, its work and its need for volunteers in the local newspaper, or you could consider taking paid advertising space just as you would for a paid job. A letter to the editor stating the importance of your work and your particular need is another option.

Many local radio and television stations run social action programmes with the help of Community Service Volunteers, which assist organisations to recruit volunteers. As with a newspaper, you can also try to get coverage for a volunteer recruitment campaign or a feature about your work, or ring a phone-in programme and make your request on air.

The *Guardian* runs a volunteer recruitment page in Wednesday's *Society* section on an occasional basis, which offers a low-cost advertising opportunity for those seeking to recruit a volunteer.

2 Recruiting people with specific skills

To recruit people with more specialist skills you need a rather more directed approach.

- To find an accountant you might seek the help of the local bank manager or accountancy firm; or for a lawyer, contact a local law firm.
- Professional bodies and associations are a good hunting ground for recently retired people with spare time who want to help. You could offer to give a talk, or suggest an article or a free advertisement in their newsletter.

- If you know exactly what you want, then by asking someone in that field if they know anyone who could do the job, you may eventually find someone who is prepared to take it on.

Unsuitable as well as suitable people will volunteer. So the next step is selecting from the people who have expressed an interest – which you may want to do through an interview and taking up references, just as for a paid job. Don't lower your standards simply because someone offers to help you. You need to take particular care where people are expected to represent your organisation in public or where they will be involved in handling money. Where volunteers are in contact with children and young people, other checks will be required (contact the National Centre for Volunteering for details).

You will need to agree terms and conditions with your newly recruited volunteers, and set these out in some form of 'contract' or letter of agreement:

- the nature of the job to be done
- the hours expected
- the supervision and support offered, and any training that will be given
- grievance procedures
- what expenses are to be paid
- any notice to be given on termination of the arrangement (by either side).

All these need to be discussed and agreed.

Management of volunteers

Like any members of staff, volunteers need managing.

- As mentioned above, any volunteer should have a clear job description.
- You should set them specific and achievable objectives.
- There should be an induction process, so that they see and understand the work of the organisation, meet members of staff (who will also need to appreciate the role and contribution of the volunteer) and be helped to get started.
- You should train them in what they have to do, so that they can do the job effectively, and continue to provide on-the-job training as necessary.
- You should ensure that they have enough information to do their job, and that they are briefed about recent changes and developments in the work of the organisation.
- You should supervise their work, give them feedback on how well they are doing, and congratulate them when they have made a positive contribution. Because they are not being paid, they need other forms of reward – recognition and appreciation are extremely important.

Resources and further information

See also general lists at the end of the book.

Organisations

Changemakers
Batbrook Farm
Lower Godney
Wells
Somerset BA5 1RZ
www.changemakers.org.uk
Tel. 01458 834767
Fax 01458 830588
e-mail info@changemakers.org.uk

DoIt
www.do-it.org.uk

The National Centre for Volunteering
(for courses and publications on all
aspects of volunteering)
Regent's Wharf
All Saints Street
London N1 9RL
www.volunteering.org.uk
Tel. 020 7520 8900
e-mail information@thecentre.org.uk

**National Federation for Youth Action
  Agencies (NFYAA)**
Northern Office
26 High Market Place
Kirkbymoorside
North Yorkshire YO62 6BQ
www.youth-action.org.uk
Tel. 01751 430116
Fax 01751 430122
e-mail ragar@compuserve.com

NCVO
Trustee Advice Service and Trustee
  Board Development Programme
HelpDesk 0800 2 798 798

Rank Foundation
28 Bridgegate
Hebden Bridge
West Yorkshire HX7 8EX
Tel. 01422 845172
Fax 01422 844329
e-mail rankhb@aol.com

REACH (Retired Executives Action
  Clearing House)
Bear Wharf
27 Bankside
London SE1 9ET
Tel. 020 7928 0452

RSVP
c/o Community Service Volunteers
237 Pentonville Road
London N1 9NJ
Tel. 020 7278 6601

TimeBank Campaign
www.timebank.org.uk

Youthnet
www.youthnet.org.uk

Publications

The following publications are available from the Directory of Social Change.
Prices were correct at the time of writing, but may be subject to change.

The Charity Trustee's Handbook, Mike Eastwood, DSC 2001, £7.95

Essential Volunteer Management, 2nd edition, Steve McCurley and Rick Lynch,
DSC 1998, £14.95

The Good Practice Guide for everyone who works with volunteers, NCV 2002, £12.50

The Good Trustee Guide, Kevin Nunan, NCVO 1999, £20

A Management Companion, Tim Cook and Guy Braithwaite, DSC 2000, £12.50

The National Survey of Volunteering, NCV 1998, £22

APPENDIX 1

Institute of Fundraising Codes of Practice, Guidance Notes, and the Charity Donors Rights Charter

The Institute of Fundraising Codes of Practice and Guidance Notes aim to act as a guide to best practice for fundraisers, and as a benchmark against which the public can measure fundraising practice. They cover a wide variety of issues and aim to address both practical and ethical concerns.

The Codes are drawn up by working parties composed of representatives of the various interested constituents in a particular field, and undergo an extensive consultation process through the charities affiliated to the Institute of Fundraising, regulators and government.

As new areas of interest are identified, so new Codes are drafted, often at the rate of two or three each year, under the supervision of the Institute of Fundraising Standards Committee. Both Charity Commission and Home Office are represented on this committee and play a major role in the development of any new work.

The Codes are endorsed and observed by fundraising organisations throughout the UK. They are recognised as demonstrating the commitment of the voluntary sector to the promotion of best practice.

The Charity Donors Rights Charter has been developed as a compact between fundraisers and the supporters of the organisations for which they work. It aims to address the expectations that a supporter has of the organisation they give to, and to articulate the commitment the sector makes to them.

Codes of Practice

Charity Challenge Events

UK Charity Challenge Events

Fundraising in Schools

House to House Collections

Telephone Recruitment of Collectors

Personal Solicitation of Committed Gifts

Legacy Fundraising

Outbound Telephone Support

Payroll Giving

Reciprocal Charity Mailings

Guidance Notes

The Acceptance and Refusal of Donations

Data Protection Act 1998

The Management of Static Collection Boxes

The Use of Chain Letters as a Fundraising Technique

UK Charity Challenge Events

New Codes for 2001

Raffles and Lotteries

Fundraising on the Internet

Copies of the Codes of Practice, Guidance Notes and Charity Donors Rights Charter may be obtained from the Institute of Fundraising at:

Institute of Fundraising
5th Floor
Market Towers
1 Nine Elms Lane
London SW8 5NQ
Tel: 020 7627 3436
Or from:
enquiries@institute-of-fundraising.org.uk

APPENDIX 2

Fundraising and the 1998 Data Protection Act

Many people are concerned about the uses to which information about them may be put, and in particular about 'junk mail' and 'junk phone calls'. Annoying people is never a good way to raise money from them, so it is important to take these concerns seriously. It is also a legal requirement. As well as being the law, the 1998 Data Protection Act provides a sound framework for good practice in the way you handle personal data. This framework is set out in the eight Data Protection Principles (see box).

The Data Protection Principles

1 Personal data shall be processed fairly and lawfully and, in particular, shall not be processed unless –
   (a) at least one of the conditions in Schedule 2 is met, and
   (b) in the case of sensitive personal data, at least one of the conditions in Schedule 3 is also met.

2 Personal data shall be obtained only for one or more specified and lawful purposes, and shall not be further processed in any manner incompatible with that purpose or those purposes.

3 Personal data shall be adequate, relevant and not excessive in relation to the purpose or purposes for which they are processed.

4 Personal data shall be accurate and, where necessary, kept up to date.

5 Personal data processed for any purpose or purposes shall not be kept for longer than is necessary for that purpose or those purposes.

6 Personal data shall be processed in accordance with the rights of data subjects under this Act.

7 Appropriate technical and organisational measures shall be taken against unauthorised or unlawful processing of personal data and against accidental loss or destruction of, or damage to, personal data.

8 Personal data shall not be transferred to a country or territory outside the European Economic Area unless that country or territory ensures an adequate level of protection for the rights and freedoms of data subjects in relation to the processing of personal data.

This appendix looks at the main implications of the Data Protection Act for fundraising, but it is only a summary and is not necessarily a full statement of the law.

It is the 'Data Controller' that is responsible for complying with the Act. Where you are working for an organisation, the Data Controller will almost always be the organisation, not an individual staff member or volunteer. In the discussion below (unless the context indicates otherwise) 'you' generally means 'your organisation', or you as a representative of the Data Controller.

You must assume that any database used for fundraising is covered by the Data Protection Act. This applies wherever the people on the database come from – your own members, a list of people who have made enquiries, a list taken from a reference book, or a bought-in list. It even applies in most cases if you are taking the names from paper files, rather than computer ones. Once you start to compile the list, even before you use it for fundraising, Data Protection will apply.

The key points are:

- Did the people on the list know you might use it for fundraising? If not, your use of the information is unlikely to be 'fair'.
- Were people on the list given the chance to opt out of their data being used for fundraising? If not, again your use might well be 'unfair'.
- If people have ever told you not to use their details for fundraising, are you sure that you have 'suppressed' their names from the list before you use it?
- If you are using someone else for part of the work – such as an agency that will do tele-marketing on your behalf, or a mailing house – have you got a suitable written contract in place with the other agency?
- If you are phoning people to ask for support, have you checked that their number is not on the Telephone Preference Service register? It is an offence to call a number on the register for any sort of marketing.
- If you use a website, or if you share information with organisations overseas, are you complying with the special rules about transferring data abroad?

Fair processing

Any use you make of people's data must be fair (First Principle). The Act says that it is unfair if you collect information from someone without them knowing who you are and what you will use the information for. These facts may be completely obvious; in that case you don't specifically have to make a Data Protection statement. However, things that are obvious to you may not be so clear to the Data Subject. So it is usually best to leave no room for doubt by saying clearly what you will use the information for. You do not have to use any specific language: 'We will keep your details on file so that we can contact you in future about our activities' is friendlier than 'We will hold your data under the Data Protection Act for Direct Marketing purposes'.

It is particularly important for you to consider data that will be shared:

- *within an organisation*, for example transferring it from the membership department to the fundraising department;
- *between organisations*, including passing it on from a charity to its associated trading company or sharing your list with another voluntary organisation.

In both cases you need to make sure that all relevant purposes are identified. In the second case you also need to indicate the type (or even the identity) of any organisation the data will be passed on to.

If you obtain the data from someone other than the Data Subject, you must make sure the Data Subject knows what is going on as soon as possible. This means that in your first contact with them (whether by phone or in a letter) you should make it clear who you are and *all* the uses that you will make of the information you now hold.

You may also want the organisation you get the data from to guarantee that they have told the Data Subject about the actual or potential disclosure to you. (It may well be their responsibility if they didn't, but it's you that will get the irate phone calls and letters.)

Once you have obtained data, you must only use it in ways that are 'compatible' with the purpose(s) specified when you obtained it (Second Principle). Although some may wish to argue that fundraising is 'compatible' with membership, for example, you will avoid any future misunderstanding by having it clearly as a purpose in its own right.

You must also meet at least one of the 'conditions' for fair processing (in Schedule 2 of the Act). For fundraising or marketing you will generally be best able to meet either:

- the first condition – consent from the Data Subject, or
- the sixth condition – that it is in your legitimate interest and doesn't infringe the rights, freedoms or interests of the Data Subject.

If you decide to seek consent, note that you need a response from the Data Subject. A letter saying 'we will do this unless we hear back from you' meets the requirement to provide *information*, discussed above, but you cannot assume *consent* from those who do not reply.

The right to opt out of direct marketing

Data Subjects have an absolute right to opt out of direct marketing, which includes fundraising and probably includes approaches seeking support of any kind. The basic right is that they can 'require' you in writing not to use their details for direct marketing. However, you cannot leave it entirely up to the Data Subject to take the initiative, because of your responsibility to be 'fair' when obtaining information.

If you are obtaining the information directly from the Data Subject, in order to be fair you should give them the opportunity to opt out there and then, preferably through an opt-out tick box. With information obtained from someone else, make sure the Data Subject knows clearly how to exercise their opt-out right.

Approaching someone who has given money in the past to ask for another donation counts as direct marketing, but following up a previous transaction does not – for example going back to someone who sends a donation without giving Gift Aid authorisation.

The opt-out only applies where the material is unsolicited. If you advertise something in your newsletter and someone phones up to ask for more information, you can, of course, send details even if they are marked on your database for 'no direct marketing'.

You must ensure that if you pass information to other organisations for marketing purposes, you exclude from your list anyone who has opted out. If you obtain a list from elsewhere you need guarantees that they have excluded those who have opted out.

Restrictions on tele-marketing

A separate piece of legislation, the Telecommunications (Data Protection & Privacy) Regulations 1999, gives additional rights in respect of marketing carried out by phone.

In particular the Regulations make the Telephone Preference Service (TPS) mandatory. You must not make a direct marketing call to any number that is on the TPS register. It doesn't matter whether the number is from your own database, from someone else's list or from the phone book. The only time you can make marketing calls to a number on the register is if you already have specific permission for this from the person you are calling.

The Regulations also forbid sending unsolicited faxes to individuals and offer a Fax Preference Service (FPS) to businesses.

The TPS and FPS registers are run by the Direct Marketing Association. See www.tps-online.org.uk

Using a Data Processor

If you employ another organisation to process personal data on your behalf they are likely to be a 'Data Processor'. Examples might include:

- sending names and addresses on disk to a mailing house;
- passing your donor database to a fundraising agency which will carry out a telephone appeal;
- using an external service to handle incoming donations in response to an appeal;
- using an agency to run an event for you, including issuing invitations and processing bookings.

In these circumstances, all the Data Protection responsibility remains with the Data Controller. In order to underline this, the Act says that there must be a written contract establishing this relationship. In addition the Data Controller must be satisfied that the Data Processor has satisfactory security, so that the data can only be used for the agreed purpose(s) and in the agreed way.

If the Data Processor cannot show that their standard contract meets the Data Protection requirements you should take legal advice.

Transferring information abroad

The Act imposes, under the Eighth Data Protection Principle, additional restrictions on transferring data to countries that do not have equivalent Data Protection provision to the UK. Certain countries are automatically acceptable; these include:

- those in the European Union;
- others in the European Economic Area (Norway, Iceland and Liechtenstein);
- those assessed as adequate by the European Union (at the time of writing Hungary and Switzerland, with Canada and others under consideration).

For countries not covered above, you may be able to meet one of the conditions that over-rides the Eighth Principle. These include:

- the consent of the Data Subject;
- transfers that are necessary in connection with a contract involving the Data Subject.

Failing that, you would probably need to secure adequate Data Protection through a contract with the recipient organisation.

The use of the internet is, by definition, world wide. Placing personal details on a website is therefore almost bound to require consent.

Additional points

Other provisions of the Act you may have to consider include:

- Is your data of good quality? The Act requires that it is accurate and up to date, as well as adequate, relevant, and not excessive.
- When you have finished using the data, do you have a policy for what happens to it? Under the Act you must not keep it longer than necessary.
- Are you confident that your data is not used in unauthorised ways and that it is kept secure? Again, this is a requirement of the Act.
- Have you checked whether your use of the data needs to be notified to the Information Commissioner?

Specific issues

One activity which might fall foul of the Data Protection Act is compiling speculative databanks on potential wealthy prospects. The whole point is usually to build up a profile in secret before deciding what is the most appropriate way of approaching them. This could well be a breach of the First Principle, especially if the material collected is not already in the public domain. Anyone engaged in this activity is recommended to take further advice.

Another common sticking point is the fear of putting people off getting in contact if you tell them up front that their details will be used for fundraising or marketing. Best practice is clearly to give the opt out as soon as possible, but it may be legitimate to capture details for one purpose (a request for information, for example) and then to inform the Data Subject about future marketing *before any use of the data is made for this purpose.*

[*This appendix was provided by Paul Ticher, author of* Data Protection for Voluntary Organisations, 2nd edition, *DSC, 2002.*]

Directory of Social Change (DSC)
24 Stephenson Way
London NW1 2DP
www.dsc.org.uk

Publications
Tel. 020 7209 5151
Fax 020 7391 4804
e-mail books@dsc.org.uk

Courses and conferences
Tel. 020 7209 4949
Fax 020 7391 4808
e-mail training@dsc.org.uk

Liverpool office
Federation House
Hope Street
Liverpool L1 9BW
Tel. 0151 708 0117 (courses and
conferences); 0151 708 0136
(research)
Fax 0151 708 0139
e-mail north@dsc.org.uk

Publishes a full range of titles for
charities and voluntary organisations,
including a large number of directories
and handbooks for fundraisers. For a
complete booklist, contact the
Publications department, or go to the
DSC website. Bookshop and library
open Monday–Friday near Euston
Station.

Comprehensive training programme
covering all aspects of voluntary sector
activity, including fundraising. For a
copy of the latest Training Guide,
contact the Courses and conferences
departments or visit our website.

Organises Charityfair, the largest annual
event for the UK voluntary sector, with
a three-day programme of events and
training. For full details, contact the
London Courses and conferences
department or go to the DSC website.

Charities Aid Foundation (CAF)
King's Hill
West Malling
Kent ME19 4TA
www.cafonline.org (gives access to all
other CAF websites)
Tel. 01732 520000

Provides charitable and financial
services to help donors make the most
of their giving and non-profit
organisations make the most of their
resources, both in the UK and
overseas. All CAF publications except
those covering international research
and some UK research are now
available only via DSC (see above).

Charity Commission
Harmsworth House
13–15 Bouverie Street
London EC4Y 8DP

Woodfield House
Tangier
Taunton
Somerset TA1 4BL

Second floor
20 Kings Parade
Queens Dock
Liverpool L3 4DG
www.charity-commission.gov.uk
Tel. 0870 3330123

The Giving Campaign
6th Floor
Haymarket House
1A Oxendon Street
London SW1Y 4EE
Tel. 020 7930 3154
Fax 020 7925 0985
www.givingcampaign.org.uk
e-mail admin@givingcampaign.org.uk
The campaign is a partnership
between government and the charity
sector to encourage a greater culture
of giving in the UK and to increase the
number and amount of donations to
charity. It provides a range of free
materials for charities to help them
make the most of all forms of tax
effective giving. All materials can be
seen on the website. They include a
toolkit for charities on Gift Aid
branding, guidance booklets for both
charities and donors on gifts of shares,
and toolkits for employers and
charities on Payroll Giving.

Institute of Fundraising
Central Office
Market Towers
1 Nine Elms Lane
London SW8 5NQ
www.institute-of-fundraising.org.uk
Tel. 020 7627 3436
Represents and supports the
professional interests of fundraisers at
all levels. Membership open to all
those working in a fundraising role.
Publishes good practice guidelines (see
Appendix 1) and runs a training
programme and annual conference.

**National Council for Voluntary
Organisations (NCVO)**
Regent's Wharf
8 All Saints Street
London N1 9RL
www.ncvo-vol.org.uk
Tel. 020 7713 6161
Fax 020 7713 6300
e-mail ncvo@ncvo-vol.org.uk
HelpDesk 0800 2 798 798
e-mail helpdesk@ncvo-vol.org.uk
The umbrella body for the voluntary
sector in England. Provides
information and advice to members via
the HelpDesk. Programme of
publications and events.

Other useful organisations

Use the page references in this list to find the page where full details of the
organisation are given.

INDEX